woodhall press

woodhall press

Woodhall Press, 81 Old Saugatuck Road,
Norwalk, CT 06855

WoodhallPress.com

Library of Congress Cataloging-in-Publication Data available

ISBN 978-1-949116-45-8 (paper: alk paper)

ISBN 978-1-949116-44-1 (electronic)

First Edition

Distributed by Independent Publishers Group

(800) 888-4741

Printed in the United States of America

The views expressed in this book are solely those of the author.

Advance Praise for Seven Drafts...

Allison is one of the most gifted writing teachers I know. She's like a friend privately taking you aside, delivering the honest truth you need, in a way that makes you enthusiastic to keep on going, even when the work gets very hard.

- Jane Friedman, publishing expert and author of *The Business of Being a Writer*

Finally, a guide from the beloved teacher who has been changing writers' lives for years. Written with her famous firehose-style delivery of crucial, clear, and inside-secret information, every page feels like her urging, "Here's what you need. Take my hand. Come on." And then she flings you ten feet in the air like the circus acrobat she (also) is. To take a class with Allison K Williams is to be lifted up and catapulted into writerly community. Now her guide is here to elevate our grammar, style, and storytelling with that same kind of precision and joy.

- Diane Zinna, author of *The All-Night Sun*

I've been lucky enough to be one of Allison's students for several years. Allison coached me from first-ever—very shitty—sentence all the way through publishing my debut novel with Knopf. She taught me everything— from writing how-to, to prioritizing my writing time (yes, I was allowed to let the dirty dishes stack up in my sink!) to navigating the publishing industry. Anyone, whether experienced writer or complete novice novelist, will find an abundance of Allison's wisdom and tender loving (motivating, no-nonsense, but sometimes laugh-out-loud funny) care in her wonderful new book, and we will all be much better writers for it.

- Rhiannon Navin, author of *Only Child*

Why self-edit when you can pay someone to edit for you? Well at some point, dear writer, we each need to figure out how to tell our stories well. In Seven Drafts, Allison K Williams is your partner in shaping your writing into something that is worth buying. Delivered with hilarity, highlight-worthy tips, and her characteristic love-filled-but-never-sugar-coated style, in Seven Drafts you'll barely notice that Allison K Williams is holding your feet to the fire as you forge a story that is worth telling and selling.

- Ashleigh Renard, author of *Swing*

Allison understands at a molecular level what makes prose work. As a sounding board, beta reader, and drop-everything-I'm-doing-to-meet-her coffeehouse workshop partner, Allison has made my writing better. Let her do that for you.

- Christopher Buehlman, author of *The Lesser Dead* and *The Black-tongue Thief*

I had nearly given up on finding an agent when I decided to rework my manuscript with Allison's help. After the revisions, an agent who had told me I could resubmit decided to represent me, and my book was acquired by Penguin Random House!

- Karen Fine, author of *The Other Family Doctor: A Veterinarian's View of Love, Loss, Mortality and Mindfulness*

There are many stellar craft books to choose from, but few are both comprehensive and fun to read. Allison K Williams does both, creating a clear and engaging path through the writing process. Read Seven Drafts once to understand the writing landscape, then refer to it again (and again) as you make the most of every draft. As an editor and coach, this book is one I wish I'd written and one I'll refer to and recommend for years to come.

- Lisa Ellison, Editor and Writing Coach

Seven Drafts is a must-read for ALL writers! The structure makes it easy to skip to the advice most needed—at any stage of the manuscript journey. Incredibly well-written, funny and filled with great examples to help writers improve their craft.

- Jessica Jarlvi, author of *When I Wake Up* and *What Did I Do?*

People also kinda liked
Get Published in Literary Magazines...

Allison K Williams separates myth from fact to provide crucial, no-nonsense advice on the practical side of being a writer, and she does it with deft humor. You couldn't ask for a better coach.

- Dinty W. Moore, Editor-In-Chief of *Brevity* and author of *Between Panic and Desire*

Engaging and straightforward—useful, concrete advice.

- Amy Fish, author of *I Wanted Fries With That*

A straight-talking guide to finding your market, calibrating your skill level and getting in print. She knows the game, she knows the rules. She knows every shortcut you'll want to take, and will tell you which ones might work and which will come back to haunt you. Part motivational essay, part how-to bible, part resource treasure-trove.

- Christopher Buehlman, author of *The Lesser Dead* and *The Blacktongue Thief*

Allison Williams' no-nonsense advice on this daunting aspect of the literary life is bright, thorough, and practical. Williams offers guidelines and encouragement with engaging self-awareness. I will follow her anywhere.

- Robert V. Hansmann, Bennington Writers Group

CONTENTS

INTRODUCTION **15**

HOW TO USE THIS BOOK 16

WHO AM I 21

ABOUT EDITING 23

TYPES OF EDITING 26

THE VOMIT DRAFT **33**

SHOULD YOU WRITE WHAT YOU KNOW? 36

CHOOSING WHAT TO WRITE 37

ORIGINALITY 39

MEMOIR: FIRST DRAFT **42**

MEMOIR IS NOT THERAPY 42

TRUTH & FAIRNESS 44

WRITING TIME **45**

WRITE FIRST 46

INSPIRATION 47

PROCRASTINATION 49

DON'T EDIT AS YOU WRITE 51

WHAT IF I SUCK? 53

RESTARTING 55

THE STORY DRAFT **57**

STORY VS. PLOT VS. STRUCTURE 58

STORY, PLOT & STRUCTURE IN A SERIES 59

MEMOIR: STORY **60**

STORY **64**

OBJECTIVE 66

STARTING WITH SUCK............................68

THE PASSOVER QUESTION 72

DRAMA...73

MEMOIR: DRAMA **76**

CONFLICT 78

MYSTERY..80

MEMOIR: MYSTERY **85**

THEME 86

PLOT..**92**

MEMOIR: PLOT **96**

STRUCTURE....................................**99**

THE CRAZY EIGHT..............................101

MULTI-ACT STRUCTURES 108

MEMOIR: STRUCTURE **113**

TIMELINE 118

PHYSICAL EDITING 120

PICKY STUFF 121

THE CHARACTER DRAFT **123**

CHARACTERIZATION...........................123

MEMOIR: CHARACTER **129**

PASSION/FOIBLE & ABILITY/WEAKNESS..........130

KILL MARY SUE 132

VILLAINS 134

CHARACTER THROUGH DIALOGUE 136

HIGH & LOW-CONTEXT COMMUNICATION......139

WORLD-BUILDING...........................**145**

BACKSTORY: THE CURSE OF KNOWLEDGE 149

FACT-CHECKING.................................151

LYRICS...153

THE TECHNICAL DRAFT 155

WORD COUNTS................................158

VOICE 161

POINT OF VIEW 166

SHOW DON'T TELL 169

SUMMARIES & DETAILS......................173

MOMENTS NOT THINGS 174

JARGON & FOREIGN WORDS 176

SEQUENCE OF ACTIONS....................177

SEX & FIGHTING...............................177

TRIMMING SCENES............................ 180

WHAT IS A SCENE?............................180

GET IN LATE, GET OUT EARLY............181

PACING & DETAILS............................182

ARRANGING TEXT ON THE PAGE........184

CHAPTER BREAKS 186

LINE EDITING 188

HOUSTON, WE HAVE A PROBLEM: LINE EDITING IN ACTION 189

STRONGER SENTENCES.......................197

WORD ORDER..................................197

SENTENCE LENGTH 199

FILTERING 203

PASSIVE VOICE 204

WHAT'S HAPPENING 205

METAPHORS 206

DIALOGUE TAGS..............................207

TEXTS & THOUGHTS 210

WORDS & HOW TO LOVE THEM..............212

VERB TENSES...................................212

MODAL VERBS.................................213

ADVERBS 214

ADJECTIVES 216

REPETITIVE MODIFIERS 219

THAT 220

AWHILE, ANYMORE & ALL RIGHT 221

PHYSICAL EDITING (AGAIN) 223

FINAL CHECK OF TECHNICAL DRAFT 225

THE PERSONAL COPYEDIT **227**

FORMAT & STYLE 227

PUNCTUATING FOR POWER **230**

EXCLAMATION POINTS 230

ELLIPSES 230

DASHES 232

COMMAS 233

COLONS & SEMICOLONS 234

INTERMISSION **239**

KNOW WHEN TO QUIT 241

ENVY 243

THE FRIEND READ **245**

CRITICISM IS RESPECT 246

HOW TO GET USEFUL FEEDBACK 247

HOW TO GIVE GREAT FEEDBACK 249

WRITING WORKSHOPS 251

THE TIME IT TAKES 254

THE EDITOR READ **259**

WHAT WILL IT COST? 260

HIRING AN EDITOR 262

USING YOUR EDIT 266

SAMPLE EDITING WORKFLOW 268

PUBLICATION 271

MEMOIR: PUBLICATION 273

WHAT IF I GET SUED? 275

THE PUBLISHING TIMELINE 278

SELF & HYBRID PUBLISHING 279

AWARDS & PRIZES.. 284

QUERYING.. 286

REFERRALS... 291

DEFINING YOUR BOOK 293

WHAT IF SOMEONE STEALS MY BOOK?........... 296

REJECTION IS NOT FEEDBACK........................ 298

MAKING A WRITING LIFE 301

READING BETTER... 306

WRITING BETTER... 307

MAKING A WRITING LIFE 308

THE WRITER'S TOOLBOX 311

WRITING GROUPS 312

USEFUL APPS & WEBSITES 314

SELF-EDIT CHECKLIST 317

BOOKS & MEDIA MENTIONED 323

ACKNOWLEDGMENTS 327

ABOUT THE AUTHOR 329

LIST OF EXERCISES 330

INDEX.. 330

INTRODUCTION

Do any of these sound familiar?

I've got a great idea for a book. Now what?

How do I create a fictional protagonist who readers will love and identify with?

I don't know when to stop writing, when to say my book is "done."

Maybe you've been writing for a while and you want to get to the next level:

I just finished a draft and I know the next step is editing. Ummm...how?

I want my manuscript to be polished enough to attract an agent.

I want to improve my feedback skills for myself and my writing group.

Maybe you've got a more existential problem in your book or your writing life:

I need help tapping into the universal—how do I address the "so what?" factor in my memoir?

How can I get helpful critique when my friends don't want to hurt my feelings?

I'm having trouble getting my ass in gear. My project has stalled. My work is unfocused.

This book will help you with those. Any of them. All of them. Plus, it will help you dispel that lingering doubt about whether you're really creating anything worthwhile. By the time you've gone through seven drafts, your manuscript will be in the best possible shape before querying, self-publishing, or hiring a professional editor. You'll know, one way or the other, if it's worth trying to publish your book.

That's a little ominous, right? If you're worried, that's a good sign. The Dunning-Kruger effect helpfully covers this: the more competent someone is at a particular skill, the more self-critical they're likely to be. The less someone knows about a skill, the better they think they are at doing it.

You're going to raise your writing skill level no matter where you're starting. Right now, you don't know what level of craft you're capable of—and that's a great place to start.

HOW TO USE THIS BOOK

(with apologies to Bob Dylan)

How many drafts must a writer draft

Before you call it a book?

How many times must you read the text

Before your editor looks?

Yes, how many times should it be revised

To get a reader hooked?

The answer my friend is...seven.

As a freelance editor, I work with writers throughout their careers, from beginners with an idea to award-winning, full-time authors. I see many of the same challenges in everyone's essays, stories, memoirs and novels:

* Technical issues like wrongly formatted dialogue tags or overused words.

* Voice issues like stiff, unnatural narrative or characters who sound the same.

- Point-of-view issues like head-hopping or characters who see or understand things beyond their emotional range or physical ability.
- Structural issues like too many subplots, final acts without enough set-up, and stories that start too many pages into the book.

As an editor, I can identify these issues for authors who want to revise their own work, or address them myself for authors who prefer to throw money at the problems. But most of these writing missteps can be found and reworked by the writers themselves before spending money on professional editing or using up a "please give me feedback on my manuscript" favor. This work is time-consuming and thinking-intensive, but it's not a secret or a talent—it's a set of skills anyone willing to go through seven drafts can acquire.

The Seven Drafts are organized from big-picture elements of story and structure to narrower areas of line-by-line writing craft. If you're starting from a rough/first draft (or no draft at all!), go in order. Working on the big picture first helps keep story continuity through subsequent sentence-level tinkering—there's no point in fixing the spelling in a scene you discover isn't needed. If you're already in a third or fourth draft, you may want to flip to the Self-Editing Checklist, which shows how you might group some of these tools.

If you're at the "I can't believe I even started this crazy project" stage, revive your enthusiasm by picking a smaller element from the Technical Draft, like dialogue tags or chapter endings. Work through those challenges to feel some progress and get back into the writing groove.

Whatever order you use, try to make it through a whole draft. One of the biggest challenges of writing a book is distraction. Committing to a series of steps and persevering through boredom, frustration, and shiny new ideas (write them down and get back to the current book!) will help you finish your manuscript and feel good about your creation.

1) The Vomit Draft

Get it out get it out! It doesn't matter if all the words are spelled rite. Don't worry about complete sentences because. Sure, there's a plot hole big enough to drive a truck through, and in the second-to-last chapter you realize you really do have to put in Aunt Ermintrude. Just finish. If you hit a creativity wall, put in a placeholder like "NEED SCENE WITH MOM HERE SOMETHING HUMOROUS," or "SWORDFIGHT RAKA WINS," or write *about* what belongs there:

> *Write scene about that time they were in the kitchen and Patricia just knew they were going to fall in love because of the way Malik's fingers wrapped around the saltshaker.*

Then let your manuscript rest for at least a week. Don't let impatience or your drive to finish cut this resting time short—fresh eyes help us see issues that our enthusiasm sped past.

2) The Story Draft

Summarize your story with "In a World" format (described in Chapter 2), with a clear problem, protagonist/hero,[1] action, obstacle, stakes and goal. If you're missing any of those elements, go back to the Vomit Draft and pour forth more words.

During this draft, fill in placeholders and discover any missing events, random extra scenes (why does my hero get a haircut?) or places where the plot doesn't make sense. Raise the level of conflict in your novel. See if anyone cares about your memoir.

After the Story Draft, let your manuscript sit for another week.

3) The Character Draft

Does each character want specific things and work to get them? Are the protagonist's actions and reactions motivated and urgent? You may discover that a character needs more on-page time or doesn't belong at all.

In the Character Draft, make sure the bad guys have clear motivations that make sense to themselves and (eventually) the reader, even if they're a mystery to the protagonist. Characters are treated fairly and the reader judges their actions and speech rather than being told who the "good guys" are (this is especially important in memoir).

Point of View (POV) gets a careful edit. Physically, a four-year-old child can't see the top of the kitchen counter. Mentally, a

---

1 The protagonist is the character whose goal drives the plot. Usually that's one person, and it's the person who changes the most. In a memoir, that's you. We'll use "protagonist" and "hero" interchangeably.

character can guess at other people's thoughts but cannot omni-sciently know them.[2]

Review the dialogue character by character. Make sure that each person sounds like themselves and that it's pretty clear who is speaking even without dialogue tags.

Examine your world-building. Is your setting clear in time and place? Is there a clear way of life, even if it's one the protagonist is defying or abandoning? Can the reader discover societal customs, history, technology and backstory from the action, without needing a lecture from the narrator? Do any elements feel anachronistic or out of place?

Revise; let sit. Waiting is key, so if you can't stand not writing for a week, draft an essay or a short story to clear your palate. If you write in multiple genres, work on a manuscript in another genre—pick a task that won't plunge you in so deeply you can't come back to this book.

4) The Technical Draft

Working chapter by chapter, ask:

Does each chapter start with a compelling action or image? Does each chapter end with both satisfaction and forward motion?

With each scene, have you gotten in as late as you can and still set the scene, and have you ended the scene as early as you can and still have it feel complete? Are the physical actions possible and in logical, realistic order? Are you showing more than telling, and choosing when telling is needed?

Check sentence structure. Have you carefully placed the strongest words? Do paragraphs end with strong sentences? Do chapters end with strong paragraphs?

Purely technical corrections happen at this stage: searching for -ly and removing unnecessary adverbs; eliminating most "was verb-ing" constructions; and removing or replacing overused words.

By now you know what you want to say—the Technical Draft refines how you say it.

Revise; let sit.

---

2 If your premise involves telepathy or deep empathy, set the rules of what those powers allow and observe your own world's limitations.

5) The Personal Copyedit

A nice, easy draft. This is a once-over for cleanliness.[3] Run spell-check with the grammar turned on. Print the manuscript and see what shows up when you're turning a physical page. Read your book out loud or use a text-to-speech program to catch errors your eyes got used to.

The Personal Copyedit is the be-kind-to-your-reader draft. Yes, it's still a work in progress, but you want reading your work to be a pleasant experience for the next step....

6) The Friend Read

Sometimes called a beta read. Exchange manuscripts with a writing buddy or call in favors from the people who keep offering to read your book. Arm your friends with specific questions: Did the story make sense? Where did your attention wander? Which character do you want to see more of? Try to get readers' comments in writing, even if you're taking notes while they talk. **Do not defend your book. Do not assume their lack of understanding means they missed something.**[4]

Set the notes aside for a few days. When your feelings have cooled down, go back and see what rings true. Revise accordingly.

7) The Editor Read

This doesn't have to mean forking out cash. The Editor Read can be exchanging manuscripts with someone you know to be harsher or more technically demanding than the previous reader. Or this could be the first time you share your manuscript with your agent. And yes, it can mean hiring a professional editor or writing coach.

This draft is where it's worth paying to have just your first three chapters edited, then applying those changes throughout the rest of the book before getting any more full-manuscript reads. Chances are good that problems in the beginning are problems through the whole book.

---

3 A professional copyedit will catch things authors miss. The Personal Copyedit is free—and will make you better at spotting future errors.

4 You asked for their opinion. You won't agree with everything. Listen respectfully, or they won't read for you again. More on this in "How to Get Useful Feedback."

Read your manuscript one more time before you send it out. Knowing that an Editor Read is imminent, you'll see more issues.

Uu

The Seven Drafts often take more than one revision each. You might repeat the Story Draft when a Character Draft uncovers a plot hole. A second Friend Read is useful after incorporating the first round of feedback. Some drafts take days, some take weeks or months. You might backtrack and revisit the Technical Draft after an on-paper Personal Copyedit.

Let your book sit for a week or more between drafts.[5] At least once, print out your pages; edit the manuscript by hand on sloppy, satisfying paper; and *retype the whole thing*[6] so you can feel the flow.

I've found this method to work for everything from essays to memoirs, short stories to novels. Drop me an email or DM and let me know how it goes for you. And if you've got a different method or a variation, please tell me about it.

WHO AM I...

...and why am I telling you all this? How does someone get to proclaim, "Do it this way!"

As The Unkind Editor,[7] I've spent ten years editing for money, and longer still editing for friends and classmates. I've worked on books published by Big Five publishers[8] and small presses, self-published books and just-for-family-and-friends projects. I'm a published author myself (credits in the bio at the back of this book). As an editor, I'm thrilled to have contributed to some prestigious literary and commercial books. I'm prouder

---

5 "I have a life and it needs me" is also worth a break.

6 Every writer I have ever told to retype the whole thing has looked at me with horror. Every one of them has told me later, "Good grief, that's exactly what I needed to do." I dare you.

7 Why "Unkind"? Because praise makes you feel good, but direct and specific feedback makes your work better.

8 The "Big Five" traditional publishers are (as of 2021): Penguin/ Random House, Hachette Book Group, Harper Collins, Simon & Schuster, and Macmillan.

still of helping first-time authors go from the roughest of rough drafts to publication, while learning how to write a book.

I'm an editor by nature. As a seventh-grader writing bad middle-school poetry, I copied poems over and over by hand before inscribing final drafts in a hardback journal.[9] For each draft I asked, "Does every word belong?" The poems got shorter, and I learned to write with economy, to make every word the right word in the right place.

In college, I studied theatre and earned an MFA in playwriting. Ten years as an actor/director and ten more as a circus and street performer taught me how fast audiences get bored—how only genuine, meaningful connection keeps their attention.

Writing for live theatre showed me the challenges every editor must watch for and helped me develop skills every writer needs:

Playwrights write better dialogue. The audience doesn't hear adverbs written in the stage directions and the writer doesn't dictate how actors say their lines. If you want "angrily" or "joyfully," the words out of actors' mouths must take them there.

Scripts must show instead of telling. Onstage narration and voiceovers are rare. Information the audience needs must be in the scene. World-building happens as characters interact with their surroundings and embody their culture. Backstory ("exposition") is death on stage. When one character tells another something they both already know, you can *feel* the audience start rustling.

The writing is actively questioned. Yes, we receive feedback in writing groups and workshops, but it's a whole new level of pain/ wonder to see your characters get up and act out the scene. This shows immediately which parts work on stage and which only make sense in your head.

Rehearsals mean fast revision. Maybe you hated the feedback. But there's another rehearsal tomorrow night and unless you show up with new pages that solve the problem, the same actor will give the same exasperated look and sigh, "I still don't know why my character is in this scene."

But most of all...

Playwriting is about structure. Most plays have clear dramatic arcs. The protagonist has a problem or lives in an untenable situation. She takes actions toward a specific goal. She must change in order to reach the goal. She has specific internal and

---

9 With a silver unicorn on the cover, of course.

external obstacles. The audience knows if the protagonist has succeeded or failed. Every character has an arc, and there's a person playing that character who is paying attention to whether it makes sense.

Spending so much time in dark rooms hearing people question my (and other playwrights') work, watching them act out my words, seeing audiences fidget when they're bored or confused, and focusing intensely on structure has given me specific tools and techniques for writing and editing. They're precise. They're detailed. And they are the foundation of all my work.

ABOUT EDITING

When I'm reading a good book, the story plays like a movie in my head. If a book drags or is poorly written, I become conscious of individual words, aware of sentences and paragraphs. Editing your manuscript streamlines the reader's experience so they can read immersively instead of noticing words on the page. Unpolished writing yanks the reader out of the world of the book. They are not moving forward in the story. They're seeing typos or noticing what they "should" be feeling. Or they're just plain confused.

If you wish to publish, either independently or through a traditional publisher, editing marks your work as *finished*. Your book is sharply dressed and well-groomed, ready to make a good impression and engage the reader. Sloppy books—with incorrectly formatted dialogue or story continuity issues or a hero whose quest just doesn't pay off—insult the reader. Sloppy books say, "The author didn't care enough to make me great." They say, "I'm not ready...but I took your time and money anyway."

Your work deserves better than that.

When should you edit your manuscript?

Write your first draft without judgment. Fixing and cleaning a whole first draft is much easier than staring at the empty page silently mocking you, thinking, *Mom was right, I should have gotten a real job.*

After the story is fully on the page, go back and edit. Start with the big picture: story and structure. Move through character and dialogue. Refine the voice. Accentuate the themes. Then get picky about punctuation and spelling. Clean as much as you can before asking outside readers to spot the things you missed.

Why is it hard to edit your own work?

Because you already know what you want to say. The story, the characters, their voices, the personal truth of what happened (whether real or fictitious), *you were there.* Your brain naturally fills in gaps between the story you want to tell and what's actually on the page. You have turns of phrase, regionalisms, slang, and cultural knowledge about the world you're building, or the one you lived in.

The reader does not have that background. They need a careful mix of hand-holding, prodding, education, mystery, and maddening deception. You must make the reader the detective who turns every page thinking, *I must find out what happened,* giving them just enough information to sustain that desire without satisfying them prematurely. So to speak.

But you can edit your own words with the reader's experience in mind. You can sidestep your own knowledge and focus on improving what's actually on the page. Each time you thoroughly overhaul a manuscript your craft will increase, and your next draft (and your next book!) will be better written and a little easier to finish. If you commission a professional edit, it will cover deeper issues and/or cost less, because manuscripts in better shape are less time-consuming to edit. When you've gotten your story as tight as you can, the editor can focus on more subtle elements.

Don't despair if you examine your manuscript and discover a great many issues you'd like to fix. Truly bad books are fast to edit because there's only so good they can get. When your book has potential, it takes more time. Why stop at "a quick proofread" when you could revise heavily and make your work really amazing?

But isn't editing just a bunch of stupid "rules" like in English class? Isn't creativity all about breaking the rules?

Nope, and yes but nope.

Editing isn't about getting an A from your teacher—it's about ushering the reader into a world where they can imagine with abandon, knowing they're in competent hands. The rules of writing[10] make the words themselves invisible. Think about walking down a well-maintained sidewalk in a beautiful, pedestrian-friendly area, earbuds in, or having a conversation. You can look around, listen, and enjoy the journey. Smooth writing is that sidewalk, taking you someplace cool and exciting. Rough writing is like crossing the street to avoid construction, every half-block, against the light. You'll still get there, but the journey's no fun.

Sometimes the writing is an obstacle course on purpose, but even then, consistency allows the reader to feel the "rules" of that particular book. Going against the reader's cultural expectations about the way stories work, and the ingrained rules of language, requires knowing the craft of writing and making deliberate choices. As in fashion, breaking "rules" through ignorance is not useful. Lady Gaga rocked that meat dress, and Björk made an amazing powder-puff swan. I, personally, could not pull off either of those looks. Nor do I write hundred-word sentences like James Joyce, move fluidly through points of view like Hilary Mantel or telescope time like Tayari Jones. That doesn't mean you can't—as long as you do it beautifully.

Editing is not bending your words to a generic form. Editing is wedding your passion, creativity, and imagination to technical tools so the reader connects deeply, personally, and viscerally with your story.

This book will stock your toolbox.

Every toolbox has a hammer and a screwdriver. You don't have to use them, and they won't be the right device every time, but you don't want a pipe wrench to be your only tool. Writers spend their lives adding techniques and skills to their toolbox. Not every technique is right for every book. You'll have tools you prefer—maybe you're a structure person, or a language person, or a myth-masking person. But the more tools you know, the easier writing gets, and the more options you have when a chunk of words isn't responding to your usual process.

---

10 Yes, yes, James Joyce, Cormac McCarthy, William Faulkner, Jane Austen, etc. If you're that good, put this book down immediately and go finish your own.

TYPES OF EDITING

Editors use different terminology, but there are four main types of editing:

Developmental/Structural/Substantative Editing

Big-picture commentary and analysis, focusing on story, structure, characterization, and continuity. The editor may note craft issues, writing habits, or grammar challenges appearing throughout the book. Sometimes this level of editing includes helping a memoirist focus their material, or assisting a narrative nonfiction writer's research. A **manuscript evaluation** or a **read and respond** is a lighter version of developmental editing.

Loosely in this category, a **beta read** is a basic overview identifying major strengths and weaknesses, usually done for free by a fellow writer but also available from professionals. Beta readers respond from the perspective of a reader rather than an editor.

Developmental editing is an informed, professional opinion, but an opinion nonetheless. The editor isn't looking for "bad writing," but for what is and isn't working in this book.

In the Seven Drafts, this editing happens in the Vomit, Story and Character Drafts.

Line Editing

Sentence by sentence, a line edit catches awkward phrasing, extra or missing words, clichés, too many adverbs, overused words, and inconsistent voice. Editors have personal taste priorities when line editing—for example, I tend to suggest reframing sentences beginning with *It was* and *There were* constructions.

Line editing is strongly rooted in an understanding of the mechanics of language—how words work on the page. Again, this is not following arbitrary rules, but enhancing the reader's experience. A good editor will pay attention to any nonstandard choices the writer has made and make sure the manuscript's style is consistent rather than "correct."

This work is in the Technical Draft.

Copyediting[11]

Not an opinion. The copyeditor finds typos, missed words, and purely technical issues. Most publishers have a "style sheet" dictating their conventions. What country's spelling is correct? What format for texts or letters? Do we spell out numerals up to ten? Up to one hundred? Are thoughts italicized?

Many freelance editors make a unique style sheet for each manuscript, including proper names, foreign words, variant spellings, and invented words. For fantasy, science fiction, and series books, the style sheet keeps continuity of names and terminology.[12]

You'll do this work in the Personal Copyedit.

Proofreading

Errors and omissions: one last check for spelling, extra spaces, anything the printer has not copied exactly from the file they received. If you're self-publishing, proofread a physical copy before putting your book on sale.

Enlist an editor or a sharp-eyed friend, because after seven drafts, it's hard to see the last few errors!

The next pages have examples of each type of editing demonstrated on Kathryn Rose's work-in-progress, *Ojas*.

Author's Note

Throughout this book, examples from published books are attributed. Selections from unpublished works are used with permission of the authors. Nonattributed text has been invented. URLs for many of the websites, resources, books and media are available at **www.sevendrafts.com**.

I am free with inclusive pronouns because we are all both readers and writers, and we're all in this together.

---

11 Yes, line editing is two words and copyediting is one. Only Benjamin Dreyer knows why.

12 Making your own style sheet as you go will help your eventual publisher, and remind you that Caileigh's name changed to Caitlin and then Katelynn until you gave up and just called her Maude.

DEVELOPMENTAL: Focus on story and characters

Ojas had lived 13 harvests. It would be at least three more before he could be freed from sitting in school on a morning like this. From his favorite hiding place on the roof he could hear Preceptor Sera scold a young boy for running in the door. She would be ringing the first bell at any moment, and Ojas knew he should climb down to avoid being late. But from this spot he loved to watch the Sun find the mountain mist, and the mountain called to him, like a song in his bones, inviting him to climb.

Ojas knew learning was important. Nenna was very serious about his studies. Nenna was the eldest person in the village. She was the mother of his mother, and he had lived with her since his parents' death, before he could remember.

Nenna worked with Ojas after Sun rested each day, to renew his school lessons and to teach him other things. She sat with Ojas in meditation after Sun rested each day and told him the stories of Sun and Stars, of Sea and Stone and Wind. She had told him the stories for as long as he could remember, and no matter what other things might have happened in a day, there were always the stories. Ojas wondered if there was a story about the mountains song. He dared not ask, because Nenna might see in his heart the reason for his question and know he had left school to answer it.

Commented [AW1]: Start here? We can find out about the environment of school later when he goes inside

Commented [AW2]: Nice job setting up the voice at the beginning

Commented [AW3]: Needed? Maybe just the last sentence, start with "Nenna was"?

Formatted: Strikethrough

Deleted: him

Commented [AW4]: "Sun" or "the Sun" in this world?

Commented [AW5]: Needed?

Commented [AW6]: OK, so this implies he's run away from the schoolhouse but we haven't seen him take that action. What if this scene started with him sitting down with Nenna? Or he shows up at home with an excuse? Like, if he left school when he wasn't supposed to, wouldn't Nenna notice he's home early?

Or what if you started with him running away from school? We're getting the routine, and the voice is beautiful, but can you start the story with the break in the routine that kicks off the plot?

LINE EDITING: Focus on sentences and flow

Ojas had lived 13 harvests. It would be at least three more before he would be freed from sitting in school on a morning like this. From his favorite hiding place on the roof, he heard Preceptor Sera scold a young boy for running in the door. She would be ringing the first bell at any moment, and Ojas knew he should climb down to avoid being late. But from this spot he loved to watch, Sun find the mountain mist, and the mountain called to him, like a song in his bones, inviting him to climb.

Nenna was very serious about Ojas' studies. The eldest person in the village, she was the mother of his mother's mother, and he had lived with Nenna since his parents' death, before he could remember.

After Sun rested each day, Nenna sat with him in meditation and told him the stories of Sun and Stars, of Sea and Stone and Wind. She had told him the stories for as long as he could remember, and no matter what other things might have happened in a day, there were always the stories. Ojas wondered if there was a story about the mountain's song. He dared not ask Nenna might see in his heart the reason for his question, and know he had left school to answer it.

Commented [AW7]: Removed extra spaces, not technically line editing but it's easy with find and replace so most line editors go ahead and do it.

Deleted: c

Deleted: could

Deleted: the

Deleted: Ojas knew learning was important.

Deleted: his

Deleted: Nenna was

Deleted: t

Deleted: .

Deleted: S

Deleted: her

Deleted: Nenna worked with Ojas a

Deleted: to renew his school lessons and to teach him other things. She....

Deleted: ,

Deleted: because

COPYEDITING: Errors and omissions, style sheet compliance, could include fact-checking

Ojas had lived thirteen harvests. It would be at least three more before he could be freed from sitting in school on a morning like this. From his favorite hiding place on the roof, he could hear Preceptor Serra scold a young boy for running in the door. She would be ringing the first bell at any moment, and Ojas knew he should climb down to avoid being late. But from this spot he loved to watch Sun find the mountain mist, and the mountain called to him, like a song in his bones, inviting him to climb.

Ojas knew learning was important. Nenna was very serious about his studies. Nenna was the eldest person in the village. She was the mother of his mother's mother, and he had lived with her since his parents' death, before he could remember.

Nenna worked with Ojas after Sun rested each day, to renew his school lessons and to teach him other things. She sat with him in meditation and told him the stories of Sun and Stars, of Sea and Stone and Wind. She had told him the stories for as long as he could remember, and no matter what other things might have happened in a day, there were always the stories. Ojas wondered if there was a story about the mountain's song. He dared not ask, because Nenna might see in his heart the reason for his question and know he had left school to answer it.

Commented [AW8]: Extra spaces removed

Deleted: 13

Commented [AW9]: NOTE: Fixed all to "Serra"

Deleted: the

Commented [AW10]: Copyeditor did not add a comma here because it's not incorrect; the line editor thought it flowed better with a comma

PROOFREADING: Errors only

Ojas had lived thirteen harvests. It would be at least three more before he could be freed from sitting in school on a morning like this. From his favorite hiding place on the roof he could hear Preceptor Serra scold a young boy for running in the door. She would be ringing the first bell at any moment, and Ojas knew he should climb down to avoid being late. But from this spot he loved to watch Sun find the mountain mist, and the mountain called to him, like a song in his bones, inviting him to climb.

Ojas knew learning was important. Nenna was very serious about his studies. Nenna was the eldest person in the village. She was the mother of his mother's mother, and he had lived with her since his parents' death, before he could remember.

Nenna worked with Ojas after Sun rested each day, to renew his school lessons and to teach him other things. She sat with him in meditation and told him the stories of Sun and Stars, of Sea and Stone and Wind. She had told him the stories for as long as he could remember, and no matter what other things might have happened in a day, there were always the stories. Ojas wondered if there was a story about the mountain's song. He dared not ask, because Nenna might see in his heart the reason for his question and know he had left school to answer it.

Deleted: 13
Deleted:
Deleted:
Deleted:
Deleted:
Deleted:
Deleted:
Deleted:
Deleted:
Deleted:
Deleted:
Deleted:
Deleted:
Deleted:

FOR SMARTASSES

Yes, this book has typos. All books do. An amazing copyeditor will be 95-98% accurate, because they're a human being. Even professional editing software misses errors. Please let us know and we'll fix them in the next edition.[13]

If you spot a typo and post a review (of the book! Not of the typo!), let us know. We'll send a free copy of *Seven Drafts* to your best writer friend.

---

13 CMOS; Merriam-Webster. Check **http://www.sevendrafts.com** for the style sheet and errors already found. We're pro-comma splices, and we've used the Oxford (serial) comma when it clarifies meaning, so don't @ me with the Stalin/Kennedy meme.

THE VOMIT DRAFT

You have an idea that sounds fun to write. Or you feel compelled to tell a particular story. Or you're a nonfiction writer or memoirist with hours of taped interviews, a pile of research, or powerful memories.

Maybe you're a "plotter" who has laboriously outlined scenes, drawn a map, filled out character information sheets and documented the history of your world.

Perhaps you're a "pantser,"[14] staring at a blank page with only an idea.

Get the words out. Your first draft might be disorganized, poorly written, or missing information you still need to invent or corroborate. Your words might be meticulously planned, yet somehow still difficult to write.

What matters is words on the page.

The Vomit Draft isn't dainty, but it's a relief. Better out than in. Fixing a messy first draft is much easier than writing from scratch—you can't revise a blank page. As a more delicate metaphor, Jenny Elder Moke, the author of *Hood*, tweeted a wonderful concept:

> *Y'all stop calling your first drafts garbage. Garbage is what you throw out when you're done with the meal. What you have there is a grocery run—a collection of*

---

14 From "flying by the seat of their pants." Most writers don't fit neatly into either category, but it's useful to know which method speaks to you.

items that will eventually make a cohesive meal once you figure out which flavors go together.

In this draft, the plotters went to the store with a list (ordered by aisle) and a wallet full of carefully trimmed coupons.[15] The pantsers grabbed whatever was on sale, looked fresh, or had a free-sample tray. But they both *bought stuff.*

The first draft is putting your ingredients on the counter to see what they'll make.[16]

Writing a first draft involves a lot of realizing midway, *This isn't working,* then deciding to keep going and fix it later, or to go back and rewrite. Not everyone finishes a first draft before editing. Many writers edit yesterday's work to get into today's groove. I pants the beginning and end of a novel from an idea, then outline the middle. Whatever your process, get what you need on the page before poking at it.

This is easier said than done.

The idea of the shitty first draft has been around for many years. Ernest Hemingway told Arnold Samuelson, "The first draft of anything is shit."[17]

Maybe you know the concept from Anne Lamott's *Bird by Bird*:

> *Shitty first drafts. All good writers write them. This is how they end up with good second drafts and terrific third drafts.*
>
> *...I know some very great writers, writers you love who write beautifully and have made a great deal of money, and not one of them sits down routinely feeling wildly enthusiastic and confident. Not one of them writes elegant first drafts.*

But it's still hard to believe. Famous authors say they write shitty first drafts—but we don't see those pages, so it sounds like

---

15 They used the pinking shears because they like the pretty edges.

16 If you really want to push the metaphor: Story Draft=cooking, Character Draft=side dishes, Technical Draft=seasoning, Personal Copyedit=plating and table-setting, Friend Read=family meal, Editor Read=restaurant critic arrives.

17 As Samuelson claims in *With Hemingway: A Year in Key West and Cuba,* a posthumously published book of memories. But hey, I'd probably remember if Hemingway said that to me forty years ago.

something they say to make crappy writers feel better about themselves. Like telling us to believe in Santa Claus.[18]

Before I was a writer, I was a circus performer. I spent hours in the gym falling into mats, watching people I respected and knew to be far more skilled than me also falling into mats. In a museum, I can see Picasso's sketches. Musicians hear each other's wrong notes in practice. But once out of school, writers rarely see the process of our peers.[19] Writers, too, need to see how others work, and work near them. We need writing buddies to share shapeless early drafts with and reading partners who can encourage and critique.

Shitty first drafts aren't the only way to write. Some writers prefer revising as they go. Perhaps some writers think through their stories so thoroughly, or outline so precisely, that when they sit down, the right words come out in more or less the right order. But for most writers, the first draft is telling the story to ourselves. Thinking on the page. Finding the heart of the story way down in Chapter Ten; a single beautiful sentence on page five; the perfect opening line in the final paragraph. Finding those words, the ones we really need, means writing a bunch more words we'll cut in the next draft. Even if you're a plotter, write first drafts of scenes with wild abandon. See what comes out unjudged.

The point is not that the first draft should be bad, but to not let fear of badness stop you from writing. A sloppy, disorganized first draft is not a failure, but a necessary first step. First drafts are barre exercises before ballet, scales before singing, charcoal on newsprint before oils on canvas. Taking the time to assemble the materials of events, characters, plot, and themes; letting the jumble show us what to say, trusting we can pull a shining thread of story from the mess.

Yes, Virginia, wherever there are writers, there are shitty first drafts. And just as presents and nibbled cookies prove Santa showed up in the night, the very existence of finished, glorious work means someone, somewhere, wrote a terrible first draft.

---

18 There is *absolutely* a Santa Claus and your winter holiday of choice is in your heart.

19 If you're still in school, become better friends with the people whose writing you like now—they're your future critique partners.

SHOULD YOU WRITE WHAT YOU KNOW?

Perhaps the most famous piece of writing advice ever: "Write what you know." A maxim right up there with "Don't quit your day job," and "Vampires are done."

But should you?

One of my favorite writers is Dick Francis (the when-he-was-alive version, not the posthumous-brand version). Francis wrote horse-racing mysteries and thrillers. Early in his career, they were about skullduggery around the track: doping, blackmail, sabotage, family conflicts. All the things that happen when wealthy people get together for a competitive hobby. Francis knew that world. He'd been a jockey for many years. But as his books became more popular, they also became more diverse. He still set each one in the world of racing, but added a layer that drove the story. Racecourse catering (poison!); racecourse architecture and renovation (explosions!); glassblowing for fancy race trophies (domestic abuse!). Francis did his research to build each new world, and readers got to discover that world as well as enjoy a gripping read.

Whole genres—fantasy, science fiction, romance ending Happily Ever After—are based on experiences we wish we could have or are excited to dream up, not "what we know." Memoirists must piece together family history and speculate or investigate why people behaved as they did. For narrative nonfiction, writing what we don't already know is the whole point.

Writing what we *want* to know can be even more powerful than writing what we already know. Research beyond a novelist's experience opens doors for interesting characters and new plot twists. For memoirists, genuinely considering a question like *Why did my mother treat me like that?* can allow us to resolve the past as well as creating a complex, nuanced picture of our personal history.

Research is time-consuming, but it's not difficult. Libraries, the internet, and specialty podcasts are goldmines (verify your facts with multiple sources!). People often love to talk about their job or hobby to an eager listener taking notes. Older relatives are usually delighted to regale you with family stories; asking the right nonaggressive questions can dig out truths that make sense of your own life.

Even if your story springs from what you already know, examine your own assumptions and see what you can disprove. As you build the world of your book, notice where your curiosity draws you. What excites you to discover will also engage your reader.

CHOOSING WHAT TO WRITE

The first, of gold, who this inscription bears, "Who chooseth me shall gain what many men desire;"
The second, silver, which this promise carries, "Who chooseth me shall get as much as he deserves;"
This third, dull lead, with warning all as blunt, "Who chooseth me must give and hazard all he hath."
How shall I know if I do choose the right?

The Merchant of Venice, Act II sc. VII

Last year, before NaNoWriMo[20], a writer friend was in agony. She had three ideas for novels but also wanted to write a memoir; should she pick something fun or something that felt more purposeful? And an acquaintance lamented in a Facebook group,

How do y'all decide what project comes first? I write free-lance, blog, and am toying with two memoir ideas. I love personal essays the most, but I keep feeling there's something I "should" be doing instead. Do I forget blogging and pitch magazine essays? Stop writing copy and finish a memoir? Write more copy and make more money to have time off?

I've felt this myself. It's pretty common to have a couple of half-finished or barely started projects jostling for attention in your head: that murder mystery twist you thought of in the bath; the Young Adult novel premise that came to you in the gym; that conversation with your grandmother about the craziest family story you've ever heard. Maybe one feels easier to finish and "get out of the way," but you're more excited about another idea. Or someone you'll need to interview is in ill health. Or a friend is writing in the same genre and you could talk through ideas together.

---

20 National Novel Writing Month. In November, many writers take up the challenge to generate 50K words in 30 days. It's an excellent exercise and some bestselling novels have emerged from NaNoWriMo projects. But remember that your 50K will need revision. Every December 1, literary agents brace for a flood of shitty first drafts. Don't add to the pile.

Like Portia's suitors in *The Merchant of Venice,* you're faced with (at least!) three caskets, all valuable, but one of which you're sure contains the prize.

How to choose which project deserves your focus today? For that matter, how to fill your precious, limited writing time, all the time?

As a freelance writer and editor who also speaks at conferences and online, teaches webinars and workshops, and leads retreats, I face that question a lot. Should I spend the day planning a future retreat or editing the manuscript in front of me? Coding a webpage or attending a literary event? Should I add a chapter to a novel that may never be published, or write a blog I can post tomorrow? Where does service to my literary community fit? I do work I love, work for prestige, and work for money, and while those things often overlap, they are rarely congruent.

I've also discovered I usually already know the answer—and I bet you do, too. You can think about which project gets you closer to a big life goal, or envision boarding a lifeboat, only allowed to bring one project. But if you look at your list, or your pile, or your laptop, you probably know in your heart. Part of every artist loves to dither, loves to see infinite potential in every project *(Well, yeah, but if I work on that other thing, maybe...)* But that dithering part of us is basically a three-year-old negotiating between a sundress or their superhero suit for preschool today. Mother Creativity doesn't care, as long as we get out the door.

As long as we *get going.*

- Pick the project you're excited about, especially if it's your first book.

- If you make money as a writer and you need money now, pick what makes the most money the fastest.

- If you make money as a writer and you don't need money now, or if you write for fun but want to make money eventually, pick the one you're excited about, because you're going to get to the murky middle and a project you're half-hearted about won't inspire you to push through to the end.

Once you've chosen, your other ideas will spend a few days waving for your attention. This is normal. Your brain is afraid of a big commitment without guaranteed success, so it generates distractions. I am never so good at coming up with great new ideas as when it's time to focus on one project. Every potential writing-related job that I'd be good at (but don't actually want to do) pops up. Every project sounds more fun, more interesting, more exciting than sitting down and doing the work I've chosen.

Stay committed. Write down those shiny new ideas in a designated place. Maybe start a new page in your notebook for each book idea. Remind your brain those ideas will be safe until you get back to them.

In *The Merchant of Venice*, the casket with Portia's offered prize isn't shiny gold or sparkling silver, it's (spoiler!) the casket of lead, inscribed not with a promise but a warning: "Who chooseth me must give and hazard all he hath." *Pick me if you're ready to go all in.*

Hazard all you have. Risk all your eggs in one basket. You will feel opportunity cost, as if you have given up something else valuable. That's OK. Choosing a project doesn't make it the last thing you'll ever write. Not choosing means not starting, or starting without full focus on the task at hand. Not choosing makes writing harder and slower.

Whichever casket Portia's suitors choose, the end result is the same: Shakespeare has written a play. Then he wrote more. Your choice doesn't actually matter. It only matters that you make a choice.

What are you going to write?

ORIGINALITY

It's common to be inspired with a fabulous, new, *original* idea for a book...and then see another book published with almost exactly the same premise. It happens in movies, too—remember *Antz* and *A Bug's Life*, released within six weeks of each other in 1998? *Friends with Benefits* and *No Strings Attached* in 2011?[21]

Many writers worry they don't have anything to say that hasn't already been said. What story can they offer that's new, different, *worth reading?* Who's going to buy their fantasy about thieves and magic in pseudo-Amsterdam after *Six of Crows?* As a memoirist, I've felt that sharp stab when seeing an essay gone viral, about an experience I've had, too. The feeling of *That should be mine.*

---

21 *No Strings Attached* was originally titled...*Friends with Benefits.*

At the literary website *The Millions*, Kaulie Lewis writes,

> *When we say, "all of my ideas have already been had," what we're expressing isn't jealousy, it's doubt in our own creativity, in our worthiness to write about anything at all. Never mind that originality in the broadest sense is hardly possible.... When we say "I should have written that," what we mean is "How unjust, unfair, unkind that you were faster, smarter, and more fortunate than I. How terrible that I have nothing more to offer."*

But no one else can tell our particular, unique, specific story. It's why showing is so much better than telling, why details are better than generalities.

There's room for *Wild* and *A Walk in the Woods*. For *The Hunger Games* and *Battle Royale*. For *Romeo and Juliet* and *West Side Story*. It's not originality that makes an idea compelling, but the specific expression of that idea. I went for a hike—why? I have to kill a bunch of my peers—how? My family won't stop fighting so I can find love—swords or guns?

Traditional publishing's long timeline means your book will not likely be in competition with another just like it that came out while you were writing. Nimble self-publishers can capitalize on similarity to a big-deal book because readers often want more of the same.

For memoirists it is not our story's singularity, but the individuality of our voice that makes our work "original." A truly one-of-a-kind story might not even resonate with readers; part of the value of memoir is seeing ourselves in someone else's world. True stories show *you're not alone. You're not the only one who felt like that. You're not the only one that thing happened to.*

Don't actively copy. Writing to the latest trend is only useful for self-publishers writing in specific, high-consumption genres like Category Romance. The books on today's bestseller lists were written, agented, and sold two or more years ago. But don't let knowing that a trend will pass stop you from writing what excites you. It's entirely possible we'll have cycled right through vampires, or books with *Girl* in the title, or working-class memoir, and come around to those books again by the time you finish, polish and publish.

Writers are seldom original. But we can always be rare. We must discover not only the general appeal of our work but also the nature of the story that is so personal, so intimate, it can only be told by one person.

Cancer memoir but I'm the doctor!

Sword and sorcery but pseudo-Mayan!

M/M Romance but ninjas!

Here is an already-fascinating topic/genre/plotline, and here is a new way to think about it.

My way.

MEMOIR: FIRST DRAFT

Good memoir shares many elements with good fiction: a compelling protagonist, on an interesting journey past powerful obstacles and/or against a fully realized villain, who experiences permanent change within herself, while changing her world.[22]

Yes, you're going to do all that on the page. I have faith in you.

As you work through the Seven Drafts, you will

- find distance from emotional trauma.
- be fair and truthful while honoring your own truth. Present the other people in your story honestly and without fear.
- create a dramatic arc using actual events and find greater meaning in what happened.
- know where and when to start and finish your story. Understand whether your story is "done" yet in real life.
- understand and address the So What Factor.

You're still going to write a wild, free first draft. Get your truth on the page before you fiddle with it for the reader's benefit.

MEMOIR IS NOT THERAPY

...so you must find distance from emotional trauma while writing.

We've all been at *that* reading. The one where our fellow memoirist clears their throat, steps to the podium, and shares with us the graphic details of their sex life. Or molestation. Or domestic abuse.

---

22 If you're writing fiction, you can skip this and the other Memoir sections (I won't be mad). If you're writing a traumatized, first-person protagonist, you may want to read those sections anyway.

We've all cringed that cringe. We've all felt, *I'm so sorry this happened to you, but maybe a roomful of strangers eating dubious cheese cubes is not the place.* We've all walked up after the reading and said, "Wow, that was so brave!"

And sometimes we've been that author. Possibly oblivious, or possibly aware that the room has gone quiet in a not-good way and only our workshop leader is making supportive, professional eye contact.

But sometimes that's the memoir you have to write.

How can an author approach "difficult material" in a way that engenders applause and a box-wine-fueled craft discussion at your book release party, instead of people hugging you and offering their therapist's number? Because "You were so brave!" is nice, but "That was amazing!" is better.

* Remember that therapy gets your feelings out and lets you process. Memoir brings out the *reader's* feelings and inspires them to personal growth.

* Ensure the dramatic arc of your story is made of actions and choices, not just the existence of a terrible situation.[23]

* Include lighter scenes, even if your story is somber. You might use black humor or wry humor or cynical humor, but even a few reasonably funny sentences let the reader breathe.

* Polish your craft to give your story power on the page. Weak writing feels like a teary confession, or worse, listening to someone talk about their summer vacation. Strong writing finds meaning in the moments, ushers readers through your experience, and surprises them on the other side with passion, joy, tragedy or enlightenment.

* Make sure you're ready to tell this particular story. Time and physical separation between you and the problem lets you focus on your story instead of your pain. You can see a larger journey, beyond a series of "things that happened."

Memoirist Dani Shapiro described it beautifully in an interview at *The Millions:*

> As memoirists, the ability to summon up the immediacy
> of our trauma without being sucked into it as we write
> is valuable. It's difficult to walk that edge of telling what
> happened vividly enough for the reader to be in the

---

23 If this is your challenge, flip ahead and read the Drama section in the Story Draft.

moment of happening, while maintaining enough remove to use our writing craft and sense of structure, but that edge is what divides memoir from therapy, what makes a story powerful and life-changing for the reader as well as the writer.

Reconsidering our trauma can indeed be cathartic. Writing it with confidence and purpose makes it worth reading.

Don't be "brave."

Be amazing.

TRUTH & FAIRNESS

How can we be faithful to our own truth while treating others in our book fairly?

By assuming we are part of a larger story and we're only able to see our part.

Imagine Protagonist-You is a character in a play. That character only knows the action of their scenes. A whole world of Hamlet happens behind Ophelia's back: Hamlet's dad's ghost just turned up to say the uncle murdered him and it's up to Hamlet to seek revenge, and now Hamlet's faking mental illness. All Ophelia knows is that her boyfriend's acting like a jerk.

To write a truthful memoir, we must speculate—or ask—what happened when we were offstage. We must seek out what we don't know. This means taking our family, friends, and antagonists seriously. Assuming there's method behind their madness. Make some phone calls. Get snoopy. Ask, "Why did you behave that way? What made that your best choice at the time?" and don't judge the answer.

Don't tell them specifically what you're writing before you're ready. "Oh, I'm really into family history right now," is plenty. Write the book before negotiating the content with yourself or anyone else. First drafts are private. You can choose who to protect in the second draft.

ᴄᴜ

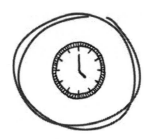

WRITING TIME

Eventually, you're going to have to put down this book (or crawl back out of your research rabbit hole) and start writing.

Many of us think we need an idyllic writing situation: the perfect coffee shop; a quiet, clean house; enough sleep and the right coffee.

Very few of us have a level of privilege that gives us those things regularly. Waiting for ideal writing circumstances means rarely writing.

Or we're hoping for inspiration: an idea will appear that excites us enough to get to work. But if we sit down and start typing, inspiration often shows up to meet us.[24] And then we put one word down after another until we reach the end.

It is absolutely not that simple.

It is exactly that simple.

Get to know your own writing process. I thought, upon retiring from my non-writing job (circus aerialist and fire-eater), that my days would be wide-open vistas. Start the morning with some freewriting, spend an hour or two on a project, break for lunch, edit for a client, wrap up and have a "normal" evening like people whose work is done at five. I thought this would make me "professional" and "grown-up."

Nope.

Turns out I run on a "theatrical" model: several months of rumination, then a panicked rush before a hard, nonnegotiable deadline, followed by some post-deadline tweaking. This is exactly the process for rehearsing a play. Since I spent twenty years training for, staging, and participating in theatrical events, it makes sense that this is how I work. A fellow

---

24 If it doesn't, we'll give inspiration another chance in the Story Draft.

performer/event-planner told me, "I'm going to do about the same quality of job if I do it all at the last minute or if I agonize about it for six weeks. I'd rather concentrate on it all at once." As a writer, I do plenty of drafts—but finishing any single draft needs that sense of urgency, or I don't get it done.

The crunch-time method is not for everyone. I don't have a day job, a child or a pet; my husband cleans; I don't live near my family. But we can all honestly confront our focus as it is, acknowledging the restrictions on our process. We can't change the laws of physics or the behavior of our family and colleagues, but we can limit the writing tasks we set ourselves to fit the time we have. Planning three hours of writing and stopping after fifteen minutes to settle a fight about who's cleaning up cat barf is frustrating and discouraging. But the feeling of *Hey, I set out to edit two pages and I did*, makes us want to do it again tomorrow—*in the time we have.*

Let go of how you "should" work, and dive into how you *do* work.

Are you better at small bites of several things at once? Or is your work better when you gorge on a single project, then collapse exhausted when it's done?

What's your process?

WRITE FIRST

Whether you're a crunch-time person or slow-and-steady-wins-the-race, there's one big secret to getting your project started, middle-d, finished, and out the door in a reasonable (to you) amount of time:

Do it first.

Don't "clear your decks" or check a few things off the list before diving into something "real."

No matter how large your pile or list, work first on the thing you most want done, that you will feel the best about having touched today. If you have fifteen minutes, do fifteen minutes. If you have an hour, or two, do that. If you have time to finish a whole chapter/section/discrete unit, finish it. Maybe you only have five minutes. That's OK. There is nothing more urgent than doing your most important project first.[25]

----

25 If your child must be rushed to the emergency room, take your notebook because there will be waiting.

Everything else can wait.

Check your email later. (Wouldn't they wait if the power went out?)

Return your texts later. (Wouldn't they manage if you lost your phone?)

Tidy your house later. (Wouldn't you leave a bit of mess if you had an urgent appointment?)

Sit when and where you can. Drop your kids at school and pull into the nearest empty parking lot; sit in the café at the gym; wait for the next train. Write on your phone or the back of your homework or the napkins in your purse.

Writing-related-but-not-writing work can wait, too. Writers are pulled in a hundred directions. Building platform. Literary citizenship. Reading widely. Blogging. Publishing essays. Teaching (and making slides...so many slides). It's all too easy to end up with a checked-off list of tasks only tangential to the actual making of words. We are more responsible than ever for finding a home for our work in the world, with more tools and more outlets but less time and support.

While you're finishing a draft, let the other stuff slide. Do less of it. Do it later. All these small, busy tasks can be done after you spend the first and best flush of energy on your top project. What can you give up? Where can you carve out an hour for your words?

What matters less than writing?

INSPIRATION

Inspiration is simply getting excited about an idea. By thinking about stories, reading widely in our genre, noting ideas on scraps of paper and in our phones, we fill a reservoir of creative energy. We can drink from this well of ideas when it's not raining inspiration.

Going to the well regularly creates its own waves, as if each bucket thrown into the reservoir makes a tiny ripple. The more buckets we carry, the wider the ripples spread until we can surf them, flow with the ideas that form into words and appear on the page like dirty magic.

The most successful and published writers I know are not waiting around for the wave to lift them up; they're carrying buckets every day. They are not praying for inspiration or agonizing about the meaning of creativity, they're doing the work.

Keep your eyes open on the world for what your audience cares about and stock up on ideas. Then make a conscious choice to start work instead of waiting for the work to start you.

If you're staring at a blank page, try one of these:

- Use a prompt, but rather than freewriting, write specifically towards the plot of your book. For example, every new sentence starts with the next letter of the alphabet. Or imagine an elevator stopping at a particular numbered floor—write about the main character at that age.

- The Snowflake Method. Randy Ingermanson (he's searchable), suggests building from a simple idea and expanding outward into sentences, paragraphs, character descriptions, scenes, and eventually the whole book. For memoirists, start from what you remember and spiderweb out from those events.

- Write the book-jacket copy that would pique a reader's interest.

- Write the synopsis of the entire plot.

- Use one of the structures in Chapter 2 to rough out key plot points. Write those turning-point scenes first. (You don't have to write a book in order!)

- If you're stuck on the next scene, write the scene after that.

- Write about what you're going to write:

    Scene with Sandy and me in the kitchen, when I realized she was dating my ex and it made me really uncomfortable. She had just dyed her hair blonde and I was alphabetizing the spice rack so I wouldn't say she looked awful. She said...

And before you know it, you're writing the thing instead of about the thing. Or at least getting down the first draft, the one where you tell the story to yourself. The one you can fix in the second draft.

It'll feel weird and awkward and not like your normal happy routine of writing when circumstances are just right (rarely!).

Do it anyway.

Do it now.

PROCRASTINATION

Many people think I'm an overachiever with everything under control. If you're also an overachiever, you probably understand the hollow laughter that inspires. The symptoms of organization—paper planners, to-do apps, regular social media appearances—often mask what feels like abject laziness. Sure, I checked six things off my list...but I did them because they were easy, instead of working on a more difficult, more important goal. I sent six tweets instead of working on my proposal. Ran errands instead of analyzing the structure of my novel. Read a hundred pages for editorial clients instead of writing one of my own.

Often, what feels like "laziness" is actually

- anxiety about the outcome
- self-doubt about our ability
- not knowing where to start
- overwhelm from too many "priorities"

Writing a book is two massive tasks:

1) You're writing a book.

2) You're learning how to write a book.[26]

Here's what helps me get past procrastination:

1) Priority means one.[27]

You can't have a list of "priorities" because a priority is one thing. Sure, your priorities may change as you shift from your artist self to your family self or from the office to the studio to your home. But at any given time, you can only have one priority. Pick one and pick it on purpose.

2) Many projects=no projects.

The amount of great ideas we have and are capable of executing far exceed the number of hours available to work. Being able to do a thing well doesn't mean the thing fits our plans. It's

---

26 If this is not your first book, you're writing a book, and you're learning how to write *this* book.

27 I learned this from cartoonist Jessica Abel, who also runs workshops for creatives learning to control their time.

OK to put other projects on the back burner while focusing on one until it's done.[28]

3) Tiny steps.

Like, ridiculous-tiny. For example, one of my 2020 goals was "be healthier," which is not a doable goal, because really, what would you do if I pointed and said, "Your job right this minute is to be healthier"? *Um, I'll get right on that?*

So I backed up: I want to drink more water.

Still not a doable step. Back up more: I need a water bottle I can carry around and also wash out and reuse.

That I can do. It needs to be small and lightweight, because I won't carry a heavy one. Step one isn't even "buy water bottle"—it's "look online to see what lightweight water bottles exist," so I know what I'm shopping for.

Most of us have big ambitions, and in the long run, that's good. Setting smaller, immediate goals creates momentum.

In a workshop with Andre Dubus III, he told us about writing *House of Sand and Fog* after his three children were born. He and his wife both worked full time and the hours outside work focused on parenting. He taught as an adjunct at several schools and picked up construction work on the side. How did he write?

Seventeen minutes at a time.

Each morning, Andre started his morning commute twenty minutes early. Each night, he came home twenty minutes late. He wrote in his car, parked in a cemetery. It was empty of visitors at 5 AM and 6 PM. Seventeen minutes at a time, he wrote in pencil in a notebook. In summer, sweating with the car windows down; in winter, with the heat on until he got a carbon monoxide headache. All the way to the end of the book.

True, some writers work best with large swaths of time. Writing residencies, the privileges of a spouse able to support the entire family or household help, co-working spaces—all grant us the luxury of time. But most of us have more things in our day than our artistic time, particularly if we're not making a living (yet) at our art. It's hard to carve out substantial time in a busy family and/or professional life.

---

28 I hedge on this a little: one personal project and one client project at a time; rotating lets me rest my brain.

"Oh yes, I wrote four words a day for twelve years and then I had a book," sounds a little ridiculous. For most of us, short work periods mean rethinking our process. There's no settling-in time, no getting sucked down a research rabbit hole that somehow led to Facebook.

But there's value in touching the manuscript more often, even for shorter periods of time. Just like the atmosphere of a retreat, when our brain knows "I'll be back at the page in a few hours," we can find ourselves working through a plotline while commuting, or suddenly realizing why a character did *that awful thing* while we're in the shower.

The first week of short writing bursts usually sucks, because establishing a new habit takes time. But after ten days or so, the flow will be triggered by sitting down.

Maybe it'll work for you. Maybe it won't. But there's only one way to find out.

5) External deadlines.

I wish I could put "Finish X by this date" on my calendar, but I just don't. It doesn't have to be a deadline imposed by another person, but I need a reason beyond "I want to be done by then" to finish a project.

I want to finish my new writing retreat website before attending a festival where I'm talking about writing retreats.

I want to finish my book proposal before going to the AWP conference so I can meet small presses and be ready to send to anyone who seems interested.

Humans respond to reasons—even small, arbitrary reasons. Giving yourself a reason for the deadline makes it feel more serious, more important to actually meet.

Next time you're feeling "lazy," ask: Am I anxious about the outcome? Worried I don't have the ability to do this? Overwhelmed by where to start? Made helpless by too many "priorities"?

Then pick one tiny step.

DON'T EDIT AS YOU WRITE

"How do you stop editing as you write?"

I was a little confused when a workshop participant asked this question, because that's normally not my problem. (My problem is Ass In Chair.) But everyone else in the room nodded. How could they keep the writing flow going without second-guessing every word?

Our brain nags us to edit, because we're afraid that if we don't stop and fix it RIGHT NOW, it's going to be terrible forever. How can we reassure our tiny, frightened lizard brain, "It's OK, I'm going to come back to it, I promise"?

Online, there are some common solutions to compulsive self-editing:

- **Turn off your monitor.** I think I'd freak out and have to keep turning it on to hit *Save* every minute. For fabulous touch-typists maybe?

- **Start each day with a fresh page.** At the end of a writing session, copy the last sentence into a new document along with some instructions to yourself about what's next. Next session, start from there.

- **Write with a timer.** Don't stop or go back until the timer rings. *Bad Tourist* author Suzanne Roberts does a variation on this: she sets a timer for an hour of dedicated writing time. If she checks social media, gets lost in research, or leaves the chair, she restarts the timer. Try restarting each time you catch yourself editing.

- **Write by hand.** It's harder to delete pen on paper.

I don't do any of those things. What keeps me from self-editing too early, or letting self-doubt get in my way?

- **Edit first.** For longer projects, I spend the first 15-20 minutes reviewing yesterday's work. Tweaking words and sentences helps me get back into the story. I rarely do a massive rewrite–if something's pretty bad, I'll scrap it and write a new scene addressing the problems in yesterday's work.

- **Work on deadline.** Most of my *Brevity* blogs get written about two hours before going live. I feel worse about being late than being imperfect.

- **Look ahead.** The work I did yesterday can be bad—terrible, even. But I'm not promising every word a place in the next draft. I already know I'll be cutting whole chapters and rearranging paragraphs. That lowers the "fix it now!" urge.

- **Plan to practice.** Musicians painstakingly learn plenty of music they'll never record. Artists fill pages with drawings they'll never work on again. Dancers take class to maintain their technique for their entire career. Why should writers be exempt from skill development? Why not write pages and pages that are simply practice and not an early draft of something great? Every artist spends time on foundations that don't directly become a finished piece. Writers need skill development, too.

Whatever tips and tricks work for you, it boils down to letting go of the dream of being perfect. Inside all our hearts is a tiny hope:

I'm going to make something beautiful, on the first try, without working very hard. My emotional experience and love of story will compensate for any lack of skill or coherence. I'm entitled to have my thoughts come out exactly right on the page, the first time, and as long as I'm still messing with it, it's still the first time.

It doesn't work that way.

We know it doesn't.

Let it go.

Let it flow.

WHAT IF I SUCK?

> *Setting out to do your first draft is ultimately setting out to break your own heart. You have this magical idea in your head and no first draft will ever ever ever match that. It's so humbling. So as soon as you sit down and it's not coming out how you imagine in your head, I think that is what we identify as writers block. But it's not, it's just frustration.*
>
> Laura Jane Williams (@authorlaurajane)

What if you finish your book and it's terrible? What if your novel is boring, your memoir a festival of self-pity? What if, as a writer, you suck?

We've all read a bad book. Most of us have read a bad published book; many of us have read a bad manuscript, perhaps a friend's, that we felt obligated to read to the bitter end. And then tell the author something noncommittal and encouraging.

You just don't know what you did there!

You make it all seem so spontaneous on the page....

You...literature...wow.

Truly bad writing—rather than slickly-crafted airport thrillers or blandly-told stories that somehow tap into the zeitgeist to sell millions—is, as Toby Litt writes in the *Guardian*, "a love poem addressed by the self to the self." He calls these authors "excuse writers."

> *Bad writers bulwark themselves against a confrontation with their own badness by reference to other writers with whom they feel they share certain defence-worthy characteristics. They form defensive admirations: "If Updike can get away with these kind of half-page descriptions of women's breasts, I can too" or "If Virginia Woolf is a bit woozy on spatiality, on putting things down concretely, I'll just let things float free". If another writer's work survives on charm, you will never be able to steal it, only imitate it in an embarrassingly obvious way.*

Imitating the greats—consciously or unconsciously—is a wonderful exercise. But most of us can't truly pull off another writer's style in our own work. Anyone good enough to accomplish that likely has their own voice they'd rather write in.

Bad nonfiction and memoir often happen because a writer wants to tell a particular story about their experiences. Until they've told it, they feel they can't move on. But because the content is so important, they don't mess around enough with the execution to learn how writing works. They can only tell what they experienced, rather than giving larger meaning to the reader. Ultimately, they lack the will to betray the material sufficiently to make it true.

For novelists, bad books happen when we love the story or the world we have created so much, we're blind to gaping plot holes, cardboard characters, or wooden dialogue. First novels at 150K+ word counts are often the product of writers who love their own work too much to be able to improve it.

Bad writers think they're good. That's why their work doesn't get better. Good writers learn to analyze their own work, and revise until they're proud to show it to the world. They are willing to accept that it isn't enough to have a powerful story—and they remember that every time someone at a party says, "I have a great idea! You should write it and we'll split the profits!"

Good writers know an idea isn't enough. Good writing comes from craft plus compelling story plus the will to shape the story into something considered, focused, interesting, and beautiful.

And along the way, a lot of messing around to learn how writing works, and how to make it work better every time.

You may not write a *publishable* book the first time, or every time. But you're probably not going to write a truly bad one. The primary way to know you don't suck as a writer?

You're asking the question.

RESTARTING

What if you're trying to restart a project that's languished, unfinished, for months or years? The one you keep thinking:

one day...

when I have the time...

and can dig out my notes...

and have a few solid hours to really dive in...

Newsflash: that day is never coming. The calendar isn't going to magically pop up "Today You Can Focus Entirely on That One Project." If there's a book, or an essay, or a story on the back burner, and you want to finish it, you must choose to bring it into your daily work.

Take some low-pressure time to assess what's in the files and think about what you really want to finish. Ask of your project, *What am I waiting for? What's holding me back?* Without the stress of "I have to write something good right now," scribble a bit about the steps you'll need to take to move forward.

If you need to generate some personal excitement, choose your most supportive and least critical reader and share a couple of passages that you liked when you originally wrote them. For one project restart, I read aloud pages from the work-in-progress to my decidedly non-literary husband. I kept finding more bits I liked and wanted to read to him. His questions and his "That's not too bad" (he's British, so that's practically seventy-six trombones of enthusiasm) made me excited to dive back in.

Restarting a chosen project doesn't have to be from the beginning. You don't have to rethink the whole project or make a huge plan or set aside two weeks when your decks are clear (let me just pencil that in for never).

Start small, by "touching" the manuscript almost every day. Not a minimum number of words or pages, but taking five minutes on the bus or in the shower to actively think about the project.

Open up the file and read one page. Tweak the grammar in one chapter. Make a playlist that brings you back to the mood and voice of the story. Keep touching it, gently renewing your interest and energy until you're ready to write.

Not finding that energy? Give it your best try. Set aside a day or a week or whatever interval works for you to finish your shit. Sit your ass down and decide if you want this book or not. If you want it, finish it. See what it feels like to do whatever it takes, to revise or seek help or break it apart and rebuild. And if that feeling sucks, let the project go.

Let go of the hundredweights of half-pages that once seemed like a good idea. Trust that in your head, in your heart, in your skill, there are more ideas—multitudes of them. Your next beautiful book may be hiding under the weight of that thing you feel obligated to finish. Be grateful you learned what that piece taught you and commit fully to something else.

Sometimes the space for what you want is filled with what you've settled for. Don't settle for half-finished.

THE STORY DRAFT

The Story Draft is creative work done technically. This is where you take your beautiful pile of words (your grocery cart!) from the Vomit Draft and organize them into a delicious book.

In this draft, you'll use "In A World…" to see if you actually have a story, and the Passover Question to determine if that story is starting in the right place. We'll talk about the difference between story, plot, and structure and analyze which events belong in your plot and why.

Memoirists will tackle the So What Factor. Both novelists and memoirists will consider whether your story has dramatic action or is merely a dramatic situation, and how all books are mysteries—even memoirs.

You'll be able to "try on" a couple of different structures for your story, uncovering plot holes and missing set-up, or even discovering that the story doesn't end where you stopped in the Vomit Draft.

The Story Draft finishes with a round of basic technical editing, making the next draft more pleasant to work on and keeping you in touch with your book on days when time or creativity is in short supply.

Start the Story Draft by taking some quiet time with your favorite beverage[29] and your notebook, and considering these questions:

---

29 Something fancy—you're about to start a big draft and you deserve it. Garnishes are always encouraging.

- Why are you telling this story? What's your connection to the material?
- Who needs to read it? Who is going to love it? Who will be moved by it? Why are they waiting for your book right now?
- Do you love this book enough to finish it? Even when you need to go back and do yet another draft?
- Write down some things you love about this story, so you can remind yourself why you're here when the writing gets tough.

The Story Draft may be the hardest of the Seven Drafts, but once you've learned and internalized these tools, they'll serve your writing forever.

STORY VS. PLOT VS. STRUCTURE

There are plenty of lists of "writing rules." Many of the world's great writers are breaking them—or subverting them so well it looks like breaking the rules. How do you know which rules to follow and which to violate? How can you make rule-breaking a choice, rather than ignorance or sloppiness?

By knowing the conventions of story, plot, and structure.

Story is the actions characters do, why they do them, and how they change.

> We robbed that bank to get Mariel's sister's leukemia treatment, but the real heist was the friends we made along the way.

Stories are not meant to "send a message" or "educate the reader." Even if you're writing narrative nonfiction or a journalistic exposé, reader learning comes from engagement in a fascinating story.

Plot is the events happening to or around the characters, or resulting from their actions.

> First, we needed a getaway car. Then Mariel had to get to the gun range and learn to shoot. When we got to the bank, we screwed up and got trapped in the vault. That's where I realized I was in love with Mariel's sister....

Plot has to make sense. The events must follow each other as cause and effect, while also surprising the reader with unexpected but absolutely logical outcomes. The events must change the characters permanently. Events trigger emotions and actions, and those actions create more events.

Structure is how the plot is revealed through the order and format you use to tell the story.

> *"Wanna know why I'm on this Caribbean island, married to this beautiful woman with a full head of hair? Well, this one time, me and Mariel robbed this bank..."*

Structure can make a story simple, or more complicated. Mysteries depend on structure, because the writer must decide which clues to reveal when, about what has *already happened,* so that the final clue completes and reveals a pattern the reader couldn't see until that moment. Fairy tales are stories, and modern retellings add more plot, deeper characterization, and often use a new structure to surprise the reader who already knows the story.

As Paul Ashton from the BBC Writersroom puts it, "Plot is the route you take, story is the journey you make." And I'll add, "Structure is the map."

STORY, PLOT & STRUCTURE IN A SERIES

If you're writing a series, each book must also stand alone.[30] In each subsequent book, the reader must know enough about the past to get what's happening, but not so much that it bores people who finished Book One yesterday. Each book must end with a strong, satisfying conclusion, while also advancing the larger conflict stretching through the series.

Many authors convert an overlong Book One into a trilogy rather than undertake the pain and tedium of cutting events that felt key on first writing. It's frustrating to the author to rethink the plot book-by-book, but more so to the reader who gets lost in backstory they don't need until Book Three.

Rather than writing blindly into 193,000 words and then deciding "Sure, it's a trilogy!" plan out the big-picture journey the characters will make. Divide that journey into logical book-length sections, each with a goal that must be achieved to get to the big ending. Then focus on your first section as Book One.

---

30 Plenty of YA trilogies end Books One and Two on cliffhangers and plenty of online reviews complain about that.

MEMOIR: STORY

Memoir already lacks suspense. We lose the novelist's standby of "will this character make it?" Readers know you survived—you wrote a book about it.

Most of us are not such brilliant writers that our shining prose fascinates regardless of the subject. Most of us are working hard to raise our storytelling skills to the level of the story's own power, because raw trauma is not enough.

An interesting story also isn't enough.[31] Interesting stories make newspaper and magazine articles. As Bloomsbury Press Publisher and Editorial Director Peter Ginna points out at Nieman Storyboard,

> *The most critical difference between a book and a magazine or newspaper article is that the publisher has to convince someone to part with twenty-five dollars or more for this story and this story alone, and perhaps more important, to invest several hours of his or her life in reading it. That's a pretty high threshold. To get across it, you need a topic that is more than merely interesting and a narrative that's more than well-wrought. **You need a story that has a significance beyond itself, and you need to convey that significance to the reader.** [emphasis in original]*

That's the secret to writing a publishable memoir: write a book that does something for the reader.

Write the book that beautifully expresses the pain of your addiction, or the trauma of your childhood, or the desperation of your divorce...

---

31 Unless your story made national/international news for more than a week, in which case write that sucker because the agent will help you make it relevant to the reader.

...but revise it to directly help the reader.

Beyond "My story is universal."

Beyond "People need to know this situation exists."

This is the **So What Factor.** Asking "So what?" isn't dismissing a writer's achievement in committing their story to the page or diminishing the importance of their journey. Answering "So what?" moves your story from personal to universal and makes your journey powerful and life-changing (or a beautiful reflective experience) for your readers.

Yes, the great gift of memoir is showing readers, "You're not the only one who felt like this." But unless we are writing National Book Award-level prose, our personal pain is not enough, no matter how honestly we express it. Sympathy for a stranger's problems doesn't last 285 pages.

As an editor, when a promising manuscript veers from story into eulogy, I sometimes howl internally, *Why are you telling us this...*

...nobody cares about your kid!

...nobody cares about your pet!

...nobody cares about your dead relative!

Transforming your painful (or joyful!) story into a book that sells means using your writing skill and personal credentials to tie your problem directly to the reader's own experience. This does not mean writing self-help, but showing specific, actionable steps the reader might be inspired to take.

What does doing something for the reader look like in practice?

- **Medical memoir:** My dad died and it was horrifying and Mom was no help at all and here's how I navigated a medical system designed to rip us off, and what I learned about myself and about Medicare.
- Also, I'm hilarious.

The reader gets: OMG my parent had funny death stuff too and I felt so bad laughing but it's OK to laugh, and wow, I don't have to pay that bill!

- **Death of a child memoir**: My kid died and it was horrifying and here's how I lived in a fantasy world where drug abuse didn't look like my kid, and what I learned.
- Also, I'm a brilliant writer.

The reader gets: I'm not the only one who missed the signs and I don't have to feel dumb and guilty because I see why she did too, and wow! That paragraph puts my grief into words!

- **Death of a pet memoir**: My dog died and it was sad and here's what I learned about alternative pet medicine, when to stop medical intervention, and how I knew it was time to let her go.
- Also, I'm a veterinarian with stories about how others knew when to treat their pet or let them go.

The reader gets: I'm not a terrible pet owner for not buying another kidney for Princess, and wow! Now I have specific ways to process my grief without hearing "It's only a dog"!

- **Family memoir**: My grandchild is precocious and I taught myself how to talk about climate change and human destructiveness without crushing a child's spirit.
- Also, I'm an educator and will fill you with hope.

The reader gets: I don't have to be a scientist to have an age-appropriate conversation with my six-year-old about human extinction, and wow! I'm a little more hopeful myself!

H is for Hawk teaches readers about falconry and processing grief through new experience. *Wild* inspires taking a physical journey to purge our past. *How To Be Black* examines race in America through a personal lens, and the lessons are truly absorbed through comedy.

Pour out your love and tragedy and joy in words. Maybe you'll have a 285-page eulogy. Maybe it'll be the first draft of a book you'll sell. For readers, your triumphant physical achievement, crazy childhood, or journey through recovery is not enough. Honoring your dead is not enough. Not your dead mom, your dead kid, or your dead dog. Write to honor your love, yourself and your kin. Revise to do something for the reader.

EXERCISE: WHAT'S IN IT FOR THE READER?

Take a look at your own manuscript:

1) Is the first chapter backstory and exposition because "No one will understand my family if I don't tell our history"?

We are not as unique as we think. That's why memoir is "universal." Cut those pages. Get the reader hooked emotionally. Identify your problem that might also be their problem. Fill in backstory later as needed.

2) Got more than two pages in a row about how great someone was, or what living with them was like?

A eulogy is not a story. Cut to the best paragraph or the most significant gesture. Show them through actions. Put their greatness in context with your problem:

My husband was so thoughtful; when I was widowed I didn't know how to pay the electric bill and here's how I navigated that.

My dog was so amazing I had to learn how to grieve an animal when she died and here's what I did.

3) Is how you tell your story inspiring, hopeful, or educational? Not textbook or self-help, but can readers productively channel your experience to walk away as better people? What actions do you show yourself taking that a reader could take themselves?

STORY

In a world...where a million books are published each year...a ruthlessly caring editor must share a seven-draft process to save the world from terrible writing, stop authors wasting time and money on problems they can fix themselves, and help them become the writers they hope to be.

You have a draft. Do you have a story?

While editing a client's work, I found myself wrestling with how to say, "You have 170,000 words, but you don't have a story." They were well-written words, and some of them were interesting words...but as Gertrude Stein wrote about Oakland, California, "There's no there there." Nothing was at stake. No one was risking their health or happiness in service of a greater goal.

As writers, we're often told, "Raise the stakes." How can we tell if the stakes are high enough in our own work, even before asking for the opinions of our fellow authors or our teachers? How do we know if we have a story?

The "In a World" test.

Think about the cheesy movie-trailer cliché. There's a shot of alien-created devastation. Or a sunrise over a battlefield. Or a sunset over a castle. A deep voice[32] intones,

> *"In a world..."*

That's the stasis, the situation as it is now, that cannot be sustained. Overturning this situation is a high-risk, high-stakes problem.

> *"One man..."*

---

32 The deep voice belongs to late movie trailer narrator Don LaFontaine, creator of the phrase.

The protagonist—the person who primarily drives the story. In fiction, the hero or main character. In memoir, the author. In our imaginary movie trailer, probably a Hemsworth.

"...must..."

The quest/goal/objective. What the hero wants. The rest of the movie will be about the hero overturning the unacceptable world or situation to get to the goal.

The movie trailer usually flashes moments of the primary obstacles (including character flaws or physical challenges), shows the villains, and gives a sense of what the hero will lose if they fail.

In fiction, the "In a world" storyline is almost always in the first chapter, often in the first paragraph. The moment is usually pretty easy to figure out:

> *In a world...where Theodore is alone and on the run... one kid must locate a priceless painting before he and his friend are killed by gangsters.* (The Goldfinch)

> *In a world...where poverty can kill you and a girl is a washed-up old maid at twenty...one girl must marry a rich husband without violating her own scruples and avoid the jerk next door.* (Pride and Prejudice)

In nonfiction, the premise should be clear in the title and sub-title of the book. Seriously. Right there on the cover, expressed in less than a sentence. What's the untenable existing situation? What's at stake for the narrator (memoir) or the reader (self-help)?

> *Wild: From Lost to Found on the Pacific Coast Trail*

> *Talking to Strangers: What We Should Know About the People We Don't Know*

Within the first chapter, make the stakes clear. What's the positive effect on the reader or narrator's health and happiness if the situation is overturned, and how will they be harmed if they fail?

> *In a world...where I've screwed up my relationships, taken too many drugs, and slept with too many people...I must walk 2600 miles to find myself.* (Wild)

In a world...where my mom is rooting through a Dumpster and I just drive on by...I must make my peace with the rotten past that made me who I am. (The Glass Castle)

Chances are, if it's hard to find your "In a world..." moment, your stakes aren't high enough. The starting place isn't untenable enough. The protagonist doesn't have enough at stake to make the story compelling.

EXERCISE: IN A WORLD...

Fill in this sentence with your own story, adjusting the connecting language as needed.

Fiction/Memoir/Active Story: In untenable SITUATION, PROTAGONIST must ACTION against OBSTACLE toward GOAL or else/because STAKES.

Memoir/Literary Fiction/Quiet Story: In ENVIRONMENT, HERO must EXPERIENCE against PRESSURE toward ENLIGHTENMENT and READER TAKEAWAY needed in CURRENT MOMENT.

Now stand up, deepen your voice, and state the premise of your book. Does it sound cheesy and overdramatic? If it does, you've got a story.

OBJECTIVE

One man must...

Your protagonist must want something. Achieving their goal must require them to take action, and they must change as a person to achieve it fully. Your main character doesn't have to state her objective flat-out. But you, the author, need to know what she wants, so that she can spend the rest of the book fighting to get it.[33]

---

33 Or, if you're writing literary fiction, despairing that he's never gotten his objective while drifting slowly through a malaise of symbolic visuals suggesting his goal and the tragic personal character flaws preventing him from achieving it.

I want to challenge myself physically to see if there's a better "me" in here. (Wild)

I want to overcome my humble origins by amassing wealth and power. (Wolf Hall)

I want to survive and achieve the destiny I was born for. (Life After Life)

One more thing I learned in drama class: the objective is an *action* you can communicate in one sentence.

"James Bond wants to prove himself again on active duty" is an objective. "James Bond is sad about the death of his parents and sees M as a mother figure, needing to win her approval by taking bigger and bigger risks and lying about his physical condition—" is zzzzzzz...sorry, what?

The "I Want" Song

Musicals are terrific at establishing a main character's objective.

Usually, the opening song of a musical is the "community" song—this is who we are, this is what our lives are like. In Disney's *Beauty and the Beast,* the prologue shows how the Beast came to live in a spooky castle with dancing cutlery. In *The Little Mermaid,* "Fathoms Below" introduces mermaids and their undersea kingdom.

Almost always, a musical's second major song is the "I Want" song, stating the protagonist's main goal. The lyrics often literally say "I want."

Belle establishes more community by singing about the daily routine, then breaks out with, "There must be more than this provincial life!"

I want a life with more books and people who can talk about them.

Ariel sings that despite her wealth of physical possessions, she wants to be part of another world.

I want to live on land.

In *My Fair Lady,* Eliza Doolittle sings, "All I want is a room somewhere, far away from the cold night air," and as the song develops, she wants not only the trappings of a simple, comfortable life ("warm face warm hands warm feet") she wants someone to share it with; someone to love her.

Consider your story: Does the character establish what she wants and fight to get it? Or is a reasonably decent life interrupted by a force your hero must deal with, in order to keep what she has?

STARTING WITH SUCK

Your book must start in the right place, right away. The "In a world..." doesn't have to be perfectly clear from the first page, but there does need to be a strong sense of something important happening from the very beginning. Beginnings make readers stand by the airport bookshelf until they have to run for the gate. Beginnings make kids stay up with a flashlight under the covers.[34]

Your book must start with SUCK. An event or action that is

Simple

Unexpected

Concrete

and **K**icks off the story.

Simple

ONE "inciting incident" that is also a case study for what's wrong in the character's life:[35]

> *A bored farm boy is fixing a robot when it projects a hologram message of a woman asking for help.* (Star Wars)[36]

> *A poor flower girl overhears a man bragging that he can teach anyone—even her—to speak like a lady.* (My Fair Lady)

34 Want to raise a reader instead of a screen reader? Buy them a flashlight and pretend you don't notice them sneaking books after bedtime.

35 If you are writing epic fantasy, science fiction, or historical fiction, one SUCK per plotline. Think of the enormous and dense *Les Misérables*, with four or five major stories. But each plot starts with simple triggers: A pregnant woman is abandoned. A man steals... a loaf of bread. Two young people fall in love at first sight as a revolution starts.

36 I'm going to mix movie and book examples throughout, because it's more important that you have at least one example you know well than it is for me to be snobby about "LIT-er-ah-tyoor."

A young man sees his father's ghost. The ghost says, "I was murdered—prove it and bring the killer to justice. Also, he's your stepfather." (Hamlet)

Unexpected

The incident is different from what always happens. Start the story with the moment of change:

Most hide-and-seek games are normal; today I went into a closet and found a snowy forest where I had tea with a mythical creature. (The Lion, the Witch and the Wardrobe)

Most days I don't get any mail; today I got my acceptance letter to wizard school. (Harry Potter and the Sorcerer's Stone)

This is true even in nonfiction:

Most business books are about success; this one is about failure. (Redefining Success: Still Making Mistakes)

Most families send their kids to school; mine didn't. (Educated)

Concrete

Something specific happens. You can point to it in reality or describe it in one sentence:

We killed Bunny by pushing him over the edge of the cliff. (The Secret History)

Elle Woods was expecting a proposal but instead she got dumped. (Legally Blonde)

Ursula pulled a gun on Hitler. (Life After Life)

Kickoff

The incident results in the protagonist **taking action**. Your hero must say "yes" to the adventure and begin her journey to personal change/changing the world.

In most books, the SUCK is typically in the first two pages. Browsing my shelves for examples, I noticed something powerful. Book after book, the trigger was in the *first line*—wham! Keep reading! Something amazing just happened!

> *They say that just before you die your whole life flashes before your eyes, but that's not how it happened for me.* (Before I Fall)

Even if a story then flashes back to show what led up to the inciting incident, the incident itself was usually in the first sentence:

> *The snow in the mountains was melting and Bunny had been dead for several weeks before we came to understand the gravity of our situation.* (The Secret History)

We find out the narrator, Richard, and his student friends killed Bunny in the next paragraph. The author flashes back and whips through Richard's childhood to show how and why he's the person who needs to join a group of eventual killers, then gets the narrator off to college to meet them on page 5 (it's a 524-page book).

SUCK can happen in action, situation, or voice.

Action SUCK

> *I was sitting in a taxi, wondering if I had overdressed for the evening, when I looked out the window and saw Mom rooting through a Dumpster.* (The Glass Castle)

Simple: sitting in a taxi, dressed for a party.

Unexpected: that's *Mom* rooting in a Dumpster.

Concrete: Mom and Dumpster are both things you can touch.

The narrator takes an action—she chooses not to stop and interact with her mother—which Kicks off the story: How did I come to be the person who drives on by when my homeless mother is on the sidewalk?

Situation SUCK

> *It was 7 minutes after midnight. The dog was lying on the grass in the middle of the lawn in front of Mrs. Shears's house. Its eyes were closed. It looked as if it was running on its side, the way dogs run when they think they are*

chasing a cat in a dream. But the dog was not running or asleep. The dog was dead. There was a garden fork sticking out of the dog. (The Curious Incident of the Dog in the Night-Time)

Simple: there's a dead dog on the lawn.

Unexpected: there's a *dead* dog on the lawn.

Concrete: there's a dead *dog* on the *lawn*. Impaled with a garden fork.

Kickoff: Christopher must investigate why a dead dog is on his lawn, and that investigation drives the rest of the book.

Voice SUCK

Call me Ishmael. I won't answer to it, because it's not my name, but it's much more agreeable than most of the things I've been called. "Call me that-weird-chick-who-says-fuck-a-lot" is probably classier, and it makes a way more respectable beginning than the sentence I'd originally written, which was about how I'd just run into my gynecologist at Starbucks and she totally looked past me like she didn't even know me. (Let's Pretend This Never Happened)

Jenny Lawson breaks a lot of rules with this opening. It's rambling, deliberately "clever," and doesn't actually start the main story (how she grew up and came to be the person she is). But for the purpose of a funny memoir, this opening makes the reader want to spend time with the author.

It establishes her voice as Simple: smart, but not a lot of big words, with clarity even in stream-of-consciousness.

Unexpected: gynecologist! Starbucks! Fuck!

Concrete: she is speaking directly to the reader as if they are already in conversation.

Kickoff: she invites the reader to join her to discover how she became "that-weird-chick-who-says-fuck-a-lot."

Start your book strong, start from the first page, and start a story. Start with SUCK.

EXERCISE: Starting With SUCK

Take a moment and think about a favorite book or movie—what's the SUCK that starts the story? Now go look it up or watch it, and notice how early it shows up. If the inciting incident shows up after five pages or after the five-minute mark, why did the writer do that? Does it work?

How does the SUCK show immediately who we're with, what their problem is, and why we should care?

Now look at your own book—what Simple, Unexpected, Concrete event Kicks off the story?

THE PASSOVER QUESTION

Don't start at the beginning. Start at the interesting.

DongWon Song

"Why is this night different than all other nights?" is one of the Four Questions asked in a Jewish Passover celebration. It's also the question a writer needs to answer as their story begins. What is changing right now? Why does the story start here?

You should be able to answer in a single sentence:

This is the day my sister's name is picked in the kill-kids-on-TV lottery.

This is the day my wife went missing.

For the change to have an impact, the reader needs a sense of what the stasis was—but as the story continues. Don't start with backstory. Don't start with a "normal" day. **Establish what "all other nights"** *used to* **look like as the hero experiences the events making this one different.** Plot happens when a character's expectations are different from reality. Show us the character's surprise at the way things are now, or how the world around them reacts when the hero tries to behave "normally." Flash back later if information is needed that can't come out any other way.

Avoid starting with

* waking up[37]
* weather or physical environment
* backstory (even if triggered by something big) or information about the world or situation
* a prologue that doesn't have a major payoff later in the book
* showing off how clever or shocking the writer is
* a dream (the reader gets involved and then you rip them off by saying "ha-ha that wasn't real!")
* main character describing themselves in a reflection[38]
* too many characters (it's like getting dumped at a party with no one to introduce the reader around)
* a minor character who won't be massively important (they're lovely, now cut them and put them in another book)
* the character alone/doing a mundane action/thinking about what's wrong with their life

Maybe you are the brilliant writer who will make those scenes compelling—but why work that hard?[39] Even when "normal" sucks, look for the change. It's not that the Hunger Games kill kids on TV—that happens every year. Today is different because they pick the heroine's sister. If anyone else's name came out of the bowl, Katniss would feel bad and the story would be over at the end of Chapter One.

The Passover Question determines a book's true beginning: the story starts when the bad situation gets *personal*.

DRAMA

Are you telling a story or only recounting a series of experiences?

---

37 I have woken up in jail, in a strange bed, and from being knocked unconscious and none of them were especially surprising. The story is what got me there or how I got out.

38 Either kind.

39 For a wonderful example of showing "normal" and subverting it at the same time, watch the opening of Stranger Than Fiction. Then watch the rest of it—the movie is a brilliant examination of a writer committing fully to her established plot while writing herself out of a dead end.

Experiences happen in dramatic *situations*.

Stories have dramatic *action*.

News is dramatic situations, worthy of reporting but mostly conveying information. The reader's emotional reaction is grounded in their own experience meeting the facts, rather than empathy for the protagonist, or a desire to see them "win."

Car Crash Claims Three

is a dramatic situation. But it's not a story unless the larger picture includes a protagonist taking an action.

Crash Claims Three: Earnhardt Jr. Vows to Race Again

Crash Claims Three: Outsider Candidate Calls for Traffic-Cam Bill

It's not enough to have an intolerable situation in the larger world—drama involves an intolerable situation for the protagonist.

Take *Gone With the Wind*, a problematic book that reflects the white supremacist mindset of its time —and supported structural racism—but is useful for this example.[40] The story takes place before, during, and after the American Civil War, a dramatic situation that changes the lives of every character in the book, moving them from place to place, destroying their homes and their way of life.

But Scarlett O'Hara's story starts when she finds out her crush Ashley Wilkes is marrying Melanie Hamilton.

Scarlett survives the Civil War because she can't let go of her hope of getting together with Ashley. Every decision she makes is based on the answer to "Will this get me closer to Ashley?" Many of the book's events occur in Atlanta because it's a place where the war was especially bad, but the events happen to and around Scarlett because she moved there to be closer (by proxy) to Ashley.

Scarlett's dramatic situation is "There's a big war changing my life." But her dramatic action is "The man I want doesn't want me and I'm going to change that." The obstacles to her quest create more action: She escapes the burning of Atlanta, now how is she going to get closer to Ashley? His wife Melanie is

---

40 Read Aisha Harris's essay at Slate, "How Movie Theaters, TV Networks, and Classrooms Are Changing the Way They Show Gone With the Wind" for more on the legendary movie-vs-huge racism issue.

super sweet to Scarlett, now how is she going to get closer to Ashley?

Living in interesting times isn't enough. Inside the war/dystopia/shattered family/quest for the ring is the key moment where the issue intersects the protagonist's life and starts her dramatic journey.

MEMOIR: DRAMA

Many of us write memoirs around a dramatic *situation*. Cancer. Death of a loved one. Running a marathon. Beating addiction. Where memoirists often get stuck is finding dramatic *action*. Our lived situation felt incredibly dramatic as we navigated the hundred small actions it took to get through every day. But in retrospect, what do they add up to?

If one has been, say, an abused child, that sucks. But the hard, cold reality is that abused children have already been written about by some of the best writers in the world. Even our own honesty can be undermined by the subject of child abuse in general—no matter how bad we've had it, someone's read worse in *Reader's Digest*. What lets us write fresh truths about any horrible-but-not-uncommon situation is telling our story, rather than listing our experiences.

Your dramatic action must be more compelling than the tragedy/triumph of the situation. If your memoir were a movie, how would you describe it? Chances are it's not just "someone had cancer," or "my mom died," or "I ran a marathon." You'd say what you did to survive, how you picked that quest, or some of the obstacles along the way.

Is your dramatic event or situation the climax of the story, the kickoff, or your antagonist? Running a marathon could be the end of a triumphant journey, an incitement to a new way of life, or an obstacle that keeps the narrator tackling physical challenges on the way to emotional transformation. Knowing the place of the dramatic event guides the writer to examine their own journey: What led me to this event? What part of my life did this event start? How did I navigate this situation? How did I recover from it?

One of the reasons Anne Frank's *The Diary of a Young Girl* works is that it's not really about the Holocaust. It's about people living in a small space and trying to get along. Anne Frank mentions little about the events happening in the Netherlands and Europe—only their direct impact on her daily life. Hearing from a hungry person that Miep couldn't get in today to bring food is more dramatic than being told Nazis are bad (we already know that part).

If your memoir or essay deals with a social issue—recovery, abuse, poverty—look for the Passover Question when the dramatic situation intersects directly with the narrator's life. Where does the hero's personal breaking point lead them to take an action that eventually changes the intolerable situation?

In memoir, the dramatic change is often in the protagonist's relationship to the world rather than changing the world itself. For example, an alcoholic's recovery story isn't going to end in a world without alcohol—but the protagonist has changed their own relationship to drinking.

Writer Stephanie Andersen asked (and gave her permission to share):

> *I'm thinking about my memoir about my mother's rape and wanting to know if I should frame the story about discovering my mother's rape within the context of a world where women are often silent about their rapes or within the confines of my own world—where I long for my mother's truth, her story, and to understand her silence.*

Stephanie already knows the answer. It's right there in the question.

> *My memoir...where I long for my mother's truth, her story, and to understand her silence.*

The larger context is there, of course, but the power of Stephanie's memoir is in the intersection of her own life and rape silence in the larger world. The bad stasis is not that all women are silent—it's that she discovered silence in her mother. It's personal.

Your dramatic situation is world-building and background. Your story is how that situation *personally* changed you.

CONFLICT

Stories have two types of conflict: a larger dramatic conflict and immediate conflicts within scenes.

Large conflict:

Hamlet's stepfather wants to get away with murder.

vs.

Hamlet must find out who killed his father and get revenge.

Immediate conflict:

Is Ophelia on my side or her father's? I have to find out if she's messing with me.

vs.

The man I love, who I believe loved me, is behaving like a jerk. I need to give him back his stuff without getting my feelings (or my body!) hurt.

The larger conflict is often between the protagonist and her world, or the protagonist and a political or social force, but immediate conflicts within scenes are almost always between people.

Large conflict:

Anne Frank needs to believe in a world in which people are inherently good.

vs.

Her whole family will be killed if they're discovered in this attic.

Immediate conflict:

I'd like to be nicer to my mom but she really angers me. (Internal conflict as well as conflicting with the other person.)

vs.

I need my daughter to behave as I wish her to.

Large conflict:

Nick Dunne needs to fix or get out of a bad marriage.

vs.

Nick Dunne is the primary suspect in his wife's murder.

Immediate conflict:

I need personal comfort from someone who uncritically adores me.

vs.

I need my brother Nick to stop meeting his lover while suspected of killing his wife.

You know it's a conflict when only one side can win. Conflict is not just "bad stuff is happening," or "people don't like the protagonist."

Not a conflict:

I'm recovering from a drunk driving accident in which I killed my best friend. I'm a horrible person and I don't know how I can go on.

vs.

Our daughter is a horrible person and should be punished by feeling horrible.

Those are negative beliefs, but they are in agreement with each other. They are not a dramatic conflict.

Conflict:

> *I killed my best friend in a drunk driving accident and I want to die.*

vs.

> *We want our daughter to heal and rediscover her bonds with us.*

Those are two opposing goals. The protagonist wants to die; her family wants her to live.

Ideally, almost every scene in your book contains an immediate conflict, whether between two people, between a person and society, or between a person and themselves. The conflict should almost always involve or affect the protagonist, even if they aren't in the scene.

EXERCISE: Conflict

What's the larger conflict in your story? What does the protagonist want? Who are the opposition and what do they want?

For each scene or chapter, what's the immediate conflict? What does the protagonist hope to get in that scene, and what does the opposition want? If the protagonist is not present, how does the outcome of this conflict directly affect their journey?

MYSTERY

All books are mysteries.

In genre mysteries, it's "Whodunit? And will they be punished?"

In family sagas, historical fiction and creative non-fiction, the mystery is "Where did this thing/idea/practice come from?" or "What really happened here?"

In memoir, it's "How did I get here?" or "Can I change who I am?" or "How can I survive as the person I am in this world?"

In romance, it's "How will these two get together?"

The "fun" of reading—whether it's playful excitement or intense engagement—comes from spotting clues and making deductions. The reader needs the "Aha!" moments of "Oh no! He's a bad guy!" or "Wow—no wonder they turned out like that." The reader needs the investigative moments of "What's going to happen? Who will it happen to?" The more the reader has to assemble the clues, the more they engage in the book. The more satisfying the solution, the better the reader's overall experience will be.

More formally, think of this as asking a central dramatic question, examining possible answers, and coming to a satisfying dramatic conclusion. In a genre mystery, this is investigating suspects and collecting clues. In a memoir, this might be tracing generations of alcoholics and learning to break the cycle. In science fiction, this might be discovering which timeline holds the answer to the world's current political crisis, and what exact change will fix the future.

Sustaining mystery for the reader is part of showing instead of telling—letting the reader experience a situation with the narrator and have their own emotional reactions (not always the same as the narrator's reactions). The more the reader almost-but-not-quite pieces together the solution, the more satisfying the final revelation that fits all the clues together and confirms a hunch. Investigating mystery—in any type of story—leads readers to enlightenment, to empathy, and to catharsis.

George Saunders says, in a short film by Tom Mason and Sarah Klein,

> The idea I love is that a story is kind of a black box. And you're gonna put the reader in there, she's gonna spend some time with this thing that you have made, and when she comes out, what's gonna have happened to her in there is something kind of astonishing—it feels like the curtain has been pulled back and like she's gotten a glimpse into a deeper truth.
>
> As a story writer, that's not as easy as it sounds.

In your book, that also means don't give away the solution and then present all the evidence that adds up, which is the format of a scholarly paper. Give the reader a burning question—*What happened here?* or *What's going to happen now?*—and let them investigate with the narrator and add up clues to get to the answer. Ideally your reader solves the mystery at the same time as the protagonist.

> *OMG! The government has made them political martyrs, so if they threaten to both die, they'll beat the government at their own game!*

> *Wow...destroying his own book means Nick is stuck in this life forever. Amy owns him. Amy won.*

Once the mystery is solved, wrap the book up quickly. The reader doesn't want to be lectured about how everything adds up to a solution they just got told.

Mystery is also important for the author as you write.

When you know what the story is and you write with a fixed intention, the plot starts to feel contrived. Maybe you discovered something new about two characters, but you already outlined that scene so it's gotta end like you planned. Allowing yourself to instinctively find new moments, character traits, and events—even if you're a plotter—brings your story to life and makes your characters deeper and more interesting. The joy and wonder of learning something new about your own creation will translate to the reader.

With nonfiction, looking underneath can be imagining others' perspectives or interviews and research. It can be challenging to change our own minds, especially about an experience or situation so powerful that we must write it, but better memoir emerges when we move beyond how we felt, how we reacted, and instead look at people's actions (including our own) and ask why.

No matter how thorough your map, allow yourself off the trail when something new sparks within your journey.

Chekhov's Gun

> *[Hermione] was pointing at an enormous, grey spiral horn, not unlike that of a unicorn, which had been mounted on the wall, protruding several feet into the room. ..."But Harry, it's an Erumpent horn! It's a Class B Tradeable Material and it's an extraordinarily dangerous thing to have in a house! ...Mr. Lovegood, you need to get rid of it straight away, don't you know it can explode at the slightest touch?"*

(sixteen pages later)

...Xenophilus' Stunning Spell soared across the room and hit the Erumpent horn.

There was a colossal explosion.

Playwright Anton Chekhov wrote, "One must never place a loaded rifle on the stage if it isn't going to go off. It's wrong to make promises you don't mean to keep." Chekhov meant that his writer friend should cut a monologue that seemed to set up a subplot that never played out onstage. But the reverse is also true: Once you've found the satisfying solution to your book's mystery, you may need to go back and plant more clues to the big payoff that's coming up. Now that you know the gun goes off in Chapter Ten, go back and hang it on the wall in Chapter Two.

In a 2015 workshop, I brought pages from a Young Adult novel, hoping my fellow writers would be gripped by suspense from the first page, the start of a countdown to a terrifying conclusion.

They found it blah. It didn't grab them. Sure, the voice was nice, but it was just a teenage girl, thinking. Where was the action?

I said, "But there's this countdown..."

"Countdown to what?"

I had failed to write the most important detail: the protagonist has a gun in her bag. I'd spent seven years with this character and story in my head. For me, the gun was just there. Why wouldn't it be? But it wasn't on the page.

Editing, I often see the same quirk of a major missing piece:

Dad's an alcoholic? That's why he acted like that? It's not in here for the reader. Adult-writer-you might want to make that clear even if child-narrator-you is oblivious.

Wait, there was an implied sex scene after the picnic? Please clue the reader. Even if you just take off her shirt or stroke her hair.

The reader needs enough breadcrumbs to follow your trail. Think about rereading a genre mystery, and the pleasure of noticing all the clues you missed the first time around; how each puzzle piece falls into place, the last detail snapping into focus right at the villain's unmasking.

Writing memoir also calls for careful clues. Show the life experience on the way to discovery of illness which shows you can fight, or that you're fighting for the first time. The hints of family history overheard as children, that adult-you knows were secrets covered up.

It's counterintuitive, but don't *surprise* the reader. When we reveal the villain's hidden motivation, or show the hero's triumph, or beat the tumor, we want the reader instead to be *shocked*. Fascinated by the story's ending that can be no other way. We want our book to be a heavily laden vehicle with bad brakes, rolling downhill toward a brick wall. Bystanders are shocked at the impact—but having watched the dump truck full of chickens gather speed, they're not surprised. If the brakes suddenly worked again, stopping the truck abruptly inches from the wall, it's still a powerful shock (plus relief!) but again, not a surprise. One way or another, everything pointed to an explosion of feathers and squawks.

The illusion in our heads is of a fully realized world, provided with every necessary action and relationship to contextualize our story. The reader only gets what's on the page. Take a look at your story. What's the stunning conclusion, the revelation, the connection the reader makes at the last minute? Go back and find the clues. What logically leads to this conclusion, step by step? Is it subtle enough to still need to finish the story to find out what happens, but clear enough that a reader who doesn't know the plot already will say, "Ohhhhhhh. Yeah. That had to happen—it's the only way."

MEMOIR: MYSTERY

Every so often, I'm asked to edit a memoir that's more of a case file. A series of incidents shows an antagonist in the worst possible light, the protagonist's actions are all justified, and the narrator sums up the experience with how they bravely came into the light.

These memoirs don't work.

Not because they're badly written at the sentence level, but because structurally, there's no mystery. We already know whodunit: the person being textually crucified.

Memoirists can learn a lot from Agatha Christie. Or Dorothy Sayers. Ruth Rendell. P. D. James. Any of the stellar writers of relatively formulaic mystery novels. There's a crime. There's an investigation. We learn the villain's motive and why she feels her worldview is correct. The culprit is identified and caught, and the book usually stops right before the punishment—it's the "Law" half of *Law & Order. Chung-chung.*

Laying out the facts in a row and (often unconsciously) slanting them toward the protagonist's hurt feelings is boring. There's nothing to discover—it's all right there. Telling instead of showing, on a whole-book level. Don't show the reader how awful this villain is, or how troubled your life was, in scene after scene. Instead, lay clues carefully, and make the reader your detective.

THEME

Theme is what your story means. You may have a specific theme in mind, or the theme may gradually emerge as you write. Theme is often what you're telling someone when you start with, "Well, it's kind of about..."

> **Story:** A girl must kill other kids on TV to survive a horrible government game.

> **Themes:** Developing your own moral code by deciding what societal rules you're willing to go along with and what you must defy; staying true to yourself under stress; the power of love against cruelty.

> **Story:** A woman stages her own kidnapping to implicate her husband, then returns to control his life forever.

> **Themes:** Women's narrow roles in society; the complicated rules within a marriage that only the couple see.

> **Story:** When a storm hits Mount Everest, climbers are killed and the motivations of the expedition companies are called into question.

> **Themes:** Man vs. Nature; the evils of greed; hubris.

Theme is not a lesson you're teaching the reader, even though they may learn from your book or reflect more deeply on your theme. The "moral of the story" is a conclusion with a point of view. Theme is unsettled and the reader wrestles with questions.

Think of theme as the part of the iceberg beneath the surface.

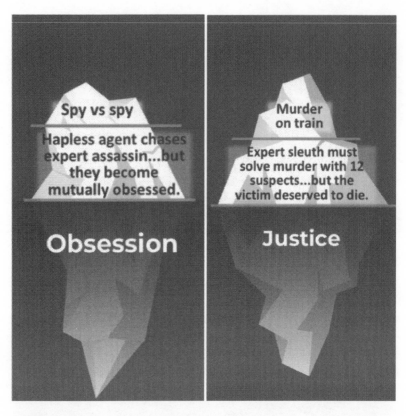

Spy vs spy

Hapless agent chases expert assassin...but they become mutually obsessed.

Obsession

Murder on train

Expert sleuth must solve murder with 12 suspects...but the victim deserved to die.

Justice

The moral of the story would be a little flag on top. In *Murder on the Orient Express* (left iceberg), you might plant "No one is guilty if true justice is outside the law." Waving atop *Killing Eve* (right) might be "Obsession destroys the obsessive" or "Selfishness kills innocent people."

You don't need to deliberately write with theme in mind, but when you feel "Hey, why does my character have to do it like that?" or "That's so unfair!" or "If only they could behave differently," chances are good you're developing a theme. When you identify a theme, see if you can bring that concept or idea in more strongly.

Original scene: A man with no money is refused service at a restaurant. Later, the waitress brings him another table's leftovers.

Add "the evils of greed": the leftovers are lavishly wasteful.

Add "feminism": the waitress is gradually becoming more defiant at her job.

Add "the power of love": the man speaks kindly to the waitress, triggering her to rethink her own bad situation.

Theme is subtle. Bring it in organically. When a real estate agent tells you to boil cinnamon sticks so the house smells nice, that's not the same atmosphere as a genuinely warm, familial home with weekly baking. Laying on theme with a trowel feels fake and pushy. Don't tell the reader your answers—make them ask themselves the questions.

The Short Story Exercise

Still wrestling with the timeline? Realized you have a giant plot hole? Try this exercise Charlie Jane Anders wrote on the comics, science fiction and fantasy website *io9*. As she describes it,

> *The good news is, there's one great technique to diagnose and fix the problems with your novel draft. The bad news is, it's excruciatingly painful.*
>
> *Try writing your whole novel over again, as a short story. From scratch, without looking at your novel draft. If possible, you can even do this a few times over, focusing on different POV characters or different themes.*

This is not an outline, a synopsis, or a plot summary. You are now writing a powerful, beautiful short story that packs all the punch of your however-many-thousands of words. Try setting your limit at 5000 words. See what stands out for you. What events are absolutely key and the story cannot function without them? What characters are less important than you originally thought? What do you just plain not remember?

Use this exercise as a way to determine what connections are missing and need to be added, whether the protagonist's quest and growth are clear, and to establish the clarity of your world in as few details as possible, with everything doing double duty—the religious icon that also shows the character's inner conflict; the method of communication that makes the setting's time and place clear.

When you finish, share it with a writer buddy. Ask what's missing. What don't they understand? Where do they need more information? Fill that in, again using as few words as possible.

Then rewrite the story again at half that length. See what happens.

When you revisit your manuscript, you'll find some things sticking out that didn't show up to you before. And if you're writing memoir or nonfiction, now you have an essay, too.

This may sound like a lot of hassle, and it's an exercise to try, not the Golden Rule of You Must Write Like This. You could also write your novel as a poem, or make a painting of it, or tell your story out loud in five minutes or less. Approaching your story in a different format will show you the most important moments and highlight elements you may be missing.

PLOT

How are we going to rob this bank?

At its simplest, plot=events. But the plot isn't just what happens; it's what happens that *changes the protagonist's life*. Events that are valuable to your story strongly influence the outcome of the book.

Strong Events

- add a companion, team member, or mentor
- add a villain or heighten the villain's opposition
- provide discovery or knowledge that illuminates the past, or (better) will be needed to solve the overall problem
- show learning or practicing a skill that will be needed to finish the quest
- add a tool or weapon to the protagonist's arsenal (doesn't have to be literal: "self-confidence around my crush" is also a tool)
- test the preparedness of the protagonist or team
- cause a setback to the protagonist or team, or damage the villain
- handicap the hero by causing a significant and lasting impairment (literal/immediate like "lost my hearing after a bomb" or metaphorical/set-up like "that awful date...who turns out to be my new boss")

The first four Harry Potter books are full of easy-to-see meaningful events. Harry is literally attending a school where he makes friends, has mentors, learns skills and practices with tools and weapons. Events that seems particular to one character later pay off overall. For example, in book three *(Prisoner of Azkaban),* Hermione loves learning and uses a time-turner to double up on classes held at the same time. At the climax of the book, Hermione's practiced skill with this tool is needed to save two lives.

You may well have events in your book that don't belong in the plot, because they don't create change. Whenever you come across a sentence like:

> *Both were doing fine and had nothing special to report.*
>
> *Nothing was out of the ordinary at the castle.*
>
> *The arrival of the plane had gone unnoticed and there were no new rumors about the cartel.*

That means, "Cut this bit, nothing's happening here." Novels are life with the boring bits left out. If everything is fine, don't tell us, unless it's a rare moment of rest in a headlong flight. If it's nothing special, don't put it in a book.

The events of the plot must lead to permanent change. If you can end with, "What a day!" your events do not add up to a plot. A plot may end with "We won!" or "Damn, we lost. But we learned something." Either way, the hero's life has irrevocably shifted.[41]

---

41 Some great literary fiction and literary or comic memoirs contain very little action. Instead, we're "watching the animals behave." If you are an incredible writer or your comic voice has a devoted following, just spending time with you or your characters can be a powerful book. Spend two hours watching penguins (or an aquarium's penguin-cam). If your story is honestly that engaging, put down this book and immediately begin your agent-finding process by publishing in a prominent literary magazine or receiving 1M+ monthly unique hits on your blog.

EXERCISE: EVENTS

This is a long one—doing it will take a couple of hours. Stick with it!

Part One: The List

Whether you're a plotter or a pantser, take a look at your Vomit Draft and list all the actions and events.

Arturo meets Mariel in elementary school and admires her on the monkey bars.

Twenty years later, Arturo and Mariel meet by chance in the bank. They are both broke.

Arturo and Mariel go for coffee and Mariel suggests robbing the bank.

Arturo gets a haircut.

Mariel calls Arturo—her sister has just been diagnosed.

Part Two: Reasons

Look why each action happens.

Arturo is lonely at home because his mom is sick, so he notices Mariel because she's so confident and fearless. They form a strong bond.

Mariel felt sorry for Arturo as a kid, but when she sees him at the bank, she wants to know what happened since they last saw each other.

Mariel suggests robbing the bank...but oh crap her sister isn't diagnosed until the next scene so she doesn't need the money yet, timeline problem!

Look at how each scene contributes to the character's goal or shows them choosing to move forward. You'll start noticing where a character's actions are unclear or unmotivated, or a scene is unnecessary (why the haircut?).

Not every single thing has to be spelled out—we do want to discover character motivations as we go. But making sure that most actions and events logically follow lets the reader notice, "Hey, that thing happened out of nowhere," or "Hey, this guy's actions are weird... but everything else is clear, so it must be something significant to pay attention to, not sloppy writing."

Part Three: Strong Events

Which question(s) does each event answer? If the event doesn't answer at least one question, is it needed?

Is a choice being made?

What does the hero learn in this moment?

How does this moment change the story?

Is it a step forward or a setback?

Why does the hero need this event to happen?

Why is this happening right now?

Watch for easy decisions or easy wins for your characters. Are they working hard enough to get what they want? Is there a genuine risk they might fail?

You don't need to spell out the answers in the book, but knowing them will help you convey the feeling and details the reader needs, and raise the tension of your story.

Part Four: Purposeful Scenes

Give each scene a title that shows its purpose:

On the Monkey Bars—character development

Two Broke Kids Walk into a Bank—SUCK/inciting incident, show they are friends-to-be not lovers-to-be

My Sister's Sick—raise the stakes, make Arturo decide if he's in or out

Now you have a clear list of scenes and you know why each one is in your book. Are they in the right place and the right order? The Structure section will help you find out.

MEMOIR: PLOT

Paying attention to your plot will help your memoir matter to the reader. Just like a novel, you must engage them in your problem at the beginning, then give them hope that you'll solve the problem and fear that you may not. Your memoir's dramatic arc must end with power. Choose an ending place that shows you making a choice or taking an action that will lead to a positive outcome, and a little of the hopeful aftermath.[42] Leave readers with the message, *I survived this and I wrote a whole book about it—isn't that amazing?*

If you're having trouble finishing your memoir, you may not have lived the end of the story yet.

Novelists can work out their relationship problems or unfulfilled dreams on the page. They can imagine the closure they wish for, forgive characters inspired by the people the writer can't forgive in real life. Memoirists stick to the truth, and if the truth isn't done yet, we're still stuck with it.

I've said to many people, "If you're OK with where you are, you have to be OK with how you got there." The corollary is that if you're not OK with your past, you're still on the journey. You haven't yet reached the place of achievement or success or peace that makes the past OK. Your story literally hasn't finished. The end is unwriteable because it hasn't happened yet.

Some writers discover their destination while they're writing the book. Processing before writing, following the discipline of making one's story fulfilling for the reader instead of therapy for oneself, is a kind of medicine. Setting down what happened, checking facts, realizing *that happened and it wasn't great and*

---

42 Can a memoir end without hope? How many books have you read and said, "That person made terrible choices and their life is still wretched. I can't wait to recommend this book so my friends can feel crappy, too!"

I'm not crazy to feel bad about it can be immensely comforting. Controlling the presentation of our experience, organizing words on the page, is validating. Sometimes we change our family's or friends' perception of what happened as well as our own. Sometimes we empower ourselves to walk away from harmful situations or cease our own bad behavior. And sometimes, if we're lucky, we can embrace what happened.

Here's what I remember about high school: name-calling, shoving, spitting, dating a lot of too-much-older guys. I finished, but I didn't graduate—I'd skipped too many classes, due to what I know now was clinical depression.

Here's what I wrote about high school: an award-winning, profitable one-woman show; a recently completed novel; several published essays.

I wouldn't trade.

If my conception of the Almighty Being had shown up in a burst of light and told Me-Age-Thirteen, "You know how middle school sucks right now? High school will be worse. But in twenty years you will be proud of a body of work that can only be written if you live those days." I'm pretty sure Me-Age-Thirteen would say, "I'll take the writing. Bring on the ninth grade, mofo."

Am I still hurt by the actions of those kids? Yeah, a little. But mostly, my past is a rich trove of information. I did that? What did it feel like? What sensory elements do I remember? What are the best words to make a reader feel what I felt? Every terrible detail I tease out to make a novel deeper, every bad experience I use in a good essay, puts me in control. I'm good with where I am, so I'm OK with how I got here. Taking away past pain would diminish the work I love doing now.

EXERCISE: FINDING THE END OF YOUR MEMOIR

Maybe you're in a good place and writing the past has helped you recognize and own it. Terrific!

To find the end of your memoir on the page: identify Protagonist-You's starting point, and what's wrong with her life at that time and place. Then figure out where in your personal history you fixed that problem or changed that situation. Chances are good the story ends shortly after. Revise your draft to reflect that dramatic arc. Now that you know the resolution, some scenes and characters will seem more important and others less so. Show the parts important to this resolution; cut down or edit out the things that don't contribute.

Or maybe you're still living your memoir with no end in sight.

1) Flip back through your pages. Can you tell Book-You, "Hold on, you can make it, it's going to get better when X happens"? If you can't, you're probably still living the journey. There's pain and processing and release still to come. Take notes. You'll be glad to have them when your story ends.

Meanwhile, take action. What would a satisfying resolution to your journey look like?

2) Find the end of your memoir in your life. Write an imaginary final chapter, as if your memoir were a novel. What happens to the protagonist? How has she grown or changed? How is her life different from where she started? Who and what are still in her life? What has been shed or repudiated or forgotten?

Make a list of the specific steps your protagonist took to get from the starting problem to the resolution. Include steps you've actually taken in your life, and check them off. What steps remain to get you to the satisfying resolution?

As best you can, start carrying out those steps. If they seem insurmountable, enlist a trusted friend, a therapist, or even a writing coach to help you figure out how to find the change in your life that will conclude your memoir.

Yes, this is a lot like therapy.

How much better do you want your life to be?

How much do you want to finish your book?

STRUCTURE

Whereas the story appeals to our curiosity and the plot to our intelligence, the pattern appeals to our aesthetic sense, it causes us to see the book as a whole.

E. M. Forster, *Aspects of the Novel*

Structure is how the plot is revealed through the order and format you use to tell the story.

Structure is also how we intuitively expect stories to unfold. Humans have always processed events that happen to them, situations they're in, and goals they aspire to, through stories. Stories have also been told for sheer entertainment for thousands of years. Our collective unconscious—the pool of subconscious human knowledge about how things "should" be—includes how a story is "supposed" to be structured.

For writers, this is a gift. Understanding structure lets you map out your story and figure out what's missing, as literally as "Oh, I'm about fifty pages in, we need to see a demonstration of the antagonist's[43] power here." When we choose to violate structure on purpose, a plot twist can be far more powerful and shocking—think about George R. R. Martin abruptly killing off *Game of Thrones* characters who readers believed would survive until the end of the story. Because good-guy main characters always survive, right?

Stories without structure feel disorganized. But using structure does not mean bending and squeezing your story into an exact mold. A basic story structure can be used like a tennis racket: to

---

43   The antagonist is the person or force behind the protagonist's main obstacles. The antagonist is often the story's villain, but it's their opposition to the hero that makes this character the antagonist, rather than their moral outlook. The "Perfect Storm" is a powerful antagonist, but a weather formation is neither good nor evil.

become Serena Williams or to whack the snot out of attacking preppies. Or to hit a piñata. Or to strain soup. Knowing the basic elements of structure (in our somewhat-overwrought metaphor, the tennis racket increases force, extends reach, can be used as a solid or a mesh) allows writers to twist the plot to shape readers' expectations, surprising and satisfying them. Structure is how we set up puzzles and plant clues. Structure helps quests proceed at the right pace, dishing out wins and losses without paying off too soon. Within scenes, structural choices can up the comedy level or give tragedy more impact.

In memoir, structure helps build a story with a beginning, middle, and end from our collection of memories and feelings.

Some books or stories follow a single dramatic arc—one story, more or less chronologically told. Others nest subplots or run two stories side-by-side, the incidents in one dramatic arc resulting from or triggering the incidents in another.[44] You might have a full subplot or "B-story" in which the main character is helping someone else achieve their goals, or a "mini-arc" in which the main character learns or achieves one specific thing as part of the larger plot.

For example,

Main plot: The hero wants to find the magic sword that is her birthright and overthrow the evil king.

Subplots: The hero's royal lineage is shown in a series of flashbacks about her father escaping a coup d'etat led by his best friend; the captured princess schemes against the evil king from inside the castle.

Mini-arcs: The hero gets over herself and learns to treat humble woodcutters with respect; the hero trains and masters using the sword; the hero falls for the princess and now has a more personal motivation to overthrow the king.

Using structure **does not mean you have to write an outline before you start,** but it's worth checking in with a simple structure diagram while you're writing, to see if your conflicts are paying off or if it's been too long since your last big plot moment.

We'll look at some classic structures that can overlap and interlock. Many of these structures are a simplified version of Joseph Campbell's *The Hero's Journey*, and if you're intrigued, there are

---

44 Some critics talk about "male" vs "female" plot structures. A slow build to a single climax with a single protagonist is "male." Interlocking story structures with multiple protagonists and multiple climaxes are "female"—get it? Har-har, those crazy literary analysts!

plenty of online resources that go more deeply into the Hero's Journey as it applies to planning a book.

You're probably only going to need one of these structures right now, so if you find one that fits, don't worry about knowing the rest—you can come back to them later.

THE CRAZY EIGHT

The Eight-Point Structure gives us a good overview of how structure works in a story and some key words to understand.

I'm going to use primarily movie examples in this chapter, because most people already know those stories well, they have fairly simple structures, and you can watch a movie in under two hours[45] to see these principles in action. For the advanced version, match these structure elements to a favorite book.[46]

1) Stasis. The protagonist is a certain way. Her community is a certain way. This is how things are. Things can be fine and dandy before they're interrupted, or the situation can be unsatisfying or dangerous/oppressive.

> *Elle Woods is the most popular girl in her school. She's not stupid—she calls out a salesgirl who tries to take advantage of her—but her knowledge is specialized in fashion and social mores. Elle's looking forward to capping her college years with an engagement ring.* (Legally Blonde)
>
> *Orphan Luke Skywalker wants to go to Tosche Station— ostensibly to pick up power converters—but he's stuck on the boring old farm.* (Star Wars)
>
> *After a civil war, all the people of Panem participate in a yearly kill-the-kids-on-TV lottery, but Katniss is doing OK by keeping her head down.* (Hunger Games)

2) SUCK. A Simple, Unexpected, Concrete incident Kicks off the story. This may not be a large physical action, but it upends the stasis and starts the protagonist's journey to personal change and/or

---

45 We don't recommend the Quentin Tarantino *ouevre* for this purpose, for various fairly obvious reasons.

46 If you're feeling extra-daring, buy a used book and mark up the pages. I paid fifty cents for a battered copy of *Speak* at a library sale, specifically to annotate for structure, and highlighting still feels like sacrilege.

changing the world. There is no going back. The hero hoped for or expected A but got B instead.

> *Elle goes to dinner with Warner, sure that he's going to propose, but he says, "I think we should break up."*

> *Luke Skywalker tries to fix a droid, but finds a hologram with a message to his neighbor.*

> *Katniss goes to the lottery ready to be sad and go back home, but Katniss's sister gets picked.*

In series books, each book's SUCK challenges the protagonist in a new way. Ideally, we see the protagonist grow in each book as they are challenged anew. Series books in genres where each book is a self-contained story rather than a continuation (mysteries, science fiction, westerns, thrillers) feel less sophisticated if their protagonist doesn't develop further in each book. Agatha Christie's Miss Marple is as sweet and shrewd and perceptive in *Nemesis* as she was in *The Body in the Library*, but no more. However, Sue Grafton's detective Kinsey Millhone grows and changes in response to each one-book mystery she solves.

3) Quest. What does the protagonist want, and how will she set out to get it?

> *Elle resolves that she is going to win Warner back by becoming a "serious" girl.*

> *Luke and his neighbor Obi-Wan are going to find and rescue Princess Leia.*

> *Katniss saves her sister by volunteering to replace her in the Hunger Games.*

4) Surprises. In nontechnical terms, "most of the book." Surprises are everything that happens along the way, and can include mini-dramatic arcs with their own SUCKs, Quests, Critical Choices, Climaxes, Reversals and Resolutions. We'll stick with *Legally Blonde* here for a bit, and the nested dramatic arcs can get confusing—turn the page for a diagram.

> *Elle studies hard and* (Surprise!) *she gets into Harvard.*

> *Elle gets kicked out of class* (Surprise!) *because she's not good at the kind of thinking Harvard values.*

> *Warner has a new fiancée* (Surprise!) *who is nasty to Elle.*

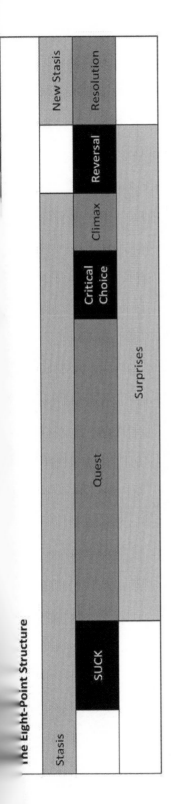

The Eight-Point Structure

Stasis — SUCK — Quest — Critical Choice — Climax — Reversal — New Stasis — Resolution — Surprises

Elle, who's used to being likable and liked, bakes muffins and brings them to a study group. They don't want her. (Surprise!) *Or the muffins.*

Elle gets invited to a party. She comes up with a great costume, but (Surprise!) *it's not a costume party. Warner tells her she's just not smart enough for Harvard.* (SUCK for Mini-Arc #1: I Am Too Smart Enough)

Elle resolves to work harder, buys a computer, and starts doing well in class. (Quest for Mini-Arc #1)

Elle shows up Warner when (Surprise!) *she can answer a tricky class question that he can't.*

Notice that Elle's overall Quest begins to shift here—*she* doesn't know yet that she wants to do well at Harvard more than she wants Warner back, but that goal is being set up for the audience so that it's a delightful but inevitable surprise later when Elle realizes that herself.

Elle gets chosen for an internship along with Warner and his fiancée. (Climax and Reversal for Mini-Arc #1: I Am Too Smart Enough; SUCK for Mini-Arc #2: A Real Court Case)

5) Critical Choice. The protagonist has changed while on her Quest. She's been affected by the Surprises. Now, she's at a crossroads, faced with the biggest decision of the plot: will she choose to be her old self and return to Stasis, or act as her new self and make a decision she could not have even conceived at the beginning of the book? (Hint: only one of these options lets you write the rest of the book.)

A few smaller Critical Choices lead up to the big one:

Elle's internship is going great—until the lead lawyer sexually harasses her. (SUCK for Mini-Arc #3: Maybe I Should Quit, which happens inside Mini-Arc #2) *Warner's fiancée overhears just enough to think Elle is complicit. Elle considers quitting Harvard. The mean-lady professor overhears Elle at the beauty shop* (Surprise!) *and reaffirms that Elle's own personal strength is valuable. Elle decides not to quit.* (Critical Choice for Mini-Arc #3)

The biggest Critical Choice triggers the Climax of the story:

Elle finds out that (Surprise!) *the defendant in the murder case is innocent, but her alibi would destroy her reputation. Elle refuses to share the alibi with the defense team because she promised she wouldn't* (Critical Choice) *and her integrity is more important than winning.*

When the defendant finds out Elle was harassed, she fires the lead attorney and hires Elle (Surprise!)*. Now Elle must win the court case without betraying the defendant's confidence.* (Now entering the Climax for both Mini-Arc #2: A Real Court Case and the main story arc)

6) Climax. As a result of the Critical Choice, the protagonist must assemble all her tools, skills and companions; add them to who she was in Stasis; and fight the biggest battle yet. The hero's original traits become unexpectedly valuable now, making her **uniquely suited** to defeat a key obstacle. The Surprises along the Quest have further developed those traits, filled in her gaps of skill or knowledge, provided her with useful companions and tools, and now she's **ready** to step up.

*Elle realizes the pool boy, a key witness, is gay, which disproves his story of having sex with the defendant. She is **uniquely suited** to discover that information from her previous fashion knowledge. After working hard, studying, and practicing by using her legal knowledge and social skills to stand up for two other people who have been wronged, she is now **ready** to fight this battle.*

The actual Climax is the trial, and Elle successfully exonerates the defendant and identifies the real murderer.

In Star Wars,

*The rebels find a hidden weakness in the architecture of the Death Star. Luke Skywalker is **uniquely suited** to be the shooter, because firing at a target of that size is*

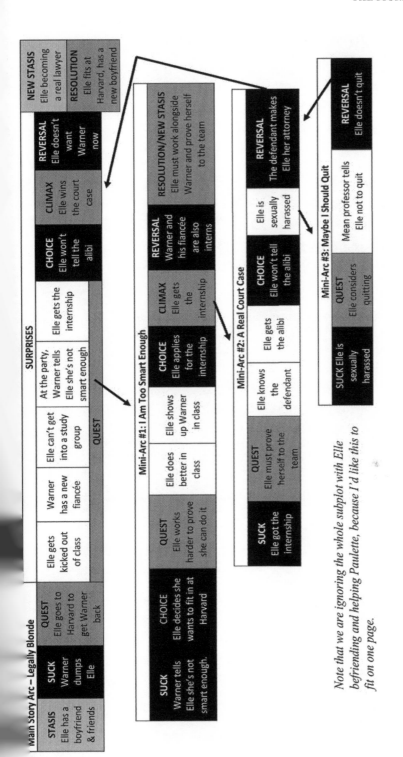

Main Story Arc – Legally Blonde

STASIS	SUCK	QUEST				SURPRISES			CHOICE	CLIMAX	REVERSAL	NEW STASIS
Elle has a boyfriend & friends	Warner dumps Elle	Elle goes to Harvard to get Warner back	Elle gets kicked out of class	Warner has a new fiancée	Elle can't get into a study group	Elle shows up Warner in class	At the party, Warner tells Elle she's not smart enough	Elle gets the internship	Elle won't tell the alibi	Elle wins the court case	REVERSAL Elle doesn't want Warner now	Elle becoming a real lawyer
												RESOLUTION Elle fits at Harvard, has a new boyfriend

Mini-Arc #1: I Am Too Smart Enough

SUCK	CHOICE	QUEST			CHOICE	CLIMAX	REVERSAL	RESOLUTION/NEW STASIS
Warner tells Elle she's not smart enough.	Elle decides she wants to fit in at Harvard	Elle works harder to prove she can do it	Elle does better in class		Elle applies for the internship	Elle gets the internship	Warner and his fiancée are also interns	Elle must work alongside Warner and prove herself to the team

Mini-Arc #2: A Real Court Case

SUCK	QUEST		CHOICE	REVERSAL
Elle got the internship	Elle must prove herself to the team	Elle knows the defendant	Elle won't tell the alibi	The defendant makes Elle her attorney
		Elle gets the alibi	Elle is sexually harassed	

Mini-Arc #3: Maybe I Should Quit

SUCK	QUEST	REVERSAL
Elle is sexually harassed	Elle considers quitting	Mean professor tells Elle not to quit
		Elle doesn't quit

Note that we are ignoring the whole subplot with Elle befriending and helping Paulette, because I'd like this to fit on one page.

*like "shooting womp rats" back home. After getting off the farm, rescuing Leia, working with mercenaries, and learning how much is truly at stake, he is now **ready** to fight this battle.*

The actual Climax is the dogfight that leads to the destruction of the Death Star.

The Climax itself is exciting, but the moment of truth leading directly to the Climax is more important to the dramatic arc. When the hero decides to step up, we already know whether they'll win or lose. In a movie, loss or victory is in the tone of the trailer, or you know that this actor isn't going to play a loser. In a genre book, the hero is probably going to win.[47] In literary fiction or serious memoir, the hero will likely either lose in a way that supports personal growth, win a hollow victory, or learn something deeper and more important than the actual victory.

7) Reversal. With a change in circumstances and character, the protagonist has moved from ignorance to knowledge. She discovers the new person she has become, and adds that new self to the good parts of who she was at the beginning of the book. This means rejecting her original Stasis and becoming ready for a new quest.

> *Warner wants to be Elle's boyfriend again, but Elle now knows that Warner is unworthy of her. She wants to be a respected attorney, and to be with someone who will value her true self—blonde hair, love of fashion, kind heart, and integrity.*

> *The Capitol now views Katniss as an active threat. She wants to go home and provide for her family, but must stay politically wary and navigate an unresolved love triangle.*

The hero must permanently change after accomplishing the Quest. In *My Fair Lady*, Eliza Doolittle doesn't just act like a lady at the end of the story—she *is* one. She has learned to think differently, stand up for herself, and demand to be treated well. The Climax is that she successfully passes, but the Reversal is that now she can't go back to her old life.

8) Resolution. A "happily ever after" or "happy for now" scene that ties up loose ends. Structure tells us the right place to end, and what Resolution will leave the reader satisfied.

---

47   Lots of readers hated the ending of the *Divergent* trilogy, but a hero choosing death on her own terms still counts as a win.

Beginning: *Popular, fashion-smart Elle Woods can't wait to get engaged.*

Resolution: *Book-smart Elle Woods fits in at Harvard, has dumped a bad boyfriend, and is ready to use her skills and smarts to help other people.*

Beginning: *Orphan Luke Skywalker is stuck on the farm, in a life that doesn't seem to matter.*

Resolution: *Luke Skywalker has saved the world, discovered the Force, and is ready to train as a Jedi and defend the universe.*

Beginning: *Katniss stays out of politics and protects her family, despite the yearly kill-the-kids lottery.*

Resolution: *Katniss is stuck in politics whether she likes it or not, but now she has the power to inspire change.*

Originally, *Legally Blonde* ended with Elle triumphantly leaving the courtroom and kissing her new boyfriend. But in early screenings, director Robert Luketic realized the story wasn't "Elle Woods becomes a successful lawyer and gets a new guy." The story is "Popular girl must start at the bottom and win respect in a new peer group." Elle's problem at Harvard is not that she isn't a lawyer—nobody there is a lawyer yet. Her problem is that people have always liked her and suddenly no one likes her. And we, the audience, like her, so we want to see her win *that* battle.

Six months later, they shot a new ending:

> *Elle is elected by her peers* (because asking the audience to believe that she's the Harvard valedictorian is too much) *to give the class speech. She's friends with Warner's fiancée—who dumped him. The hot assistant attorney from her internship, who respects her mind, is going to propose.*

Winning the court case doesn't make her popular. Getting elected to give the speech shows she's been accepted by her peers and closes the story in a deeper and more satisfying way.

If you're setting up a sequel, the Resolution is the new Stasis, and the next SUCK will interrupt that Stasis, adding higher stakes.

As *Catching Fire* begins,

> *Katniss lives reasonably happily in her home village again. But there's another Hunger Games* (SUCK), *and*

this time the Capitol is specifically out to get Katniss (higher stakes).

MULTI-ACT STRUCTURES

Five-Act and Three-Act Structures are what I use the most for fiction and memoir; Four-Act Structures work well for thrillers, mysteries, and suspense.

Five-Act Structure

Act One begins with the hero in Stasis. This is the way the world is, and it needs changing. At the end of Act One, the hero makes a big choice or has one imposed upon them. They are on board with a new plan.

> *"I volunteer as tribute."*
>
> *"You're a wizard, Harry."*
>
> *Jane fights back against her awful cousin and is sent to boarding school. (Jane Eyre)*

Act Two has one or more low points, where things aren't going well.

> *Katniss's mentor is a drunk who won't be much help. Several of her fellow Tributes are bigger, stronger, and better prepared.*

Turns out Harry's famous and it's not fun. Professor Snape hates Harry. Draco Malfoy hates Harry. Hermione is a know-it-all and Ron's a buffoon.

The school is cold, low on food, and run by a religious zealot who humiliates Jane in front of the whole school. Jane's best friend dies of consumption.

At the end of Act Two, the hero makes a conscious decision: they recognize the game they're in, and they want to win. The situation dramatically improves.

Katniss shoots the pig on the judges' table. She will not be ignored. She receives a high rating from the judges.

Harry is naturally great at broomstick-flying and joins the Quidditch team. He tries to find out more about the Sorcerer's Stone.

The consumption epidemic leads to changes in the school administration and better conditions. Jane studies hard and becomes a teacher herself. She accepts a position as a governess at Thornfield Hall.

Act Three is usually about as long as the first two acts combined, and most of the learning, growing, and changing happens here. There's usually a low point near the beginning of Act Three.

Katniss thought Peeta was on her side, but he's joined the trained-killer kids who are hunting her down.

Draco Malfoy challenges Harry to a duel, but it's a setup.

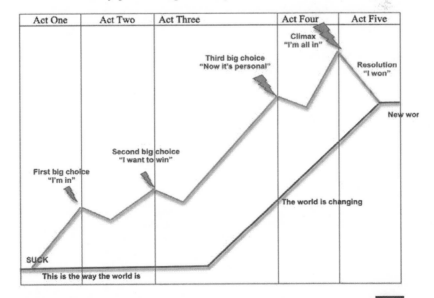

Jane's boss, Mr. Rochester, is moody and attractive, but he has a lovely fiancée. Also, the house has a weird presence in a wing Jane isn't allowed to enter.

Act Three ends with another big decision. Now it's not enough to be in the game—now the hero wants to *win*.

Katniss bonds with Rue, who reminds Katniss of her own sister. When Rue is killed, Katniss doesn't just want to survive—she wants revenge.

Harry and his friends are convinced Professor Snape is planning to steal the Sorcerer's Stone. They must try to get it first.

Mr. Rochester turns out to already be married—and his mentally ill wife attacks Jane. She must leave to protect herself and maintain her self-respect.

Throughout Act Three, the world is changing and the hero is gaining the companions and learning the tools and skills they'll need for the climax of the book.

In Act Four, the hero commits fully to the battle at hand. There's another low point near the beginning.

Katniss's friend Peeta is gravely ill. She needs to fake being in love with him to get medicine...and she's also growing feelings for him.

Harry's mousy friend Neville tries to stop their quest and they must jinx him to continue.

Jane wanders sick and alone on the moors and passes out on someone's doorstep.

But the hero is ready for the final battle, which will test their readiness and their character.

Katniss realizes if both she and Peeta die, the Capitol will look foolish. She forces the game to allow two winners.

Harry, Ron, and Hermione's unique strengths get them through the obstacle course to the Sorcerer's Stone. Voldemort shows up, but they survive and escape with the Stone.

Mrs. Rochester burns down Thornfield Hall and dies. Jane finds Mr. Rochester wandering on the moors, nearly blind. Closer to equals, now they can be together.

Act Five is the Resolution, where the story ends with satisfaction and loose ends are tied up. The characters are changed people, living in a new world. If there's going to be a sequel, the seeds are planted here.

> *Katniss goes home to her family a winner. But she's torn about her feelings for Peeta, and discovers the Capitol now owns her more than ever....*

> *Harry, Ron, Hermione, and Neville all contribute to winning the school cup. Harry goes home for the summer, and his awful foster family doesn't know he's not allowed to use magic. But Voldemort is on the loose....*

> *Jane marries Mr. Rochester, and they return to live in half-ruined Thornfield Hall.*

This also works as a Three-Act Structure. Roughly, Act One includes the above Acts One + Two; Act Two covers the above Act Three and is the longest of the three acts; Act Three comprises the above Acts Four and Five. Plot twists and big decisions happen around the same locations. Usually, Act Two is longer than Act One and Act Three.

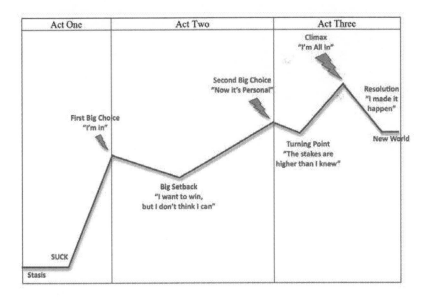

This Four-Act Structure works well for thrillers and mysteries:

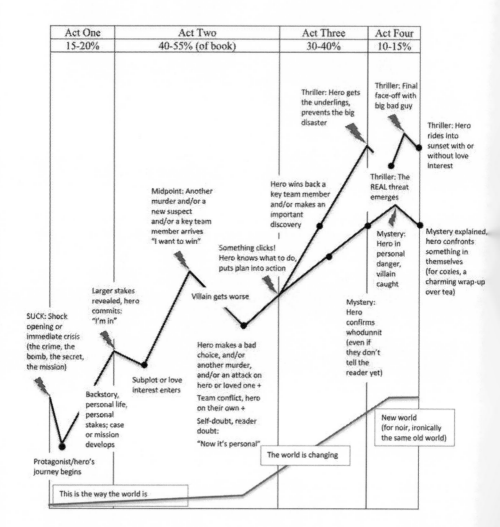

Act One	Act Two	Act Three	Act Four
15-20%	40-55% (of book)	30-40%	10-15%

Thriller: Hero gets the underlings, prevents the big disaster

Thriller: Final face-off with big bad guy

Thriller: Hero rides into sunset with or without love interest

Midpoint: Another murder and/or a new suspect and/or a key team member arrives "I want to win"

Hero wins back a key team member and/or makes an important discovery

Thriller: The REAL threat emerges

Something clicks! Hero knows what to do, puts plan into action

Mystery: Hero in personal danger, villain caught

Mystery explained, hero confronts something in themselves (for cozies, a charming wrap-up over tea)

Larger stakes revealed, hero commits: "I'm in"

Villain gets worse

SUCK: Shock opening or immediate crisis (the crime, the bomb, the secret, the mission)

Mystery: Hero confirms whodunnit (even if they don't tell the reader yet)

Hero makes a bad choice, and/or another murder, and/or an attack on hero or loved one +

Team conflict, hero on their own +

Self-doubt, reader doubt:

"Now it's personal"

Subplot or love interest enters

Backstory, personal life, personal stakes; case or mission develops

New world (for noir, ironically the same old world)

Protagonist/hero's journey begins

The world is changing

This is the way the world is

MEMOIR: STRUCTURE

It boils down to trusting our intuition with our writing, to asking if our experiences or interactions with the subject matter lead us to the truth, a "go big" where our presence brings the reader in and illuminates the story, world, or some aspect of our shared humanity.

Samantha Claire Updegrave
"Truth and First Person Journalism"
at the *Brevity* Blog

Structure makes memories into stories.

Memoirists often tackle the first draft chronologically, setting out what happened in order, or thematically, expanding from times, places, or feelings. Both are terrific ways to generate a Vomit Draft. In the Story Draft, organizing your book's dramatic structure will increase tension, determine pacing, and create reader enlightenment and satisfaction.

Structure is easier in a "quest" memoir: climbing a mountain, beating cancer, and overcoming addiction tend to have turning-point decisions and physical setbacks that map easily. Sobriety is visible—you can picture how your life will change.

In a "quiet" memoir, personal growth must be presented as dramatic action by treating your permanent change as a Climax you didn't know you were working toward. Character-you moves toward change blindly, but writer-you knows when you got there. "I'm worth more than I thought I was" is a dark goal. Structure invests events and moments with deeper meaning than they might have had at the time.

When it happened: *I had to pack all my stuff and get out and it broke my heart that I couldn't take my mom's painting.*

What you know now: *That was the first big sacrifice I made to get out of a bad relationship—I just didn't learn enough not to get into the next bad relationship.*

What you do as the author: *Leaving Jim was the turning point of Act One. Mourning the loss of the painting is the low point opening Act Two. I want to show that losing that painting cost me a lot, and when I stayed with Brad, part of my decision was not wanting that pain again.*

But![48]

Don't spell that out in your narrative. Let the reader put it together.

Look at the difference between

> *I thought about leaving Brad, but then I remembered sitting there in that crappy motel room and mourning my mother's painting. I didn't want to feel that pain again, and I guess that was enough reason to stay, or so I thought at the time.*

and

> *Brad's slap burned on my cheek like the poppies in the painting I'd left behind. But our threadbare couch was better than another night in a crappy motel room.*

Show us what's happening. Let the reader deduce what it means.

Two structures are particularly useful for memoir. They're also great for blog posts, essays, and magazine and newspaper articles. You can see letter-*e* structure in action in pretty much any travel story, and circular structure in many lifestyle blogs.

---

48 And it's a big butt, Dottie.

Letter-e Structure

The story flows like a lowercase *e*. Start at the crossbar in a moment of action or a key decision, then move forward for a short time.

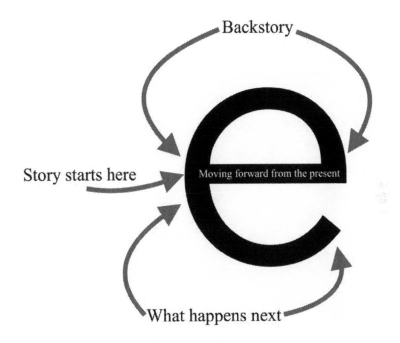

I met my gynecologist in Starbucks and she acted like she didn't know me... (Let's Pretend This Never Happened)

I lost my boot off the side of a cliff, but my feet were so screwed up at this point, I went ahead and threw away the other boot. (Wild)

Circle back around the top of the *e*—how did you end up here? Fill in just enough backstory to return us to the point of action. Give the events that are the context of your decision, not your whole life story.

I grew up in Texas in a weird family with a lot of taxidermy. Then I met Victor.

My mom died and our family splintered. I got into heroin. I decided hiking the Pacific Coast Trail would change me or kill me.

You've reached the crossbar of the *e* again. Skip to the end of the scene from Chapter One (or to the consequences of the action) and continue forward. Depending on how much backstory is needed, you might now be at the end of Act One, at the midpoint of the book, or going into the last act. If you're still early, use another structure from here.

For more letter-*e* structure in action, check out "high trash" books, like Judith Krantz's *Scruples*. Krantz is a master at reaching a turning point in the main action, introducing a new character and their backstory, then returning to the main action.

Circular Structure

Great for essay collections but tough for single-plotline books, because it's hard to make a series of attempts satisfying for that long.

However, if your memoir is "voice-driven"—people just want to spend time with your funny or beautiful writing—or a "collage" memoir of dreamy prose-poem scenes, circular structure may be enough.

Start by identifying the key challenge or question you're facing:

How did I grow into being myself as a young gay boy, and how do I still relate to the world in those ways as an adult? (Me Talk Pretty One Day)

How is who I am now rooted in being from Florida? (Sunshine State)

The first scene shows that challenge in action: how does it actually harm or impede your life? Then show the protagonist trying to change with an anecdote or action that was ultimately unsuccessful, or succeeded enough to keep moving forward. Pair this with analysis or reflection about what happened and why it didn't work, or why it wasn't satisfying enough to end the story here.

Keep repeating attempts paired with reflection until the narrator reaches permanent change. Close with a scene showing this changed self in action, often one that mirrors the opening scene. Now the protagonist can react differently.

In each scene you're searching for an answer to your main question. Each scene resolves when you find an answer and like it (or not!), or you don't find an answer but deal with the question in another specific way.

Eat, Pray, Love is a circular memoir, and Elizabeth Gilbert raises the stakes in each round: Eat to recover from a bad relationship; Pray to rediscover herself and her spirituality; Love to move forward in her life as a healed person.

Circular structure usually works best for shorter work. A circular book must actively raise the stakes in each successive repetition. Your prose must engage the reader at every turn. Even if the reader sees "Uh-oh, here we go again..." they need to feel "Oh gosh, I hope it works out this time!"[49]

⌒⌒

---

49 For an example of circular structure feeling flat, see the middle of *Harry Potter and the Deathly Hallows*: We're camping, we're talking, we're fighting, we're camping, we're talking.... The payoffs of each attempt aren't big enough.

EXERCISE: Structure

Pick a dramatic structure that suits your book and try "mapping" your story—blocking out the events on a diagram. When you need to depart from the basic structure, think about why that's the right choice for this story. If you depart often, another structure may be a better fit.

Mapping helps in a few ways. If you're working on a book with multiple plot lines, your map helps reference where you are in each story. If you're not able to write every day, the map helps you remember what you wrote last week, and look ahead to what's coming up in the storyline.

Mapping is technical, rather than creative, so it's also a great way to spend a writing session where you aren't feeling "inspired" but you need to get some active, thoughtful work done.

TIMELINE

Timeline helps establish structure. Using seasonal changes and holidays to mark the passage of time helps, and you don't need to explicitly name every day. A tighter timeline can raise the suspense and make the plot developments more important.

If you're writing a thriller, mystery, or suspense novel, include an active countdown of some kind:

> *I have to find my wife before the police arrest me for her murder.*
>
> *I have to find the killer because I'm next.*
>
> *The bomb goes off in twelve hours.*

If you need a deceptive timeline to serve your plot, pick fuzzy chronology or fuzzy action. Using both confuses the reader. Mysteries usually have fuzzy action (we don't know who started the plot in motion by murdering someone) and a specific timeline (the detectives solve the case in real time). Books with unreliable narrators sometimes use fuzzy chronology—in

Gone Girl, we read the wife's journal entries charting her failing marriage...then find out she wrote them all at once as a deliberate red herring.

If the reader not knowing *when* something happened is key to your plot, make sure that *what* happened is clear. But if you want *what* happened to be a secret revealed later, let the reader know *when* it happened, and they'll keep that plot hole in their head and watch for the answer. A great example of knowing when-but-not-what is the opening chapter of Karen McManus's *One of Us Is Lying.* We see the exact sequence in time of students coming to detention, being distracted by a car accident outside, and one of the students dying from anaphylactic shock. We don't see how the student was poisoned with an allergen, and solving the mystery of "what happened when we all looked out the window" drives the book.

However you shift in time, signal it to the reader. Don't count on putting the date at the beginning of the chapter—very often, readers skip that information, or they don't count the days. You want them lost in the story, not doing math.[50] Open scenes with a season, or a reference to what happened yesterday, or some visual cue that establishes the time relative to the previous scene if it's not immediately chronological.

EXERCISE: TIMELINE

Print out a calendar of the years your story is set or your memoir happened; or make a calendar using the date system you've invented for your world. Write your events in the order they show up—is this the closest sequence in which they can appear? Will shortening the timeline raise the tension?

---

50 This also applies to epigraphs. Quoting another writer at the top of each chapter is a nice touch, but many people skip them. Consider your epigraph, then make it a writing challenge to put the mood of the epigraph in the chapter itself.

PHYSICAL EDITING

Every manuscript needs at least one paper phase.[51] Working on a screen doesn't always show what's missing on the page, because we retain backstory and fine details in our own brain. A paper phase helps sort out a confusing Story Draft, or reorients the writer midway through a Vomit Draft. For pantsers, this is where you shuffle scenes and fill in plot gaps. As a plotter, mapping your structure thus far gives the confidence to go with an inspiration that wasn't in the plan.

Try to give yourself a week between screen and paper, to let the book settle in your subconscious. Then treat yourself to some colored pens, sharp scissors and paste, and plunge in like the first day of third grade.

At the bare minimum, print your manuscript and read it with pen in hand. Scribble notes in the margins, scratch out chunks of text, eliminate needless words. Cut up chapters and pages and shift them physically to adjust the storyline and chronology. Add sticky notes or extra sheets when you realize you're missing a transition or a scene.

For a more visual experience, use a big blank wall—put up brown paper if you need a clean surface—and tape up chunks of material in areas based on idea or theme. If you don't have a wall, use a large table or clean floor space.[52]

Sue Grafton's detective heroine, Kinsey Millhone, writes case facts and discoveries on index cards, then shuffles the cards to see what sparks new understanding or questions. Try investigating your book the same way. Physically snipping your manuscript into scenes points out repetition in a way that encountering the same scenes while scrolling doesn't.

When writer Jocelyn Bartkevicius approached her memoir-in-progress about burlesque clubs and her Lithuanian heritage (trust me, it works), she made a wall map of stories she wanted to tell, then drew lines connecting stories that seemed thematically in touch with each other. This helped her see where anecdotes stood alone and needed more support, or place a new memory within the whole structure. You could order events based on chronology, or draw out your own

---

51 For writers with disabilities that make paper hard to use, try an app like Evernote, Trello, or Scrivener that allows you to move virtual index cards and sections of text.

52 You will love your pets and children better if you keep them out of the room with your book laboriously laid out across the floor.

version of the Hero's Journey or a three- or five-act structure, and tape your pages to their places on the diagram.

In the paper phase, it helps to relocate from where you first wrote the book. Change coffee shops, change rooms, or just sit on the other side of the table. If time and money allow, check into a hotel or AirBnB for a day or two—it's amazing how much writing feels like your "real" work when you show up in a dedicated space. Some artist residencies cater to writers who need just a few days to focus in a new space.

When you've got a visual grasp on your storyline and chronology, reassemble your book in a new document. Add placeholders and notes for what needs to be written, and decide whether to tackle them now or as you reach them in the next draft.

PICKY STUFF

Nice work so far! The Story Draft is big, and you're doing great.

These steps are actually line and copyediting, and you're going to repeat them in the Technical Draft. But do a quick round here, because it gives you a little break from heavy-duty editing. You'll enjoy working on a cleaner draft, and by fixing these things yourself, you'll learn them thoroughly.

1. Proofread for spelling and punctuation. Double-check anything you aren't sure of. Many spellcheck programs and apps like Grammarly make mistakes that only a human eye can catch.

2. Check for consistent verb tenses. Is the narrative in the same verb tense all the way through? Do you need a different tense for flashbacks, memories, or when characters recount a previous experience?

3. Many books start the story too far into the book, with backstory and filler slowing down the early pages. Pick a friend who hasn't read the manuscript and ideally doesn't know the story.

   * Give them pages 50-70, without including any earlier pages. Ask them to write down what they know about the characters, place, setting, and quest.

   * Ask them to also write down questions they have, or missing information they need to understand pages 50-70.

- Review your first fifty pages and take out information/backstory that is clear later. Keep needed information—or see if it can be briefly worked in after page 50.

THE CHARACTER DRAFT

We cannot understand each other, except in a rough and ready way; we cannot reveal ourselves, even when we want to; what we call intimacy is only makeshift; perfect knowledge is an illusion. But in the novel we can know people perfectly.

...a character in a book is real...when the novelist knows everything about it. He may not tell us all he knows, but he will give us the feeling that though the character has not been explained, it is explicable.

E. M. Forster, *Aspects of the Novel*

In this draft you'll deepen your characterizations, making your characters more themselves and more powerfully driven to complete the events of your plot. We'll talk about villains— and antagonists from your life in memoir. We're going to look at world-building, too, because setting also acts as a character in your story.

CHARACTERIZATION

Characterization is how characters show who they are through action, ritual, habit, and interaction with the environment.

We don't need to see everything about a character—just the important things. And we want to learn these things mostly from their actions and a little bit from their thoughts, rather than from the narrative telling us what they're like.

("Narrative" is all the writing that isn't dialogue and thoughts—the part that's the writer or the POV character telling the story.)

Characters don't need to be fully physically described all at once. Bring in a first impression when they arrive. Drop in more characteristics as your protagonist notices them; use those characteristics to show how the protagonist feels about them.

He had a hairy mole by his upper lip.

A beauty mark sat above his full lips.

Ways to show character include

Gesture: A character unconsciously reaching to hold another's hand can tell us they're insecure...or in love.

Appearance: Are they wearing a t-shirt with a slogan or a band on it, a dress, or a three-piece suit? How groomed are they, and is that their regular routine? Did they walk in covered in blood, or dirt, or silver glitter?

Name: Income, class, nationality, ethnicity, race, and family can all be emphasized in a name.[53]

Nickname: Casual names help show relationships and levels of respect.

And of course, the characters' actions show us who they are by how they interact with the world and each other.

When introducing characters, watch out for "character parties." When the reader meets a large group of people all at once, it's difficult to know who is going to be important, who we should remember, and why we should care about each person. It's frustrating when a crowd is vague and we're not sure if we are supposed to know these people already or remember them for later.

To show characters clearly as individuals, introduce each one when they have a direct bearing on the plot. At that moment, give some sense of how they will affect the main character. When Harry Potter first meets Hermione Granger on the train to school, she's already book-smart and a bit officious. Her knowledge, and her willingness to stand up for what's morally right, define her heroism through the entire series.

---

53 Avoid character names that sound alike or share opening letters unless that's on purpose. Readers will confuse them. Yes, Annie and Amy don't sound that much alike. But most people aren't reading as carefully as you are.

Introducing a character is also the time to make them likable, if the reader is supposed to like them. You may have heard of "Save the Cat." This concept comes from Blake Snyder's *Save the Cat: The Last Book on Screenwriting You'll Ever Need*. Snyder means your character must do something in the opening pages that makes us want to like them. This can be an action or a feeling. They could literally save a cat from a tree. Katniss Everdeen feeds her family. Tris Prior *(Divergent)* is afraid to hurt her family though she desperately wants to leave them.

If you're writing an antihero—a protagonist we enjoy spending time with, but who violates the morality or social mores of their world—you don't have to make them "good," but they must have some intriguing quality that makes us want to spend a whole book with them. A moment of kindness or a glimpse of their positive motivation can be the easiest way to handle this. Antiheroes can also be likable by starting out as total badasses, like James Bond and other spies; charmers, like Scarlett O'Hara; or lovable scoundrels, like Terry Pratchett's Moist Von Lipwig in *Going Postal:*

> *Moist stared straight ahead while the roll call of his crimes was read out. He couldn't help feeling that it was so unfair. He'd never so much as tapped someone on the head. He'd never even broken down a door. He had picked locks on occasion, but he'd always locked them again behind him. Apart from all those repossessions, bankruptcies, and sudden insolvencies, what had he actually done that was bad, as such? He'd only been moving numbers around.*

Going Postal, incidentally, starts with an amazing SUCK: at the end of Chapter One, the protagonist is hanged. His Quest happens after his alias officially dies, when Moist is forced to live as his true self and must pull off a bigger con than any swindle he's ever run before.

Characters in Fantasy & Science Fiction

The biggest characterization challenge in nonreal settings is emotionally connecting the reader with the characters. No matter their alien race, strange customs, or unique living situation, your characters must still be three-dimensional beings who experience growth and change, with real concerns and real conflicts within the rules of the world you're creating.

You must also battle all the baggage the reader shows up with—they already "know" what aliens and princesses are like; they've watched *Star Trek* and *Shrek*. Dispel assumptions promptly. If your characters differ from the archetype readers know, make sure you clearly show how and why. If your vampires glitter in the sun, or love playing baseball, get that in early, and show the reader how that behavior helped them survive in a world that knows about Dracula but doesn't believe in "real" vampires. If your sorority blonde is whip-smart about marketing, show her correcting a salesgirl trying to sucker the blonde into buying last season's dress.

Series Characters

Telling only part of an epic set in a huge world can leave readers unsatisfied. Yet you want them to buy Book Two. Think of the protagonist's dramatic arc as having two parallel tracks:

1) Quest: The specific task we're trying to accomplish in this book.

> *blow up the Death Star*
>
> *win the Hunger Games*
>
> *save the Sorcerer's Stone*
>
> *join a new faction* (Divergent)

2) Objective: Why the character wants to complete the Quest (their "I Want" song).

> *save the universe*
>
> *protect my family*
>
> *escape my horrible life*
>
> *discover my true self*

Complete **only one of those tracks**—but complete it fully.
If the protagonist achieves her personal Objective
  * show which *part* of the Quest she's accomplished
  * leave the overall Quest hanging for Book Two
  * start a new Objective
If the Quest resolves in this book
  * leave your protagonist's Objective unfulfilled

- start a new Quest—ideally, a larger one revealed by finishing this book's Quest

Luke Skywalker is off the farm and ready for more adventures, and he blew up the Death Star...but Darth Vader didn't die.

Luke's Quest and Objective have both resolved, but the audience sees a loophole for the next installment. The larger Quest, "defeat the Empire," is hinted at.

Katniss won the Hunger Games...but now the politicians own her life.

Katniss' Quest to win the Games has resolved. Her Objective, "protect my family," is unresolved. The larger Quest, "defeat the Capitol," is revealed in the next book.

Harry Potter is a wizard and has saved the Sorcerer's Stone...but Voldemort is out there.

Harry's Objective, "have a better life," is unresolved but he's made progress—his life is significantly less horrible. This book's Quest has resolved and the seven-book Quest has been revealed.

Tris and Four have shut down the make-people-kill simulation and escaped their faction...but there's a larger plot behind the simulation.

Tris' Objective has resolved—she's confident in who she is independent of her faction. Her Quest has renewed and expanded.

Imagine instead that a character resolves neither the Objective nor the Quest:

Katniss' sister joins her in the Hunger Games as a new contestant in the final round. They stare at each other in the arena and...end of book.

Harry Potter's relatives found out he can't do magic all summer, so going home is going to suck. But he found the entrance to the Chamber of Secrets! He opens the door and...end of book.

Find out what happens next in Book Two: My Editor Let Me End on a Cliffhanger. And don't miss Book Three: I Swear I'll Finish a Story This Time!

I've read a few books that finished on cliffhangers without resolving either track of the dramatic arc. I returned one, and wrote a negative review for another, because I felt ripped off. I'd invested my time in exchange for fulfilling entertainment, and what I'd actually bought was a game of keep-away.

Don't do that to your readers. Unresolved endings are lazy writing. Please-buy-Book-Two cliffhangers are poor customer service. Resolve at least one dramatic arc to leave the reader satisfied and ready for the next book.

At the end of each book in a series, your character needs to achieve what they set out to do, and/or have grown as a person. Then reveal a bit of the larger Quest or greater personal change coming up, and renew their dedication to their Objective.

EXERCISE: Character Purpose

Consider why each character is in your story:

What does this character add that we must have to complete the Quest? Can this character's physical contribution or dramatic purpose be given to any other character?

What skills do they bring to the team, whether that's *knows how to slay minotaur* or *wields curling iron to make hero feel beautiful*?

Where does that needed quality show up in the book?

Readers more readily attach to characters with a clear reason to be in the story. If a sense of their unique contribution isn't shown the first time the character appears, carefully consider why not. If you don't have a specific reason for holding back why someone's in the story, get it into their first scene. If they are a double agent or secret enemy, clearly show their fake purpose when they first appear.

MEMOIR: CHARACTER

For memoirists, the Character Draft is the draft in which you are even more honest about yourself than you are about everyone else. How do you reconcile your own behavior with the situation or the end result? Who deserves the benefit of the doubt? Where did you screw up? Self-hagiography is boring. Very few situations truly involve a wronged innocent.[54]

The best memoirs lead us down a winding path and make us wonder how it will turn out—can we trust the narrator? Were they truly right? Reward the reader with heroism and relief at the end. But through the murky middle, show us the moments when the paths not taken looked a lot like the right choice.

Memoir often springs from a grudge. That's not a bad thing. If life had turned out exactly right, as your due, there would be no story to tell. But you must know your own anger and bewilderment, and that you are probably not a hero (if you are a hero, let someone else write you). You earn the right to write the pettiness, the silliness, the nasty selfishness of others, as you write your own.

Shaming is for editorials. A genuine attempt to understand and justify the behavior of those who "done you wrong" goes a long way toward a rounded and interesting memoir, instead of a litany of complaint.

Don't make your mother/father/ex-lover the villain—ask *why* they did what they did and show the reader that, too. Not just explaining kindly that they meant well or quoting the defense

---

54 This does not apply to child abuse. However, your memoir will still be more interesting if your abusers are presented as flawed humans, unless "faceless villain" is a deliberate choice you're making. Abuse of both children and adults gets covered up in part because many of us don't know what it looks like, so also show the part that looked like a lovely relationship to everyone else. Your story will have more tension and your book will have more impact.

they yelled at us too many times. But walking in their world, looking with their eyes. Seeing what they saw—however twisted, however rationalized—and *agreeing to believe them.*

There's plenty of time to show the reader our side, why they were wrong/lying/horrific, show why we survived, why we deserved to win. But victory is sweeter when it was in doubt. Survival is more meaningful when it's fraught with conflict, when we're still questioning, *Was I right to react that way?*

Think of yourself at this stage not as the writer, but as the fact-checker. It's hard and uncomfortable to examine our hurt feelings from the point of view of the person who hurt us, but it can deepen our writing to ask the person, "Why did you do that?" and see if their stated motivation belongs in there, too. The villain's side of the story may become a turning point for protagonist-you.

If you can't ask them, spend some time thinking about their motivations, just as you would for a fictional villain. Genuinely try to understand. If you dislike your antagonist so much you can't do this, enlist your most fair-minded and compassionate friend, your therapist, or your yoga teacher to brainstorm why someone might behave like that.

PASSION/FOIBLE & ABILITY/WEAKNESS

I'm not a character-chart person. I don't spend time on their astrological signs or childhood memories, though I sometimes discover those elements while I write. Instead, I consider two sets of contrasting characteristics:

1) The character's primary Ability and main Weakness.

The Ability makes the character the Chosen One—the right person to undertake this quest.

The Weakness is what they need to learn and why they need a team/sidekick/mentor, and gives the reader genuine suspense about whether the character can accomplish the goal.

2) The character's Passion for what they want most, and the Foible[55] or personal failing that stops them from getting it.

---

55   Say it "FOY-bull," and credit to immersive theatre director Gary Izzo for this pairing.

Passion drives the character to undertake the Quest. Foible helps the reader sympathize with them on the way—no matter how powerful the character is, they have a human (or human-ish) failing. They screw things up in ways that are their own darn fault.

These pairs of characteristics balance each other. Too much Ability and not enough Weakness gives a too-good-to-be-true Mary-Sue-perhero.[56] The story will lack suspense, because of course the protagonist is going to get what she wants, and she'll get it in exactly the way her Ability suggests. The story will lack drama and conflict, because the protagonist has no true challenges.

> *Harry Potter is naturally pretty good at magic* (Ability), *but Professor Snape holds institutional power that lets him genuinely challenge Harry no matter how good he is. Meanwhile, Harry can't control his impulses* (Weakness) *and keeps getting detention for sass.*

> *Katniss Everdeen is an amazing shot and a hard worker* (Abilities), *but her temper gets the best of her and she has a hard time seeing the big picture. Her quick anger and lack of trust in anything she doesn't fully understand* (Weaknesses) *create self-sabotage, including injuring her primary ally right before they enter the Games.*

In both cases, the characters' Weaknesses directly threaten their Ability. Harry can't look for the Sorcerer's Stone while in detention. Katniss can't get medicine she needs without playacting a love story she doesn't trust, which also gives her feelings she doesn't understand.[57]

A protagonist's Passion and Foible pair the same way. The thing they want is directly jeopardized by who they are.

> *Harry wants to hunt down the guy who killed his parents* (Passion). *But he's impatient and believes he can do the job alone* (Foible). *Whenever he tries to do something alone, he gets caught and punished, or creates a larger problem.*

> *Katniss wants to survive the Hunger Games* (Passion), *but realizes she wants Peeta to come out alive, too* (Foible).

---

56 We'll get to the fabulous Mary Sue in a moment.

57 In many ways, Katniss is Hulk-smash! Every time an emotion confuses her, she breaks something or hits someone.

Planning for two people to survive wrecks her solo survival plans.

Passion/Foible and Ability/Weakness must balance each other. Without her Foible, Katniss's Passion could have made her the sole winner of the Hunger Games, but then we'd hate her. Without Harry's Weakness of individualism, he might have told a responsible grown-up his problems and wrapped that sucker up by Book Four.

Balanced characters are more interesting and realistic, and create conflict and drama wherever they go. Give your character Passion for their Quest, and almost (but not quite!) enough Ability to attain it. Give them a Foible they can't help following, and a Weakness they must specifically learn to overcome.

EXERCISE: ABILITY, WEAKNESS, PASSION, FOIBLE

For each main character, determine your character's Ability/ Weakness and Passion/Foible. Think about how those paired qualities continue through the entire plotline.

Then drill down. For each scene of your story, note which character directly shows their Ability or Passion. Who else does that affect? How does it advance characters on their Quest or create another obstacle?

For each scene, note who is directly hindered by their Weakness or distracted by their Foible. Who else does that affect? How does this create conflict in the scene, or plant the seeds of later conflict?

KILL MARY SUE

Why doesn't Mary Sue belong in your book?

Because she's *amazing*.

Mary Sue is beautiful—but not normal-beautiful. She's exotically beautiful with an unusual eye or hair color, or she's a tomboy who thinks of herself as plain—but no way, she's gorgeous!

Her eyes shimmer, gleam, or radiate powers. She moves like a ninja—or she's adorably klutzy.

Mary Sue is talented. She's a computer genius, picks up magic spells immediately, recognizes liars, fights like an MMA champion, bonds with animals, and always knows the secret entrance.

Mary Sue is loved. Everyone in the good-guys group adores her and makes her the center of attention. Anyone who dislikes Mary Sue is obviously a villain or only around so Mary Sue looks good by comparison.[58] No matter how shy or socially awkward Mary Sue is, everyone is drawn to her and immediately trusts her with their deepest secrets.

Mary Sue's only flaws are stubbornness and/or a bad temper. But she's always right, so if she's yelling at someone, they deserve it. If she demands her own way, it turns out to be right.

Poor Mary Sue has a tragic backstory. After her parents were killed, she was raised by wolves or magicians or a cruel guardian who took away her rightful inheritance.

A Mary Sue may be named Anastasia or Lumina or Raven, or anything else so sparkly-special she can't get a personalized keychain to save her life. But she doesn't want that keychain, because she's *not like other girls*.

All of Mary Sue's struggles are in her tragic backstory. She starts the actual story as a badass, visits some literal or metaphorical battlefields, and finishes as the same badass, plus love interest, plus trophy.

Meh.

Many early drafts contain a Mary Sue: a character so special and perfect and amazing, she's boring as hell to read about. Often, Mary Sue (or Gary Stu) is the character the author wishes they were themselves. We all want special powers, skills to overcome all obstacles, and great hair—but stories are about struggle, conflict, and change.

In the Character Draft, you must remove most of Mary Sue's amazingness, talents, and strengths. You must give her genuine problems, now, in this plotline. Problems she actually has to learn and grow and acquire skills to overcome. If you're

---

58 If your novel features an evil ex-girlfriend, you get back in there and give that girl a personality and some reasons to believe she's been wronged. Reasons a normal person believes.

writing memoir, you must show the protagonist's—your—flaws and faults.

Too-perfect protagonists, or an unexamined memoir self, are boring and disingenuous. Readers invest more in an ordinary person with normal flaws and normal skills,[59] working hard at the limits of their abilities to physically or mentally survive the plot.

As a writer, your craft will get better if you give your characters real problems, and not quite enough tools to solve them.

VILLAINS

Just as heroes aren't Mary Sue, villains aren't the Big Bad Wolf.

Even when the story centers on good versus evil, the bad guy doesn't wake up in the morning, twirl his mustache, and cry, "I've got some oppressing to do today!"

What do your antagonists want, that—if the book were told from their POV—would make them the good guys? What does your villain believe in?

> *I've spent my life building a successful intergalactic organization with immense power and resources. It hurts me deeply that my son spurns his inheritance.*

Darth Vader has feelings, too. Or imagine *The Wizard of Oz* from the other side:

> *My sister was killed in a tragic architectural accident. Seeking an heirloom that's rightfully mine, I must defend myself before I'm murdered by the thief.*

Maybe the mad scientist thinks the country needs smart people to run it and having cyborg soldiers is proof you're smart. Maybe the billionaire thinks rich people should run things because they can't be bribed. Maybe the dictator wants a class of people who labor, collect their check, and go home, and everyone's employed because no one makes waves.

Or maybe they're suffering, too. My yoga teacher used to say to herself, when someone was horrible to her, *That person must be in a lot of pain to be behaving like that.*

---

59 "Normal" for the world you're writing.

In another life, I was an actor. I miss that work schedule—in some ways, the immediacy of "Be at rehearsal at 7 PM, we open in two weeks," is a lot easier and more comfortable than "Write 1000 words today. Or just 300 good ones. Or maybe do some research...which project am I working on again?"

That comfort, plus loving Shakespeare, plus being a huge ham, is probably why I auditioned for a local production of *Macbeth*, thinking to myself, *I'd love to play Lady Macbeth but I'll probably be a witch (again!). It'll be something fun to do a couple nights a week.*

Instead I won the title role in an all-female cast and spent the next six weeks living on takeout and not writing very much. I also learned to play a man—I live in Dubai, where casting Mac and Lady Mac as a power lesbian couple is not an option. I put on facial hair and stuffed my groin. But the biggest help was the shoes. Big, solid oxford brogues, half a pound each, with a blocky inch of heel.

I took longer steps. I shook hands hard and softened my grip with ladies. I touched people without their permission and interrupted everyone but my boss. I manspread like a champion. The show was an immersive production set in modern Dubai, and the audience followed actors through the venue to boardrooms and bedrooms and banquet halls. Between the official Shakespeare scenes, we improvised in modern language. The audience chased us upstairs and around corners. One night, I held the door to the elevator, barking at the guests following me, "Hustle! I'm not holding this door for my health!"

Suddenly, my dad was speaking through me. My gruff, angry dad.

That's why he barked. He had someplace he needed us to be. He was afraid we wouldn't get there if he left us behind. *And this is how that felt.*

Lady Macbeth spends most of Act 1 Scene 7 telling Macbeth, "If you were a real man, you'd kill the king. If you were a real man, I'd love you." In the next scene, I'd hover over sleeping King Duncan with my knife, terrified of murder but desperate to please her, to make her look at me with the same joy I imagine she used to.

That's the way I treated my ex-husband. As if nothing was enough, as if I got to define what it meant to be a man, and measure him. *And this is how that felt.*

There's power in stepping into someone else's shoes. You must ask, "In what view of the world is my villain the hero of their own story? What genuinely leads them to believe they're right?"

A villain who has some good points to make can increase the internal conflict for your protagonist—and increase external conflict, by making it harder for the hero's team to stay together through the whole Quest.

Traitors believe they're switching to the right side.

EXERCISE: THE HERO OF THEIR OWN STORY

Summarize your story from the villain's POV. Explore as fully and deeply as you can why they think everything they do is a great idea—or comes from a place of great pain, or great longing.

Make sure at least one scene in your manuscript shows why the villain behaves as they do, and why they think they're right. This could come at the beginning, as part of their origin story, or be revealed at the end as their secret motivation. Or the reader might catch glimpses of the villain's humanity and desires throughout.

CHARACTER THROUGH DIALOGUE

It's not just about vocal patterns. It's about what they're saying in addition to how they're saying it. It's about their ideas and vision and desires.

Chuck Wendig

If you haven't written much dialogue before, chances are some of your characters sound alike, or they sound like you, or they sound "writerly." Characters use vocabulary beyond their education. They speak in long sentences without a breath, or short sentences without much actual content. They sound overly formal, like the writer is trying to sound smart.

By the end of the Character Draft, your characters will each speak as themselves, and as real people, with a level of education and formality appropriate to their station and the world you've created.

Start by actively hearing and thinking about real conversation.

Most student playwrights are advised to improve their writing by going to public locations and listening to conversations. Beyond eavesdropping (fascinating in itself!)[60] this exercise teaches how much conversational filler real people use. How many *ums* and *likes* and *dudes* and *y'knows*.

EXERCISE: DIALOGUE

Go to a public place: a café, restaurant or shopping mall. Listen to conversations (walk away if it's clearly private rather than normal chatter) and note what kind of language people use, and the way their attitudes change when they talk to the servers or staff instead of talking to their companion.

If it's not safe to go out, or you aren't comfortable with this, schedule a video chat to catch up with a couple of friends. With their permission, record it. Interact normally—after about fifteen minutes people will forget the recorder is on. Then, listen to the audio and notice verbal patterns.[61]

Now, read a chunk of the dialogue in your manuscript aloud, into a voice recording app. Listen to it and pay attention to what sounds like real conversation but a little bit smoother, and what sounds fake, stilted, or overdone.

As you edit through the Character Draft, make deliberate choices about each character's speech.

What makes characters sound unique?

Sentence lengths and patterns. How long do they speak before taking a breath? People with more education tend to use longer, more complex sentences. They may include multiple ideas in a sentence, or

---

60 Earbuds that aren't playing music make this easier. Bob your head for verisimilitude.

61 If you have older characters, get in touch with older relatives. That's a good deed for the world as well as your book.

backtrack, bringing in details out of order. Younger or less-educated characters may speak in shorter sentences with simpler grammar.

People speaking a second language often bring in language patterns from their mother tongue. "Broken" English can reflect an innate cultural pattern showing in a learned language. Make careful choices.

Coherent thoughts. Some characters know what they mean and say it. Others navigate their thoughts as they speak. Often, high-status people finish a complete thought in a complete sentence, and they expect everyone to pay attention the whole time. Low-status people may pause, checking in if it's still OK to talk, or if their words are welcome.

Formality. Does anyone use particularly formal or informal language? Do they change that pattern based on who they're speaking to? Think about Britney Spears explaining to the *Mickey Mouse Club* audience, "When Ah git back home, Ah start talkin' country agin. Stuff like, 'yonder' and 'hey y'all.'" Too much dialect can be hard to read, but using a few phrases to signify the formality level can make dialogue sparkle a bit more.

Code-switching. People of color and in minoritized communities often speak differently to members of the majority than they do at home, using different speech patterns, vocabulary, dialects, and accents. If you incorporate code-switching for a character whose background is different from your own, you will need a member of that group to read your work for accuracy and appropriateness. Paid "sensitivity readers" can give insight on why certain choices may or may not work on the page.

Vocabulary. If a character uses big words or special vocabulary, think about where they learned those words. Are they using them naturally or trying to make the world see them in a particular way?

Literary devices. Do your characters use similes, metaphors, and analogies? Similes are simpler, metaphors are more complex and require more understanding. Comparisons can also add to world-building: "She jumped like a frog in a bucket" shows a different world than "She jumped like she was on Phobos without her G-belt."

Candor. Who has gaps between what they say and what they think? How does that change based on who they're talking to?

Empathy. How much compassion and comprehension does each speaker show outwardly? How self-focused are they? You can also use this in the narrative, showing what the narrator notices about other people.

Stress. How do your characters' speech patterns and word choices change under pressure?

EXERCISE: Character Voices

Go through your manuscript several times; once for each character. Each time, read only that character's dialogue and thoughts, checking for voice, consistency, slang, dialect and contractions.

Does each line sound specifically like this character?

If the dialogue tags were taken away, would it still be pretty clear who's talking?

Make conscious decisions about who uses contractions, who uses what slang, and how the adults speak differently than the kids.

HIGH & LOW-CONTEXT COMMUNICATION

People who know each other well use high-context communication. Inside jokes and shared experiences let them avoid spelling out things they both already know.

> *"Hey Gabe!" Maya said. "Doc Patel rip out another molar?"*
>
> *Gabriel cautiously touched his white-wrapped jaw. "Still numb."*

Sometimes, characters are written using low-context communication. We get trapped in overexplaining to make sure the reader GETS IT.

> *"Hello Gabriel," Maya said. "I see by the bandage on your cheek you've come from Doctor Patel's office."*

Gabriel cautiously touched the white strips covering what looked like stitches in his jaw. "Our mutual dentist? Why yes, I was there a few minutes ago."[62]

Low-context communication is sometimes called "As You Know Bob"—a joking reference to a character saying something like, "As you know, Bob, your father, the king, has died." That's not two characters in the same world talking to each other—it's the writer telling the reader, "I need you to know this information and I can't figure out how else to get it into the scene."

Trust the reader to make associations (or to read further to find out what's up):

"Let's talk about the Martin account," Bob said. "I think you're about ready to handle it alone."

James looked away. "Sure." He shuffled the papers in front of him and stood up.

Bob was still talking. "How's Marlene?"

James twisted his wedding ring. "She's—she's fine." He met Bob's eyes. "She's just fine."

For a moment, the silence stretched. Then Bob laughed harshly and slapped James on the shoulder, so hard they both staggered.

We know something happened. We may not know *what* yet, but making the reader the detective—sustaining Mystery— is much more compelling than hearing a bald explanation:

"Hello, Bob," James said, trying not to show his disgust at his boss, who'd slept with James' wife. His promotion was on the line, though—he had to be pleasant.

When low-context communication lays it all out for the reader, nothing has happened dramatically. We just got told stuff. Instead, high-context moments of "Aha! Now I know what they meant!" excite and satisfy the reader, giving them the urge to read on.

---

62 I realize it's unlikely Gabriel would have external stitches for a tooth extraction, but let's just say this tooth was really impacted.

EXERCISE: TRIMMING THE NARRATIVE

The narrative is all the writing that isn't dialogue and thoughts—basically, the part that's the writer, or the POV character, telling the story. Early drafts often have too much telling about characters in the narrative and not enough showing the characters through dialogue and action. One way to fix that is to experiment with removing the narrative entirely.

Choose a scene from your manuscript (or a book you admire) with lots of dialogue.

1) Rewrite the scene as a script, using only dialogue and the most necessary actions. Take out anything that's "narration."

For example, I've added too much narrative and screwed up the dialogue in this scene from a writer friend's work-in-progress:

An older man with thinning brown hair and a deeply dimpled chin approached us. He looked like trouble to me, but what did I know?

"Are you Mr. Kincade? They told me to look for the gentleman with the big redheaded bodyguard, and here you both are, right where I thought."

This wasn't the first time I'd been used as a landmark, my six-foot-five frame towering over most parties.

"Yes. I'm afraid you have me at a disadvantage."

That phrasing, and lack of a smile as they shook hands in cautious greeting, was my cue. Roberto did not want to be left alone with this man for any reason. And when my boss was nervous, so was I.

"I'm Charlie Camden, we already know each other because you own a chain of clubs I'm interested in acquiring."

"Ah, Mr. Camden. Your trail of slime precedes you."

Time for me to maneuver on top of the situation here. I touched Roberto's back to warn him I was primed to intervene and let him know which side I was moving to. "Excuse me, sirs. We're in a walkway and we're obstructing the thoroughfare for the ladies and gentlemen at the party. Could we step over here?"

I led them to a small round table.

As a play:

CHARLIE: Are you Mr. Kincade? They told me to look for the gentleman with the big redheaded bodyguard.

WES: Not the first time I've been used as a landmark.

ROBERTO: I'm afraid you have me at a disadvantage.

CHARLIE: I'm Charlie Camden.

(ROBERTO and CHARLIE shake hands without smiling)

ROBERTO: Ah, Mr. Camden.

(WES glances at the situation, then touches ROBERTO's back and leads the way)

WES: Excuse me, sirs. We're in a walkway.

(He gestures at, then leads them to a small, round table)

2) Now, go back and look technically at each line, adjusting them to sound even more like the character.

3) Take off all the character names and see if it's still reasonably easy to understand who is speaking.

4) Rewrite the scene from the script, adding dialogue tags as needed for clarification.[63]

An older man with thinning brown hair and a deeply dimpled chin approached us. "Are you Mr. Kincade? They told me to look for the gentleman with the big redheaded bodyguard."

This wasn't the first time I'd been used as a landmark.

"Yes. I'm afraid you have me at a disadvantage."

Roberto's lack of smile as they shook hands was my cue. Do not leave him alone with this man for any reason.

"I'm Charlie Camden."

"Ah, Mr. Camden."

I touched Roberto's back to warn him I was about to intervene. "Excuse me sirs. We're in a walkway. Could we step over here?"

I led them to a small round table.[64]

---

63 More on dialogue tags in Chapter 4: The Technical Draft

64 This version is much closer to Sky Burr-Drysdale's work-in-progress *Wes & Sava* before I messed it up to be an example.

EXERCISE: ONE LAST CHARACTER POLISH

For each character, go through the book and read only their parts.

- Do the protagonist's actions and reactions seem motivated and urgent?

- Do any supporting characters need more development? Do any not belong?

- Do the antagonists have clear motivations that make sense to themselves and (eventually) the reader, even if they're a mystery to the protagonist?

- If you're writing memoir, are you treating people fairly and letting the reader judge their actions and speech, rather than telling the reader what to think?

For each main character (and heck, do it for the minor ones, too, it'll make the book stronger), look at three things:

1) Existing state: Who were they when the book started? What were they like? How did they see themselves and how did others see them? What did they want?

2) Change: What causes them to change who they are? Is that change generated within themselves or by someone else seeing them differently? How does this change result in people treating them differently and them acting differently? What do they want now?

3) Resolution: What does this change lead to? What action do they take that they wouldn't have taken before? Did they get what they want, and how did getting it or not getting it affect them?

WORLD-BUILDING

No matter what genre you're writing, the world is another character in your story, one the reader must also know well.

But world-building is not description. As writer Chuck Wendig says, "Details are mostly boring." Readers should learn the details by watching the characters interact with the world throughout the plot. Everything a character touches or receives information from shows something about time and place.

Near the beginning of the story, get in just enough detail to show us what "normal" is. The closer your normal is to the world of the reader, the less you have to show. If trees are trees, you can focus on the single detail that matters:

> *The tree had not been on that corner the day before.*
>
> *The tree rustled, even though there was no wind.*
>
> *He drew closer to the tree. One leaf had gone flaming red. It was February.*

Contemporary novels get a shortcut: much of the world is already built. The novelist can focus on the inner world of the character, or her particular subculture or community. In Diane Zinna's *The All-Night Sun*, a grieving orphan compares her own world to that of the international students in her English class:

> *They didn't realize how much I connected with them, how keenly I felt their descriptions of not having the right words, of not being in on the jokes, of laughing along to something you didn't understand when laughter was the last thing your homesick heart could bear. Grief can feel like homesickness.*

The world is specifically one in which her support system is missing; grief colors everything she sees.

With fantasy, science fiction, and historical fiction, the reader must be plunged into the world right away. The author must quickly establish "normal in this world" so the reader can feel it when the norm is broken—why this night is different than all other nights. Show the character behaving as usual...but getting a different reaction, as when Harry Potter finds out the details of wizard school by anticipating regular school. Or the character pays more attention to things that are new or surprising, as when Laura Ingalls boards a train for the first time in *By the Shores of Silver Lake.*

Build the overall world gradually. Readers won't understand the larger importance of the protagonist's quest if they only see the part of the world the protagonist directly interacts with, but readers will disengage if there's a full-on history and culture lecture in the narrative.

When you establish baseline normal, think about time, place, politics, travel, social mores, religion, technology, communications, and the level of privacy in daily life. Historical fiction authors can look up details and choose which ones to use. Fantasy gives free rein, but be consistent within your created world so readers aren't disoriented. In a dystopia, hint at what went wrong with the world before. With paranormal elements, a clearly established set of powers shows what's new—plenty of paranormal stories kick off with "Normally my ESP works like this, but today something went wrong!"

Even in creative nonfiction or contemporary fiction, it's still important to set up the time period and the physical location—a normal day in Texas is very different from one in Paris or New York. If your Black male hero wears a natural (hairstyle), is it the 1968 Black Power natural or the 2016 hipster version?

When you build a new world, it's tempting to rely on knowing what words like "castle" or "masculine" or "loyalty" mean in our world. But they have to be defined in the world created. Without consistent, deliberate world-building, the reader gets distracted trying to figure out where and when they are, what's important and what's not, what technology exists and what doesn't. Readers must be shown, usually through the eyes and feelings of the main character, what concepts are the same as in the real world and what are different. They need to feel the author's hand guiding them through the new land.

Time

Even if you're using a date as a scene or chapter header, give details that anchor readers firmly in that time:

> *Harold ran a hand over the tail fins of his brand-new Chevrolet Impala.*
>
> *Kevin ran a hand over the '59 Chevy's tail fins. He'd pick his classic hotrod over a Prius and clean air any day.*

If you use language with anachronisms like "thou" or "ye," make sure the reader knows if you're in real history with an invented story, fake history, or a time that isn't Earth's history at all. Is this Medieval Europe? An Earth where the Brazilians are the dominant world power? Pseudo-Ancient Rome?

Time can frequently be shown by juxtaposing technology and geography. For example, horse collars + no gunpowder + Europe puts us around AD 1100 in real history. Even if you're not using a real time, learning about that historical period might give you some ideas for your political structure or details of daily life.

Physical World

Show the environment. Reading about great characters without enough setting is like watching actors filming against a green screen for the background to be filled in later. (If you're missing the physical world in your current draft, no big deal, fill it in now.)

Think about how climate dictates clothing, which dictates physical movement and personal interaction. Human reactions to weather can give emotional content to physical spaces.

Be clear on where places are in relation to each other, and what means the characters use to get from place to place. For example, in *The Hunger Games*, you travel on foot if you're poor, on a high-speed train if you're rich, and in a hovercraft if you're military. This also shows the restrictions on poor people's movement, and the terrifying power of the Peacekeepers.

Technology

How do people communicate? Letters, messengers, emails, telegrams, phones, carrier pigeons? Tech is one of the fastest ways to show the world through character interaction in a scene:

Her phone vibrated. "Yikes, it's Mom. Again."

The wallscreen blinked. Her mother's angry face came into view before she could hit "refuse."

The messenger stood before her. "Madam? Will you answer your mother's request?"

"Was that the telegram boy at the door? Did he have something from Mother?"

She clutched the paper in her hand. Her mother had to be the last person on First Earth who'd written paper letters, but now she was glad to have it.

Social Rules

What constitutes etiquette in this world? How are people polite, how are they rude, and how do they manage to express rudeness while being "officially" polite?

What's the social hierarchy? How do members of the insider group relate to each other and how is that level of formality different with outsiders? What physical contact is allowed? What's a violation of protocol?

In your memoir, is your family only polite to people they dislike? How do your own rules conflict with those around you?

Privacy

What's the distinction between how people behave in public and how they behave in private?

How is nudity viewed? How well do people know each other before sharing personal details? In Tudor England, it was an honor to be the person who held the chamber pot for the king or queen, because the position gave political access.

Religion

What's the role of religion? Is it official? Is it mandatory? How does it weave through daily life?

Are there religious icons—mezuzahs or crucifixes or crescents or home shrines—that show who belongs to what creed? A religious dress code?

Political Hierarchy

What's the world's governing structure? How do political entities (countries, kingdoms, city-states) relate to each other?

Is there a nobility, and is it hereditary? What about alliances through marriage?

How does religion affect politics? When Henry VIII wanted to marry Anne Boleyn, he had to leave the Catholic Church, create a new religion, and execute a number of advisors who tried to tell him no. In *The Handmaid's Tale*, religion and politics are one.

Where does the military fit into this? Who bosses it officially and who bosses it for real? Are defense forces their own entity or subject to another branch of government?

Names

If you're working with real names, group characters by name origin, both in place and time.

If you're inventing names, look at the patterns in real names. Names that "belong together" can show that people belong together.

EXERCISE: WORLD-BUILDING

Find a passage in your manuscript where you've spelled out details of the world. Revise to show the same information, but by the characters interacting with environment.

Check for description of more than a paragraph per chapter. Focus on your characters' interactions with the world and how we can see the world as they experience it. Limit the characters' view to what they can see.

BACKSTORY: THE CURSE OF KNOWLEDGE

Many writers do considerable work on the story around the story—where characters come from, what shaped their lives before they entered this plot, the history of the world they've built. But there's a fine line between too much information and too little.

You will fully know your details and your characters; the art is in revealing them in a way that hooks the reader. Sometimes we write "infodumps"—places where far too much information is revealed at once, and it bogs down the plot.

In this scene from *Jumpsong*, a manuscript-in-progress, the protagonist, Elzbit,[65] is signing up as a navigator. This closes the chapter where she's chosen by a space crew:

> *"Fine," he sighed and returned to the waiting group. "We'll take her."*
>
> *Provincial documents denoting her temporary Hy'lot status under Chaebol MacTavish's control were drawn up and signed by retinal scan and DNA print. A copy would be stored on ship and with the bonding office but not pushed to the broader network until she was formally bonded. Escort by a crew member any time she left the ship would also be required until she was accepted as a full Hy'lot.*
>
> *Elzbit would take the ship for two jumps and then back to the station for formal bonding provided both sides agreed. Technically a Hy'lot could refuse an assignment but it never actually happened.*

Six words of plot, a stage direction, and two paragraphs of paperwork. Do not open your exciting space opera with paperwork.

> *"Fine," he sighed. "We'll take her."*

...ends the chapter just fine.

- We know they've shown up to hire her and they do.

- Elzbit's temporary status isn't relevant. If that matters, the crew can treat her like an outsider, or later dialogue can ask if she's staying. Or we can find out later, when she desperately wants to be permanent (drama!).

- We'll find out she must be escorted if she actually leaves the ship. That could then create conflict about being babysat, or conflict about finding an escort when she wants to get off the ship, or it could create conflict if she fights with her escort but can't stomp away on her own.

---

65 Elzbit is a cuddly space iguana with a deep inner life, watch for her in Sky Burr-Drysdale's *Jumpsong*, on shelves in a couple years!

- We'll find out how long her term of service is when it's time to sign on permanently, quit, or be fired.

- *Technically a Hy'lot could refuse an assignment but it never actually happened* could actually be valuable, because it shows her race's status relative to the space crews. But it probably belongs earlier or later as a tiny extra detail in Elzbit's thoughts, possibly as she's on her way to meet the crew.

Whenever possible, avoid explaining details that can be learned from context. When there's a guidebook or a manual in the middle of the action, the reader gets distracted and mentally moves away from the characters and their immediate situation. Give only enough detail to understand the plot—let the reader make discoveries. If your writing style includes lush, lavish descriptions of setting, customs, and history, go for it, but know that you will need to write exposition extremely well to hold the reader's interest.

Finally, when your story is set in a world that readers know, or have assumptions about, you can challenge some expectations and reinforce others. For example, if you're writing dystopian fiction (or for that matter, social-issue driven nonfiction), readers already have beliefs about evil governments, technology taking over, and rebels. Without over-explaining, address and clarify those expectations—and shock readers when you go against what they think they "know."

EXERCISE: BACKSTORY

Read every section that's a description of a character or setting's past history. Ask yourself:

Do we have to know this to understand this character?

Do we have to know all of it?

Do we have to know it right now?

FACT-CHECKING

Oh, facts. Those pesky things that get in the way of a good story. Problem is, sometimes our readers know the facts, and when we get fuzzy or inaccurate, it yanks them out of the story, their inner child shouting, "Are not!" Then we have to win them back—and everything else we write is suspect. (If the writer didn't get *that* right, what else did they screw up?)

As you write, note things to fact-check. If you're still in the Vomit Draft, take a little time each day that is specifically *not* your writing time and look them up. Confirm brand names, place names, historical event dates and details, etc. Researching them may also jog new story ideas, flesh out characters, or provide interesting details to include.

Once, for an 816-word flash fiction set in the UK, I fact-checked

* the spelling of Haagen-Dazs

* the location of Sussex, England and where would be far enough from the sea to not have saltwater affect daily walking life

* the color of irises, when irises bloom and what else blooms with them

* what a small patch of municipal garden would be called in an English village

* what's a "road" and what's a "street" in colloquial British English

* whether a middle-aged man in southern England would say "bottle of HP" or "bottle of HP sauce" (checked when brought to my attention by an eagle-eyed reader)

* how the police department of Sussex is referred to in casual conversation, and in a news story

* whether holly in Britain is a bush or a vine

* which TV chef hosted "Restaurant Challenge"

* ...and quite a bit more.

Fact-checking can take almost as long as writing the piece. But if we don't care enough to get the facts, then part of the story is a lie.

It's not that we can't make stuff up. After all, "It may not be what happened, but it's the truth" is a good grounding for fiction and creative nonfiction alike. But if we deviate from the facts, or set a lie in opposition to a truth, we have to know it, and do it on purpose.

Ignorance is no excuse.

Part of the joyful drudgery of writing is our responsibility to the truth—and the delight and wonder of finding out what that truth is.

The late Dick Francis's horse-racing mysteries included other worlds. Catering. Meteorology. The trade in high-quality semi-precious gemstones. And because he cared enough to write the facts, I know a lot more about them than before I read his books. Discovering new worlds helped me enjoy his somewhat formulaic mysteries.

I like to think Francis enjoyed discovering them, too. And every time we check a technical term, or call someone who does the job we're writing about, or look up the weather in another city for our character to walk through on a sunny May afternoon, we serve ourselves, our readers, and the truth.

LYRICS

The short answer to "What song lyrics can I quote in my book?" is "You can't."

Not easily, anyway.

Songs written after 1925-ish are almost certainly under copyright. First, find the writer(s)—who may or may not be the singer or band who recorded the song. You'll need to credit them even if you don't have to pay them.

Then track down the song's publisher through ASCAP or BMI. The music publisher wants to see your publication contract or specific, written publication plans including where you'll be selling the book, the cover price, and how many copies will be printed. Then the music publisher bills you.

When Blake Morrison wrote *South of the River*, his permissions got expensive. He told the *Guardian*,

> *I still have the invoices. For one line of 'Jumpin' Jack Flash': £500. For one line of Oasis's 'Wonderwall': £535. For one line of 'When I'm Sixty-four': £735. For two lines of 'I Shot the Sheriff' (words and music by Bob Marley, though in my head it was the Eric Clapton version): £1,000. Plus several more, of which only George Michael's 'Fastlove' came in under £200. Plus VAT. Total cost: £4,401.75.*

But what about "fair use"?

Fair use is the legal principle that allows quotations from artistic works under copyright. Quotations are fair use if the number of words used is a small proportion of the total in the original work; if the quote is properly attributed; and if it's essential to the point you're making in your own work.

As of 2021, song lyrics have not yet been held to a "fair use" standard. Arguably, even a line of a song is a fairly large proportion compared to say, 200 words from a 90,000-word novel. But even short poems can be quoted in some contexts. What makes songs different?

Music publishers with deep pockets, excellent legal teams, and a strong precedent of defending their copyrights. Your literary publisher doesn't want to spend her time and money in court, so she will seek permissions or ask you to remove unpermitted lyrics.

You can obliquely quote in a way that makes knowledge of the original song unnecessary:

> *He banged his head to "Sweet Child O' Mine" and I wished hard I could like Guns N Roses.* (Titles are OK!)
>
> *On the radio, Springsteen was on fire, singing his creepy lyrics about Daddy not being home.*
>
> *We rolled down the windows and cranked up the stereo— GooGooDolls, The Cure, KLM, the bass throbbing in my chest and making me feel like I was part of everyone.*

Before gearing up for the permissions process, consider what impact quoted lyrics will truly have in your book. Does your reader associate "Janie's Got A Gun" with that beautiful night you sat in a convertible, watching the ocean roll in below the hills? Or does she remember her school's anti-violence initiative that used the literal message of the song? Will readers from another generation even know the song you're quoting? Will they think of it as "Mom's music" instead of "pulse-pounding jam"?

A single lyric conjures up a world of emotion in our heart. But it's both uncertain and a bit lazy to expect that line to do the same for every reader. You've got something important to say. Don't lean on a song to say it for you. Instead, ask yourself what emotional purpose that song serves, and put that feeling in the setting, in the narrative, in the dialogue. Trust in your power to create your own music in the reader's head.

THE TECHNICAL DRAFT

Writing has rules.

Storytelling has fewer rules, and certainly more flexible ones.

But actual writing has legit rules.

It's not math, not exactly—but things do add up a certain way and we are beholden to either apply the rules to our work or break the rules to create a specific effect.

You don't just break the rules because it's fun, or worse, because you don't know them. That latter is where a lot of new writers fall. They simply don't know that things work a certain way, and when you write in contravention to These Certain Ways, we can all smell it. It's stinky. Your prose gains the vinegar stink of flopsweat as you gallumph about on the stage of the page, not knowing how to actually do this thing you promised us that you can do.

Chuck Wendig

At this point your story is in pretty good shape. Now it's time to focus on words, sentences, and scenes. The Technical Draft is where you refine your authorial voice. It's also where you will greatly improve your manuscript by making noncreative craft fixes.

This is not a grammar book or your high-school English class. You already know the basic mechanics (or can google them). This draft is about fully understanding how words work in combination with each other and in their layout on the page. Learning generally accepted English usage is terrific—understanding why to use those rules and when to break them is even better.

The more rules you break, the better your story or your writing must be to hold the reader's attention. We've all been frustrated reading a wildly popular book that wasn't well-written...yet the story captured millions of readers. But writing a story with that much appeal is a crapshoot, so you might as well add good writing to the reasons why readers choose your book.

The writing class in which I learned the most technical craft was terrifying. In most workshops, the writer sends their pages in advance. Everyone reads and marks up their own copies to hand back to the writer. In class, the writer or the teacher reads a few pages aloud. Then there's discussion.

Not my MFA nonfiction class. There was no reading schedule— we brought our pages and lunged forward, learning to demand time and space for our work instead of waiting politely for a turn. We'd pass out copies and begin reading aloud. When our professor, J. D. Dolan, got bored or heard something that felt "wrong," he'd interrupt: "Stop! Stop there. Can you hear the problem?"

Very often this was after the first sentence.

Reading your own work, knowing you're probably about to be cut off, is dreadful. But after a couple of classes, we *could* hear when someone else's work went wrong. We discussed the problem that needed tackling before moving forward. We appreciated not having to read nine more pages with the *exact same problem*. And we fixed those problems and brought our pages back for more critique.[66]

When a reader chooses your book from a shelf or uses "Look Inside!" for sample pages, they will mentally stop when they hit something "wrong." They will put the book back or close the window.

You may be counting on hiring a professional editor. As an editor, I quote lower prices for cleaner writing, and the writer gets better and more in-depth feedback for their money. Writers thinking it's the editor's job to clean up everything cheat themselves of

---

66 On the first day, when we each shared why we'd signed up for this class, I said, "Because I heard you're a hardass and I'm tired of easy A's. I want to get better." J. D. was and I did. I was less proud of my eventual A than of one day bringing in an essay and getting through the *whole thing* without being stopped (hallelujah!).

the opportunity to improve their craft by making a thousand tedious fixes, and in the course of that work, teaching themselves new habits. If a writer must, say, re-punctuate all their dialogue, the correct way will begin to come naturally.

Writers who blow off learning craft with, "It's not the writing that counts, it's the story underneath" may be deluding themselves that they are a special snowflake for whom packaging is irrelevant. (Are they dating people who don't take baths? Are they going to the mall in their bathing suit?) Or they are too busy accepting prestigious awards for their incredible rule-breaking-but-consistent style while their publisher handles the editing.

Painters sketch—even Abstract Expressionists. Dancers learn technique—even breakdancers. Singers practice scales and learn to read music. It is the height of arrogance for writers to pretend our personal talent is somehow "above" developing our craft to clearly express our vision in a way our readers can receive.

We can do it alone.

We can hire help.

But we cannot ever pretend that writing full of errors is equal to writing that isn't.

Writing craft makes great storytellers into great writers.

In the Technical Draft, you'll move through the four stages of learning:

- Unconscious incompetence—we don't know what's not working in our writing.
- Conscious incompetence—we feel crappy about the ways our writing is not working.[67]
- Conscious competence—we must repeat and remember and remind ourselves to write well.
- Unconscious competence—after practice, our best writing comes more naturally.

Best of all, the Technical Draft fits into your life. Not "feeling it," but need to get some writing in? Don't have three hours for the coffee shop, but you might have fifteen minutes before carpool? Much of the editing in the Technical Draft can be done in short chunks, and it's truly technical—your creative brain can rest.

---

67 It's not that bad; you're just noticing it more. It'll get better quickly now that you know.

You're also going to learn the greatest editing secret weapon in my arsenal. If you have the courage to use it, you'll be more confident in your writing than ever before.

WORD COUNTS

Word counts matter for two reasons:

1) Length can determine which agents, publishers, and readers will buy your book. This applies to online and bookstore purchases, and to both traditional and independent publishing. When faced with an overlong or too-short book...

Agents think: This author doesn't know the market; perhaps their storytelling needs work.

Publishers think: This long-ass book will be expensive to print, or This skinny book's spine will be hard to find on the shelf.

Readers think: This fat book is expensive and looks time-consuming, or I don't think I'm getting my money's worth on this skinny book.

2) Readers are accustomed to the stories in different genres playing out in familiar amounts of time. The more you violate their expectations, the better your story and writing must be to hold their attention.

General word-count guidelines, longest to shortest:

Sweeping, epic fantasy and sweeping, epic historical fiction: 120,000-150,000. A lower word count probably means not enough world-building. More may mean too many subplots or too much backstory. However, debut novels are unlikely to be this long. For your first book, max out at 120K and use every word carefully.

Science fiction: 85,000-120,000, depending on how complicated the world-building is and how close the technology is to the reader's world. Lower means not enough world-building. Higher means too much jargon or an extraneous subplot.

Upmarket, women's, or book club fiction: 80,000-110,000. Lower means the book isn't exploring an issue seriously enough that readers can talk about it with their friends. Higher probably means you're wordy at the sentence level or multiple scenes show the same idea. (More also means half the club won't finish the book before the next meeting.)

Non-epic fantasy and non-epic historical fiction: 80,000-110,000. Lower means not enough world-building, higher means too much backstory or scenes that aren't moving the plot.

Mysteries, thrillers, suspense and domestic suspense: 80,000-100,000. Lower means you're missing a twist (or two). Higher means the countdown is getting boring and your protagonist is faffing around instead of solving the crime, discovering the secret or saving the world. If the book has a unique voice (like noir), aim for 65-80K to leave the reader wanting more.

Romance and light women's fiction ("chick lit"): 65,000-90,000. Lower means the relationship is moving too fast. Higher means someone needs to get to the point and say they're in love already. "Category Romance" is a special genre in which each publisher has their own, very specific rules for each sub-genre or publishing imprint. If you're publishing traditionally, follow your publisher's guidelines. If you're self-publishing, research typical lengths in your category.

Literary fiction: 60,000-100,000. Lower might mean the book is too short; or if that's the right length, it might need a unique style element. Higher means wordy sentences, too much character development, or the narrative is meandering. If you write like a National Book Award winner, make it whatever length your story needs.

Young Adult: 50,000-90,000. Only reach the higher end with world-building. Lower means not enough plot to serve the story.[68] Higher means too many young readers will be turned off by the length. Either way, storytelling for young adults means *tell them the story* and leave them time to think about it after.

Middle Grade: 35,000-50,000. Longer is too complicated for young readers, or your book will outlast their attention spans *as determined by the teachers, parents and librarians who* buy *the books.* Yes, you were a unique flower reading *War and Peace* in fifth grade. Write for the rest of the fifth-graders and be happy that smart second-graders are reading up.

Picture books: fewer than 2000 words. And you're reading the wrong book right now. Go join the Society for Children's Book Writers and Illustrators (SCBWI) and start with their suggested resources.

---

68 Laurie Halse Anderson's *Speak* is 46,591 words. The length works because the book has a high-tension plot around a dark subject. Karen McManus's *One of Us Is Lying* is about 92K, and the length works because the book is told in multiple POVs, each of which must be fully developed.

If your book is too long:

1. Send pages 50-70 to a writer or reader friend. Ask what they know about the story from this point, and what they don't understand. It's likely you have started the story too late and can pull just the needed details from the first fifty pages, making a healthy cut of 10,000 words or more. (You may have already done this in the Story Draft; it's worth doing again if you know you're wordy.)

2. Map the structures of the main dramatic arc and subplots. Can anything be removed as a dramatic unit? Maybe only one or two subplot details need adding to the main arc.

3. Repeat the Plot exercise from Chapter 2 and make sure every event has a purpose.

4. Write a synopsis. If your book can't be explained in 1000 words, the plot is over-complicated. Trim it down by simplifying cause-and-effect sequences. (Trimming a synopsis and then editing the book to match is easier than the other way around).

5. Follow the steps in the Technical Tune-Up section of the Self-Editing Checklist at the end of this book.

6. Ask a sharp-eyed friend or hire an editor to look at your first twenty-five pages. Specifically ask, "My book is too long, can you see any reasons why?" They may tell you the story hasn't started yet, or your sentences are wordy, or you repeat ideas. Apply that feedback through the whole manuscript.

If your book is too short:

1. Map the structures of the main dramatic arc and all the subplots. Are you hitting high points and low points in each act? Are there enough Surprises? Is your protagonist facing real challenges that they must change (and work) to overcome? Is that change shown in action?

2. Check your world-building, whether that's a solar system or a high school. Are the political, social, technological and religious elements of the world clear?

3. Add a subplot that shows another significant change in the protagonist or a main companion.

4. Share your manuscript with a reader or writer friend and ask where they wanted more information or felt like things happened too quickly.

VOICE

Voice is how we know it's you.

Voice is the narrator's manner and tone while telling the story. This can be the voice of a character, an omniscient or exterior narrator, or the author.

The authorial voice in nonfiction and memoir is the writer talking to the reader. At the news site *Slate*, several writers share the parenting column. Here are fragments of three responses to different letters about sibling conflict:

Michelle Hermann:

> *He can ask as often as he wants (or needs) to; she can say no every time. It's not your 9-year-old daughter's job to reassure your 10-year-old son—it's yours.*

Jamilah Lemieux:

> *Your letter implies there may be something else that you and your family will have to confront that is much more complicated than the current rift between your daughters.*

Nicole Cliffe:

> *Your parents are just old and tired and wise enough 10 years on to know what things to let slide. The allowance? Let's call it inflation. Food in the living room? They've given up on that carpet, which likely is a lot less pristine after 10 years of family use.*

Similar advice, delivered with no-nonsense practicality from Michelle, compassionate probing from Jamilah, and snarky realism from Nicole.

That's voice.

In fiction, the narrative voice may be entirely unlike the author's. If the narrator is a character, the voice often shifts with age or experience. Here is Hilary Mantel, writing as young Oliver Cromwell in *Wolf Hall* (for bonus points, read this aloud):

> *The weather is cold but the sea is flat. Kat has given him a holy medal to wear. He has slung it around his neck with a cord. It makes a chill against the skin of his throat. He unloops it. He touches it with his lips, for luck. He drops it; it whispers into the water. He will remember his first*

sight of the open sea: a gray wrinkled vastness, like the
residue of a dream.

The last sentence is "lyrical," which means prose that's a bit poetic. The literal sight of the sea is followed by a metaphor and a simile. That sentence is also complex—Mantel stacks the literary devices so that the simile refers to the metaphor and not the original sight. Even then, the words aren't "big vocabulary." Every sentence before the last is simple, almost flat, ten words or fewer. They each start with subject-verb, even the lyrical one. Mantel isn't telling us how to feel, or even diving deeply into Cromwell's feelings. She's showing us, in plain language, what he physically experiences. Only that last lyrical sentence of twenty words shows this boy's potential for deep thoughts.

As an extra-sophisticated touch, notice how the words have fewer syllables at the beginning of the paragraph. Then the first "poetic" moment has alliteration—the medal "whispers into the water." That phrase ushers us into the lyrical ending of the paragraph, in which more multisyllabic words are used.

Grown-up Cromwell's voice is more complicated. His sentences are longer:[69]

> *Later, when he thinks back to that morning, he will want to catch again the flash of her white cap: though when he turned, no one was there. He would like to picture her with the bustle and warmth of the household behind her, standing in the doorway, saying, "Tell me when you are coming home." But he can only picture her alone, at the door, and behind her is a wasteland, and a blue-tinged light.*

The whole paragraph happens within Cromwell's thoughts. The *shortest* sentence is twenty words long. The sentences have multiple clauses. Mantel uses "thesis and antithesis": a pair of opposites, like "to be or not to be":

> *He would like to picture her...*

> *But he can only picture her...*

The contrast between what Cromwell wants and the fact that he can't have it creates internal drama.

Here is Hilary Mantel writing as herself in the *London Review of Books*:

---

69 So are his paragraphs. I hunted for this short one!

I used to think that the interesting issue was whether we should have a monarchy or not. But now I think that question is rather like, should we have pandas or not? Our current royal family doesn't have the difficulties in breeding that pandas do, but pandas and royal persons alike are expensive to conserve and ill-adapted to any modern environment. But aren't they interesting? Aren't they nice to look at? Some people find them endearing; some pity them for their precarious situation; everybody stares at them, and however airy the enclosure they inhabit, it's still a cage.

A thoughtful, modern voice with a touch of humor, writing for an educated reader, but not one with unlimited time for fancy sentence constructions. The paragraph has one simile, explored thoroughly, deftly taking the reader from "cute pandas!" to "caged animals."

Genre helps determine voice. Science fiction usually sounds smart, weaving in commentary about the reader's contemporary society by showing how the world of the book continues or diverges from the real world. Contemporary romance has an intimate conversational feeling. Historical romance weaves in archaic language: enough to set the scene, not so much as to alienate the reader (if they wanted 100% historically accurate, there's plenty of Jane Austen in print).

To find the narrative voice of your book—or yourself, if you're writing memoir—pay attention to your best sentences. What do you like about them? How many adjectives and adverbs are in them, how many clauses? Long or short? Try reading a great sentence aloud while pretending you're different stereotypical characters. Does it sound especially funny as a California surfer, or especially meaningful as Darth Vader? If there's a stereotype that resonates with your words, what other word patterns or vocabulary choices from that personality could weave into your own voice without becoming caricature?

Special Writer Voice

Many writers fall prey to writing in an elevated style, using formal and poetic language even when it's not appropriate to the narrative voice. This overwriting shows up in long descriptions full of adjectives and adverbs, heightened vocabulary, lots of characterthinking in the narrative, frequent metaphors and similes, and intentional alliteration.

This character is meant to be a party-loving, nineteen-year-old high school dropout, in mourning for his father's death, driving cross-country:

> *I drive straight through. There is no time for activities of the leisurely variety. Even if there were, I would not be interested. How could I, after what had happened?*

But the conditional "were," not using contractions, the past-perfect tense of the last line, and describing "fun things to do" as "activities of the leisurely variety," doesn't sound like that guy.

Special Writer Voice reads as if the writer is trying to show how smart they are instead of telling the story. Watch out for

- large words, such as *apprehensive* instead of *nervous,* or *well-versed* instead of *knew* or *familiar with.* Make sure your narrative voice supports bigger words when they appear.

- not using contractions, which automatically sounds more formal.

- slightly stilted language like *begin* instead of *start,* or *as if* instead of *like,* or using *of* constructions instead of possessive apostrophes (the car of my aunt/my aunt's car).

This does not mean you can't ever use those words! But be aware of how poetic and formal language serve your story, rather than calling attention to your pretty writing.

The best voice for an author, as we say in memoir, is "like you're telling the story to a friend, but better." You don't need Special Writer Voice or big words to sound smart. Find out what it sounds like when you tell the truth—even when the truth is fiction.

EXERCISE: VOICE

Voice I

Read ten advice columns from *Slate*'s Care and Feeding, noticing traits of each writer's voice. Then read five more, but scrolling directly to the first columnist answer after the first letter, without looking at the writer's byline. See how many sentences it takes to figure out who wrote this column.

(You could do this with different advice columns, but it's harder to make a blind test when they advise on different topics or are published in different places.)

Voice II

Take a paragraph from your manuscript. Rewrite it with another character narrating. How does the sentence rhythm, or word-length, or directness/indirectness change?

Rewrite this new version with the original narrator, paying attention to how they convey information differently. Compare it to the paragraph you started with. What's characteristic in your own narrative voice?

Choose an author whose book you have on hand. Take the same paragraph (original or revised) and rewrite as if *that author* is writing your book. Are they more humorous than you, or more serious? Do they write longer or shorter sentences? Is their language more flowery and complex, or less lyrical than yours?

Voice III

Read your first three pages. Is it clear who is telling this story, why they are telling it, and their perspective? Are you establishing a mood? Is your genre clear from the way the narrator tells the story?

POINT OF VIEW

Often abbreviated POV, Point of View is the vantage point from which the reader sees the story play out. Whose eyes are we looking through?

Formally, POV is usually divided into:

First person: I walked into the room.

Second person: You walked into the room.

Third person: She walked into the room.

When the narrative is from a character's first-person POV, it should be in that character's voice.

Third person can be limited or omniscient. In limited third person, we see the world from one character's perspective, but we are outside her head. In omniscient third person, the narrative shows several characters' POVs.

POV shows character traits through what they look at and how they assess what they see. The physical experience of the world changes depending on a character's priorities and mood. For example, if a band of fantasy characters walks into a room,

> *the magic-user checks for doorways to other planes, or traces of another magic-user's aura.*
>
> *the pyrokinetic girl having trouble controlling her abilities notices the walls are wood and the ceiling is thatch—uh-oh!*
>
> *the warrior looks for alternate exits and sees a big chest they could block the door with. He guides the pyrokinetic girl out of sight of the windows.*
>
> *the servant sees there's a little wood stove—maybe he has time to cook a meal for the group.*

If the writer uses omniscient POV, but moves abruptly from one character to another, that's called "head-hopping" and can disorient the reader:[70]

> *Merlin scanned the second plane—aye, another mage's skills had filled this room not long ago, he saw. Her mentor's worried frown at the thatched roof made Aliena*

---

70 Omniscient POV was common in many classic novels. Sure, you might be the genius who's going to bring back multiple POV-omniscient, but why burden yourself with that as well as writing a book?

uneasy. He stretched his arms. Thunderhof knew they'd only be safe here for a little while. Baldric looked for a bucket, thinking he'd get some water.

Pick one character. If the whole book isn't in their POV, stick with them for the length of a scene, and show what the other characters are thinking through the POV character's eyes.

Thunderhof examined the flimsy door—this cottage wouldn't keep them safe for long.

Beside him, Merlin muttered, "Another mage's skills filled this room not so long ago."

Thunderhof saw Aliena stare fearfully at the thatched roof. He put his hand on her shoulder and turned to their bondsman. "Fetch some water, Baldric."

The same information is included, but staying in Thunderhof's POV helps the reader experience the scene instead of tracking whose head they're in right now. If the reader knows everyone's thoughts, they don't have to fill in the blanks themselves and will mentally pull back. Assembling information themselves helps the reader engage more with the POV character. Head-hopping also removes tension: if we know what everyone thinks, we don't have to guess what might happen next.

If you looooove multiple POV, check out some contemporary books that use it: Jill Paton Walsh's continuation of Dorothy Sayers's work, starting with *Thrones, Dominations,* and Robertson Davies' work—try the Salterton Trilogy. Kate Atkinson's *Life After Life* uses a close third person that occasionally changes which character we're closest to. Terry Pratchett's later books, especially *The Truth,* come close to omniscient, but usually stay with one character per scene.

When choosing POV, consider the distance: how close are we to the thoughts and feelings of the character? In "close" POV, the reader is inside the narrator's head, seeing through their eyes. In *The Secret History,* the narrator-protagonist tries to remember a Greek word:

I looked down at the index and racked my brain for the case they were looking for. The Greeks sailed over the sea to Carthage. To Carthage. Place whither. Place whence. Carthage.

Suddenly something occurred to me.

We are thinking with Richard, sharing his thoughts in close first person.

But we can stay with one character and still see them mostly from the outside, as in P.D. James' *A Certain Justice*:

> *As Dalgliesh entered the court, carrying his murder bag which looked so deceptively like a more orthodox case, he wondered how a casual watcher would see him.*

We're with Dalgliesh, but we're watching him wonder, not wondering with him.

Double-check the limits of POV in your narrative. Literally, what can the character see relative to their body? Based on their intelligence and empathy, what are they capable of deducing from other characters' behavior, or from the situation they are in? Is there information the reader should know, but that the character doesn't have? If so, what details must the character observe for the reader to make their own deductions?

If the narrator tells the reader what another character is thinking or feeling, try instead showing the behavior that leads to that deduction, and letting the reader make the assessment themselves.

EXERCISE: POINT OF VIEW

If it's safe, go into the world. If not, use a photograph of a location. Imagine you are one of your characters and view the place through their eyes. For example, an alley off the main downtown street: a teenage punk sees a place to hide. A drug dealer sees a place to do business. A little kid sees a shortcut. A young woman sees a safety threat (who's hiding?). A retail worker sees a place to finally dump his bag of lunch garbage. A homeless person sees a bathroom.

Now watch the people, if you're in the world. How do people interact with their surroundings? Who walks strong down the middle? Who creeps over near the edges? Who looks in every window?

Write three short paragraphs, each one describing the same location, but from the perspective of one of the people you see.

SHOW DON'T TELL

> [The Girl on the Train] *breaks the show-don't-tell rule of cinema several times per minute. When we first see Rachel, she explains who she is and how she feels in ponderous voiceover. Then when she sees Megan (Hayley Bennett) smooching with someone who isn't her husband, the film-makers don't trust [Emily] Blunt's acting to convey her reaction, so they have her saying, "Who is that man? What is she doing?"*
>
> Nicholas Barber, BBC.com Culture

As writers, we worry our audience won't get it unless we explain. For memoirists, this hits even closer to home—what if someone reads my book and doesn't understand me? What if I sound unreasonable? Showing instead of telling means trusting your own words and your readers' intelligence.

"Telling" is explaining that doesn't serve the narrative. In early drafts, descriptions of scenes and dialogue get the story down while you're figuring out the plot. Treat these first-draft summaries as shorthand. When a character tells another character something that happened elsewhere; when you catch *He explained that...* or *They discussed...* or *I told them...* with no quotation marks in sight, mentally read those as:

Scene to be written here.

Or

This will eventually be dialogue.

Telling distances the reader. Don't lay the evidence out neatly with an explanation—let them meet you on the page to investigate the scene of the crime. Readers notice contradictory dialogue and actions and guess characters' thoughts from their gestures. They understand when someone does something shitty. When Mom slapped us or Dad came home drunk again or the doctor started with, "It's not good news..." the reader knows how they'd feel. Experiencing the atmosphere of a well-written scene is more powerful than being told the author's feelings.

"Showing" still doesn't mean "describe everything." You don't need all the furniture in the room. Thinking cinematically can help you track the reader's experience. Are you watching a scene play out in a location with people taking actions and talking to each other? Or are you hearing the protagonist's voice, *I told Ruth about the day I had, that I'd seen my boss and asked for a raise*, narrating a silent movie or a series of snapshots?

Scene by scene and moment by moment, how can you show the weather, the character's mood, the setting? The narrator noticing wildflowers on the embankment has a different mood than the narrator noticing roadkill on the shoulder, even though they both tell the reader she's walking down the side of the road.

Each scene doesn't need every element, but compare:

> *I've got basketball-star posters hanging on my cheery yellow walls.*

Not bad, but it's just the facts, ma'am. With:

> *Diana Taurasi's in midair in the poster on my wall. The me who wanted to dunk like that was the me who painted the yellow wall behind the poster, my mom saying, "This will be nice and bright in the winter," before she smacked my butt with a brush full of Dainty Buttercup.*
>
> *Maybe I'll paint my room black.*

We don't know what happened yet, but we know this teenager's in a mood.

Show emotion through action. If you're having a hard time imagining what your characters are doing, imagine yourself as a director coaching an actor: "You're jealous of Binkie's life, what actions could you do in this scene?"

Maybe the imaginary actor says back, "I want to snoop in her diary, but reading it will make me cry, so I'll hug it to my chest and wrinkle up my face to not cry."

In moments of crisis, a single action can encapsulate a character. In the Bertolt Brecht play, *Mother Courage,* the title character tries to buy back her kidnapped child before he's killed. She takes five pennies from her pocket, then puts back two and offers three, saying, "This is all I have, please give me my beloved child."

Wow.

From that gesture,[71] the audience is seared with Mother Courage's eye for a deal, always thinking about how she'll eat that night, even when her child's life is at stake.

Use action to establish the setting, too. Open chapters with active scenes that show where we are, rather than narration or backstory.

> *The tunnel echoed with crossing opinions and points of order. I struggled to keep my notes straight in the echoes of competing voices—Mavis would want them later, and I owed Mavis, owed her everything she'd refused to accept from me when I came here with my few possessions. Thanks to her, I still had most of them. Thanks to those still Souled above ground, I'd lost a few friends—and my family had lost me, when that dull, lightless orb fell from my hand.*
>
> *"Angry Angry Muttering!" said Guy Whose Dialogue Tells Us What He's Like.*

The author has established

* the characters are in a tunnel
* it's an organized society (points of order)
* there's a bond with Mavis

---

71 Brecht called this encapsulating action *gestus,* and it's worth looking up if you're digging into showing character strongly through single actions.

- the narrator's position as secretary
- what makes those above ground the enemy
- why it's personal
- that conflict is occurring between members of this group

...in under 100 words.

This does not mean "never tell." There are great reasons to tell instead of show!

1) Summarizing previous information for a character who doesn't know what the reader knows, like when a detective communicates investigation details to another detective.

> *She brought Guillermo up to speed on the cartel's plans.*

Or if we've just come out of the chapter where Prabhat asked his boss for a raise and she threw a fax machine at him, we might open the next chapter with, "He told Ruth about the day he'd had." (Though I'd still push for Prabhat walking through the door rubbing his bruised head, saying, "I asked.")

Watch for conversations, especially phone calls, that summarize previous scenes. Make sure the summary is truly needed to get to the point where new information comes in.

2) Communicating cultural information that's innate to the character or setting, but new to the reader:

> *At one o'clock, we head for the square. Attendance is mandatory unless you are on death's door. This evening, officials will come around and check to see if this is the case. If not, you'll be imprisoned.* (The Hunger Games)

3) Moving dramatically in time and place, when going through the journey doesn't add to the story:

> *In the short/long weeks between when I got news that I was leaving until I actually left, Walter hardly slept at all, talking through the night, 1,001 life lessons for the recently unincarcerated.* (An American Marriage)

EXERCISE: WRITE THIS AS DIALOGUE

Search for *explained, told,* and *discussed*—is the information cued by those words dialogue or a summary? Repeat with *thought, realized, wondered, understood, wanted.* (Use the verb tense you're writing in.)

Scan your sentences for repetitions and over-explaining. Ask in each place, "Can I make the reader work a little harder?"

SUMMARIES & DETAILS

At a paragraph level, it's common to have written a summarizing description followed by or preceding the details that make up that description:

> *Her camp was a mess. The bear had broken into her tent, torn open cardboard boxes, even made teeth marks in cans of beef stew.*

"Her camp was a mess" summarizes the details that follow, but the details are more interesting than the summary and we don't need both to get the picture. In those cases, ask yourself what is the most vivid, fresh language, and chose either the best details or the tightest summary, whichever is more interesting.

Too many details also equals telling. If you have ten good details, pick the most crucial. Think of Japanese *sumi-e* paintings, where the bare minimum of black lines suggests a running horse or a spray of autumn leaves.

Your voice may absolutely be more lavish, full of details and images. But if so, strive for details that are more than facts or physical descriptions. If you're writing fantasy, science, or historical fiction, or memoir set in a unique world, you'll need to be richer with detail. But get them in through interaction with the environment.

Only catalogs list clothing, unless it's a plot point or a character trait.

Only dating sites lay out age and marital status instead of showing them through action or dialogue.

Summarizing details happens at the sentence level, too:

He looked like an old man with his grey hair and gnarled hands.

Tell it once:

His hands were gnarled.

Better yet, show it in an action:

He ran a gnarled hand through his grey hair.

Sometimes the same thing is shown multiple times:

Jane patted my shoulder, gently massaging my arm to calm me down as she said, "Shh, there, there."

Show it once:

Jane rubbed my shoulder. "Shh, there, there."

Sometimes there's a festive riot of showing, telling, and over-explaining:

I picked up my phone and texted my boyfriend:
Mike rhutho wywugeybk ajboaubuo huhis ihi abidvyts
Although the only thing I spelled correctly was his name, when I sent him the text I thought it was very clear.

Pare it down:

I texted my boyfriend:
Mike rhutho wywugeybk ajboaubuo huhis ihi abidvyts
I thought it was very clear.

Texting implies the phone is in the narrator's hand. Juxtaposing the garbled text and "I thought it was very clear" creates comedy.

MOMENTS NOT THINGS

No ideas but in things.

William Carlos Williams

As you convert telling to showing, think about Instagram. Influencers want strangers to slow their scroll and interact, so

174

they need photos that pop, that say, "There's more to find out here."

The best photos, says Instagram expert Sara Tasker (@me_and_orla), are "moments, not things." A plate of beautiful cupcakes, pink frosting sculpted into dainty swirls is a pretty picture, but it's just a picture. Add a child's hand reaching into the frame, one finger sneaking some icing, and now it's a moment, the first sentence of a story that will be told in the caption.

This applies to people, too. What's more precious: The first-day-of-school pose stiffly against a backdrop? Or the hurried shot of the kid late for the bus, running and waving while Dad thrusts the 7TH GRADE sign into the frame?

One is a moment.

One is a thing.

> We were so poor we qualified for public assistance and had to buy the cheapest groceries. My mom was ashamed and tried to hide our broke and hungry state.

It's not bad, but it's still telling. An exercise I learned from Andre Dubus III was to take a series of abstract concepts and express them through a concrete situation or action.

Poverty:

> We made dollar-store macaroni and cheese with water instead of milk.

Andre led the workshop through Justice, Fatherly Love, Motherly Love, Betrayal, Jealousy, Sexual Deception, Shame, Pride, Loyalty and more. Every writer in the room had vivid, concrete experiences from their own or their characters' lives that could become moments in their memoir or novel.

Sometimes, pinpointing the moment led to an even larger theme:

> My mom resewed her underwear for us...but we weren't poor, it was that my dad controlled her by controlling the money.

As you learn to show more than tell on the page, look at the world in moments. The huge, shiny food court I see every day? It's very Dubai, and different from many people's experience, but it's a thing. Watching the janitor, head on his folded arms on the plastic table before the mall opens, because he's dropped off by a too-early van from his worker dormitory? That's a moment.

If I do the research, maybe it's also a story. One gesture, one pose, shows a whole life.

Find the meaning in the thing. Find the moment.

JARGON & FOREIGN WORDS

When you need technical terms specific to your world, or you're sprinkling in words in a foreign language, avoid directly defining them. Instead, don't put too many in a row, and make them clear from context.

As much as possible, add the explanations in naturally:

> *The young doctor said, "Gleeble the salpinette, stat!"*
>
> *I knew he was wrong. The gleeble was still untested, and there was no way I wanted to thread that balloon through the patient's major artery now, before the anesthetic kicked in.*

With languages, it's often enough to just cue the reader, "Oh yeah, this person is speaking a foreign language which you're magically hearing translated to English in your head."

> *"People make mannat here, sahib, and if their wishes are granted, they must visit," the driver offered in Hindi.* (from Natasha Israni's *Monsoon Gods)*[72]

Or show it in context:

> *"Yeh aapka room," the attendant declared, stopping Antara's wheelchair at the door.*

Or paraphrase quickly:

> *Amidst the clinking of instruments, she heard a doctor's stern voice. "Tumne yeh sterilize kiya hain?" Have you sterilized this?*

With foreign words, italicize their first occurrence and then use plain text when they show up again. Don't define or italicize foreign loanwords common in English, like chai, tamale or anime.

---

72 Antara's fighting cancer while encountering avatars of the Ashwini Kumars, Indian demigods of medicine and healing—watch for her on shelves in a couple of years!

It's OK to make the reader work a little to understand! Part of why they're reading is to come into your world, not to force you to explain everything at the level of their own experience.

SEQUENCE OF ACTIONS

Sometimes writers give actions in order of importance instead of smoothly continuing the action.

> *She grabbed Tania's hand after reading the note, as they sat at the kitchen table.*

But the reader is backtracking through this sentence. Having to reprocess the sequence of actions is jarring. Show the actions in order:

> *At the kitchen table, Jessica read the note and grabbed Tania's hand.*

Within scenes, imagine a camera zooming in, zooming out, or panning. Show the actions and setting in a logical order without jerking the mental camera back and forth.

SEX & FIGHTING

Sex and fighting are actions like any other. Without showing character or plot development, they're porn and violence. But scenes of physical interaction, whether conflict or congress, can deeply develop the story while engrossing the reader.

Pay attention to the physical movement within a scene. If a motion happens with particular timing, stand up and act it out with a stopwatch. Use dolls or condiment bottles to plan how bodies move around each other. Maybe even grab a buddy and walk through fight moves gently and slowly, just to see where hands and feet are and how the bodies move around each other.

If your characters have extraordinary powers, make sure their abilities are consistent from scene to scene, and that changes or growth have reasons. If they have weapons, figure out how much reach each one gives them, and how attack momentum changes their balance.

In chases and melees, clarity is key. When everything is chaos, the reader skims, looking to the next place they understand what's happening. Show chaos as contrast to clarity. Establish

- the character we're with
- the characters chasing or fighting
- a big-picture image that shows their relationship to each other

...not necessarily in that order. Watch this mental camera cut between scenes (I made these up for this example), then zoom out:

> *Björn Torrig ran through the woods, his heart pounding. The knight was behind him—but not far enough. Hoofbeats kept him running, too scared to look back.*
>
> *Sir Evilmere noted the broken branches—what a pity his prey didn't know about the shortcut to the lake. Evilmere took the next fork, branching left.*
>
> *The dungeon master looked up. "You rolled a six. The Chartreuse Knight's totally gonna beat you to the lake." He sketched a path on the graph paper on his mom's dining room table, showing how the shortcut ran like the string on a bow, Karl's bard forced onto the longer curve while Otto's dark paladin galloped on.*

From *The Hunger Games*, a melee. We start close:

> *A boy, I think from District 9, reaches the pack at the same time I do and for a brief time we grapple for it and then he coughs, splattering my face with blood. I stagger back, repulsed by the warm, sticky spray. Then the boy slips to the ground. That's when I see the knife in his back.* [Zoom out for the big picture] *Already other tributes have reached the Cornucopia and are spreading out to attack.* [Zoom in to the immediate chase] *Yes, the girl from District 2, ten yards away, running toward me, one hand clutching a half-dozen knives.*

With sex scenes, think about what giving or taking the body means for the characters. What's happening in their relationship that's being expressed through these actions? From Tayari Jones's *An American Marriage*:

> *Davina took care of me. That's the only way that I can tell it. Two days after I got out of prison, she laid me out on her bed and took care of me. With hand and mouth, she touched my entire body, leaving no small parcel of*

skin unloved. She moved over, and under, and maybe even through me. Whichever part of me she wasn't loving was on fire, hoping it would catch her attention next. You don't know what you need until somebody gives it to you exactly the way you need it gave.

The sex scene is fairly explicit, but Jones focuses the scene so clearly on the man's need to be accepted after being in prison, it reads as hungering for validation rather than lusting for physical experience. Lust is great, too—but consider what each person wants. What emotional need is being satisfied, or left hanging?

Most important, consider how a character is changed by the physical interaction. How does their relationship with the other person evolve through sexual interaction? How have they hardened or softened after a fight? Are there key moments of decision, where a character's next action reflects their mindset after this encounter?

TRIMMING SCENES

You have some good stuff and some great stuff. Cut the good stuff.

Old vaudeville saying

In the Vomit Draft, we told the story to ourselves:

> *Reuben leaves his driveway, shutting the garage door with the clicker that never works right. He drives down Maple Street and Main Street and Park Street, parks in the Employee of the Month spot and uses his key card at the back door.*

The author needed to know how Reuben gets to work, because when she wrote the scene, she didn't know what was going to be important. The reader doesn't need to spend all that time on the road. If the scene is a fight with his boss, start in the office. The garage door detail is cool—maybe it belongs somewhere else, when Reuben can't stop his wife running down the driveway yelling at him, or the garage door closes in the middle of a conversation—but get to the action of this scene, now.

In the Technical Draft, it's time to trim the excess. Cutting doesn't mean a detail is bad, or that it wasn't useful to learn about the character—it just means the reader doesn't need to know that particular detail right this minute.

WHAT IS A SCENE?

A "scene" can be as short as a paragraph or as long as a chapter, but each time the narrative shifts location, time, or POV, it's usually a scene change.

EXERCISE: Scenes

Start by going through your draft and noting each scene. You can mark this on a paper draft, or highlight blocks of text if you're working onscreen.

For each scene, answer these questions:

- What is physically happening in this scene? Is that physical action directly related to moving the plot forward?

- What emotional discovery is a character making about themselves or someone else? Is that discovery directly related to moving the plot forward?

- What information is the reader learning in this scene? Is it shown? If it's told, can I show it instead? If it has to be told, can it be told while an action or emotional discovery is happening?

- Does this scene duplicate information or action that's also in another scene? If so, are both scenes needed?

Go ahead and cut any scenes that aren't providing information the reader needs. Next, you'll trim within the scenes you're keeping.

GET IN LATE, GET OUT EARLY

Each individual scene needs to be as engaging as possible. Lighter, more comedic writers might call that "lively," but if you're writing a quiet memoir or literary fiction, go with "compelling." If you're writing mystery, suspense or thriller, think of it as "tension."

One way to find that liveliness is by starting scenes as late as possible in the action and ending them just after the peak action. How far in the timeline can the reader enter and still "get it"? How early can they leave?

> *Scene opens with Reuben waking up and brushing his teeth, he gets in his car, messes with the garage door clicker, drives*

*to the office. He gets called in by the boss, the boss is cranky
and upset, he's fired, he packs up his desk, security walks him
out to the parking lot where he discovers his car has been
towed.*

Or

*Reuben hears the boss call him in. The boss is cranky and
upset. Reuben is fired, security walks him out with a box,
in the parking lot he discovers his car has been towed.*

Or

Reuben hears the boss yell his name.

*Holding the box of his stuff, Reuben stares in disbelief
at his empty parking spot. The security guard shuts the
door behind him.*

Note the empty line denoting time has passed.[73]

If your intention is to show the crushing minutia of Reuben's
life, you might want the first version. (The movie *Stranger
Than Fiction* is a great example of establishing a boring daily
life that is key to the plot.) If you're writing a comedy, the last
version, with the quick juxtaposition of before and after, could
serve you better. If you're writing the mystery of who killed
Reuben's horrible boss, maybe you need him being walked out
and noticing the guard's gun or the convenient fire extinguisher.

It is rarely necessary to lay out the physical action step by step.
If you do, make sure it's on purpose. The reader trusts that what
you show them is important—don't confuse them and use up
their attention span with pages of extraneous detail.

PACING & DETAILS

Pace is how fast plot moves and story develops. "Slow" means
spending a lot of time in one scene, whether that's through lots
of setting and details, deep internal narrative, or a long conversation. Bad slow pacing is when scenes don't show change or
bring in new information. "Fast" means actions happen close
to each other on the page; scenes are shorter, without much
thought in the narrative, and we only get necessary details. Bad

---

73 Next time you watch a movie, notice how a blackout/jump cut can
bring the audience smoothly into the next scene, which might already
be in progress.

fast pacing whips through scenes without enough time to process what happened and wonder what it all means, or, missing information confuses the reader.

Thrillers often have a "ticking clock" that drives the pace of the book—the hero must take a specific action before a defined deadline, like finding the bomb before it goes off, or uncovering the assassination plot before the political parade. But even books without countdowns need momentum to pull the reader along and slower scenes that allow the reader to reflect and assemble information.

Hopefully you've already cut most of your no-new-information events. Now, take a look at the speed of each scene:

- How long does it take in literal time? Is this a five-minute conversation or an all-night sleepover?

- How fast are you moving the reader through the events or information? Do you provide more than one new piece of information? How close together are the revelations? Does a character learn these things as the reader does?

- Have you had several fast or slow scenes in a row? You might need a fast montage to pick up the energy, or some reflection time for the hero that also allows the reader to breathe.

Pace can be sped up or slowed down by controlling both the length (word count) of a scene and the amount of detail revealed about the setting, characters, and action.

> *The throne room was decorated in gold and silver, with flagged stone floors in shades of grey and black forming a tesserae pattern and ornate embroidered hangings along both walls. Some of the hangings covered doors, and servants moved in and out, carrying trays of delicacies or paperwork or merchandise for inspection. The footmen wore red trousers and blue tunics with brass buttons—perhaps they were gold?—shined to a high finish. The prince waved his arm, reminding me of the peremptory way my dad summoned me to his side.*

In this made-up example, the pacing is uniform. It's hard to get a sense of what's important and what's less important, because it's all unhurried and detailed. The reader thinks, *We're spending a lot of time in this situation...it must be really important. No, it wasn't, it was just a lot of actions...OK, we're spending a lot of detail on what they're carrying, so there's going to be something important about that...no....*

Too. Many. Details. When everything is detailed, when every-thing is worthy of an excursion into the past or into the char-acter's psyche or the emotional weight of their actions, then nothing is important. Maybe what the writer actually needs to establish here is a hidden door that will be key to the climactic fight scene. But the fact that there were doors behind some of those tapestries got lost in all the surrounding detail.

> *Ornate hangings decorated the throne room. One tapestry swished aside, and a footman emerged, buttons shining gold on his blue tunic. He carried a tray of drinks—was that a passageway to the kitchen? The prince waved impe-riously, and Alyk dismissed the door and moved forward with a grimace, remembering his father's lordly ways.*

We see the door, we wonder with the hero where the door goes, and we actively move on from the door. Stripping away excess detail lets the door be mentioned three times in three ways. We're not bogged down wondering what's significant in this scene, because the writer has focused our mind on what they want us to remember for the big escape at the end of the book.

ARRANGING TEXT ON THE PAGE

Take advantage of the visual aspect of your words by arranging them on the page to heighten meaning.

How does each example feel when you read it?

> *Silence, then the sound of a prayer bell.*
>
> *Silence. Then the sound of a prayer bell.*
>
> *Silence.*
>
> *Then the sound of a prayer bell.*

The slightly longer or shorter pause created by comma, period, or new paragraph subtly changes the scene's timing. This visual timing can replace words like *suddenly, just then, now, next,* and *then.*

> *They sidled down the corridor, ducking Eyes. Suddenly, an alarm shrieked. Marina called, "Plan B!" and then she pulled her blaster.*

We know the alarm is sudden because it interrupts a quieter moment. We know she drew her weapon "then" because it's next on the page.

> *They sidled down the corridor, ducking Eyes. An alarm shrieked and Marina pulled her blaster. "Plan B!"*

This version runs faster, and the actions overlap. For more tension, try a different text arrangement that feels more one-beat-at-a-time:

> *They sidled down the corridor, Marina watching for Eyes and signaling them to duck.*
>
> *An alarm shrieked.*
>
> *"Plan B!" Marina pulled her blaster.*

Text arrangement removes the need for some dialogue tags, too.

> *"I'd like to hike the blue trail," she continued, tracing the map with her finger. "We'll climb the peak for sunrise."*
>
> *"I'd like to hike the blue trail." She traced the map with her finger. "We'll climb the peak for sunrise."*
>
> *"I'd like to hike the blue trail"—she traced the map with her finger—"we'll climb the peak for sunrise."*

Because the dialogue goes on, "continued" is self-evident.

> *...cleared her throat and began to speak. "Welcome, friends."*
>
> *...cleared her throat. "Welcome, friends."*

We know she starts speaking because there is dialogue.

> *He wrote about his father as follows:*
>
> *He was not the kind of man who invited confidences or offered advice*
>
> *He wrote about his father:*
>
> *He was not the kind of man who invited confidences or offered advice*

"As follows" is unnecessary: the writing physically follows the introduction on the page.

Text arrangement also applies to scenes as dramatic units. Comic or tragic irony can come from juxtaposing scenes that contradict each other or that show circumstances that would change a character's actions if they knew the whole story.

CHAPTER BREAKS

When ending chapters, consider using a "button," punchline, or cliffhanger.

Buttons sum up the mood of what we've just experienced and leave us with pleasant tension. From a work-in-progress, *Life After Life,* and *The Curious Incident of the Dog in the Night-Time:*

> *"Fine," he snapped. "We'll take her."*

> *"We have been tested," Sylvie said, "and found not wanting."*
> *"This time," Bridget said.*

> *When I got home I said hello to Father and went upstairs and fed Toby my rat, and felt happy because I was being a detective and finding things out.*

Punchlines do the same, but with humor. From *Wolf Hall* and *Where'd You Go, Bernadette?:*

> *A little later, he hears that Anne [Boleyn] has taken the wardship of her sister's son, Henry Carey. He wonders if she intends to poison him. Or eat him.*

> *What choice did I have? I boarded the shuttle. Pablo did bring me back an order of salt-and-pepper calamari, but it didn't travel well.*

Cliffhangers drive the reader into the next chapter to find out what happens. From *The Hunger Games* and *The Curious Incident of the Dog in the Night-Time:*

> *Peeta blushes beet red and stammers out. "Because...because...she came here with me."*

The policeman took hold of my arm and lifted me onto my feet. I didn't like him touching me like this. And this is when I hit him.

If a chapter's last lines are an explanation or description, look back. There's often an action or line of dialogue a few sentences previous that would end the chapter more strongly.

LINE EDITING

Congratulations on getting to this point! This is subtle work within the Technical Draft, examining what you're trying to achieve on a word-by-word level.

I'm ruthless when editing a client's work. For developmental editing (similar to the Story and Character Drafts), I often ask if a scene is needed or a subplot is serving the story as a whole. During line editing, I chop unnecessary words and phrases:

> Driving ~~in the car~~...
>
> That night I ~~fell asleep in my bed and~~ dreamed...
>
> He ~~got out of his car, walked across the lot, and through the front door of the apartment building, where he~~ pressed the elevator button for the tenth floor.

Not all editors have this near-ridiculous focus on using the fewest words needed, and I do curb this instinct with writers whose natural style is wordier, or who write in a more descriptive cultural tradition. But usually, cutting every possible extraneous word sharpens the manuscript's focus. Keep the reader's focus on what matters instead of losing them in a thicket of less-important language.

Line editing is something you already do all the time. When you rewrite a sentence six times to find the exact right word order, that's line editing. But self-editing at the sentence level as you write is still different from line editing a full draft. Working as your own editor, you must keep the big picture in mind, and choosing a specific voice/style/mood on purpose makes this work easier.

To define your voice, consider these questions:

- What's the voice? Who's telling this story and how do they talk?

- What's the tone or mood? Funny, serious, romantic, tense?
- What's the style? Commercial or literary? Magical realism or Hemingway-esque? What style choices are other books in this genre using?

Consider your publishing intentions. Of course you've been reading widely and noticing who is publishing books like yours and which self-published authors are succeeding in your genre. If possible, go to a physical bookstore and see where your book will be shelved. Dip into the books that will be next to yours. If your research is primarily online, search for books like yours and others "recommended" or "also bought," and read the sample pages. Describe your book to an avid reader or librarian—what books do they remember that are like yours? Read at least a few pages.

- What tense are they written in? Past tense is the most usual. Present tense, commonly used for thrillers and suspense, goes in and out of fashion for novels, so check publication dates.
- What's the POV? Young Adult, romance and domestic suspense tend to be written in first person. Thrillers and mysteries are often in third person, or have multiple POVs.
- How formal or flowery is the voice? Lots of description? Terse and to the point?

Look at your own manuscript. Do you want to contrast with those books, or fit into the crowd? Make specific, thought-out choices. Being a different voice in a genre is terrific—as long as you can pull it off through careful writing and painstaking editing.

Line editing well takes practice. But the more you line edit, the more you internalize the skill of writing great, voice-driven sentences that show the reader what you want them to see. Your next book won't need as much line editing. Every first draft you write will be better.

HOUSTON, WE HAVE A PROBLEM: LINE EDITING IN ACTION

Here's a sample line edit, and what my editorial brain thinks (shouts!) as I work through a client's paragraphs.

The author has written:

Jake, pulling on his ratty sneakers, bellowed with the full lung capacity of a ten-year-old boy, "Hey Ma! I'm going to the marsh!" and not waiting for a reply burst through the screen door.

The editor shrieks:

TOO MANY THINGS HAPPENING AT THE SAME TIME! Jake is pulling on sneakers, he is bellowing, he is not waiting, and he is going through the door. The author is going for a sense of urgency and quickness at the beginning of the story, and that instinct is good. But the scene is muddy and confusing when everything happens at once. Plus, try bending over to pull on your shoes and bellowing at the same time. Forward crunching makes it hard to yell.

This sentence also switches between verb tenses:

pulling=present continuous

bellowed=past

not waiting=present continuous

burst=past

Technical elements to watch for in your own work: Actions happening simultaneously or out of sequence; mixed verb tenses.

The fix: Break up the actions into a logical sequence and choose one verb tense.

> *Jake pulled on his ratty sneakers and bellowed with the full lung capacity of a ten-year-old-boy, "Hey, Ma! I'm going to the marsh!" Not waiting for a reply, he burst[74] through the screen door.*

* The *and* in the first sentence clues the reader on the sequence of actions. This happened, and then that happened, but the sequence feels faster without *then*. Eliding *then* honors the author's intention to create speed.

* By starting a new sentence, the reader processes the dialogue before moving to the next action.

Next sentence:

---

74 My brilliant agent argues that this signals a boy-shaped hole in the screen, but I'm going for colloquial use. Or perhaps Jake is related to Bugs Bunny. Imagine this whole sequence with adorable animated rabbits and we're both right. Plus, bunnies!

He snagged his bucket and net from the back porch and took off across the yard, in search of boyish treasure.

Nothing's wrong here, but part of line editing is shifting clauses and ideas that already work just fine, for the sake of fixing something else that isn't working. This could combine with the previous new sentence to continue the sense of Jake's speedy movement:

He burst through the screen door without waiting for a reply, snagged his bucket and net from the back porch, and took off in search of boyish treasure.

Now we have continuous motion outward from the porch. Or what about:

He burst through the screen door, snagged his bucket and net from the back porch, and took off without waiting for a reply.

What's more important? "Across the yard" or "without waiting for a reply"? Maybe there isn't room for both of them. I'd choose:

Jake pulled on his ratty sneakers and bellowed with the full lung capacity of a ten-year-old-boy, "Hey Ma! I'm going to the marsh!" He burst through the screen door without waiting for a reply, snagged his bucket and net from the back porch, and took off in search of boyish treasure.

* We want the reader to focus on "treasure," so let's end the paragraph with that word.
* Longer sentences with fewer conjunctions give a sense of continuous speed. The next visual takes us to a more important setting, so we don't need the yard here.

The next few sentences have a different challenge:

Jake loved the quiet wooded creek, with its lollipop pines and the trail that meandered alongside, leading to the marsh and river. This was Jake's favorite kind of day. Storms had passed through in the night, driving away baked on dust and enlivening the hues of wildflowers and trees. Spiderwebs, having survived the watery assault, were now cloaked in rainbows as reward, and Jake could never resist touching them to watch the prismatic droplets dance and fall. The pungent reek of the marsh would be dispelled by the winds, and for a day or two leave only the earthy, astringent scent of the pine forest behind.

First, "summary/details" is one of my most frequent editorial comments. The author has given a summary of the situation:

This was Jake's favorite kind of day.

But she has also written evocative details that support the summary—storms, dust, flowers, trees, spiderwebs, rainbows, reek, winds, pine forest. That sensory imagery really works. This author has done a great job bringing in touch, sight, smell, and a little bit of hearing (depending on how the reader processes "winds"). But the details are more interesting than the summary, and there are too many individual things to take in at once.

Watch for in your own work: Details that are also summarized.

The fix: Pick the tightest and sharpest summary OR the most evocative and interesting details. Give the reader fewer details of greater importance. This also changes telling to showing. The summary *tells* us this is Jake's favorite kind of day, but the right details *show* it.

Watch for in your own work: Defining a character's emotional response instead of letting the reader deduce it from the character's actions and dialogue.

The fix: Create a "favorite kind of day" feeling by showing the surroundings and letting the reader have their own emotional reaction.

> *Jake loved the quiet wooded creek, with its lollipop pines and the trail that meandered alongside, leading to the marsh and river. Storms had passed through in the night, driving away dust and enlivening the hues of wildflowers and trees. Spiderwebs were now cloaked in rainbows, and Jake could never resist touching them to watch the prismatic droplets dance and fall. The pungent reek of the marsh would be dispelled by the winds, leaving only the earthy, astringent scent of the pine forest behind.*

The next challenge in the same passage is Special Writer Voice.

These words are supposed to be a little boy's POV. Know any ten-year-olds who say "enlivening," "prismatic," "pungent," "dispelled," and "astringent"? All in the same sentence? Maybe if the character is Young Sheldon, but not a Tom Sawyer-esque scamp. Jake's dialogue is suited to his character, but the narrative should be closer to his voice. We want to look through Jake's eyes—not watch the writer show off beautiful vocabulary.

There's another Special Writer Voice issue in the sentence structure. The author has moved nicely from past tense to past perfect tense to show the storms that happened before the immediate past tense of the story. But that gives us a weird verb construction:

> *Spiderwebs, having survived the watery assault, were now cloaked in rainbows....*

"Having survived" is a verb form called perfect gerund or perfect participle. It's not incorrect, but it's a sophisticated construction, showing a subtlety about time that feels out of voice in a folksy story about a small boy's adventures.

Watch for in your own work: Special Writer Voice. Words and sentence constructions that show how smart you are rather than the character's level of intelligence and experience.

The fix: Simplify! When in doubt, imagine someone you know similar to your character (for Jake, maybe a young cousin, or a kid you knew in fourth grade). Imagine them speaking the words aloud. Does it work?

> *Jake meandered through lollipop pines along the quiet wooded creek. Last night's storm had washed away the dust, leaving bright flowers and trees. He touched a spiderweb to watch a rainbow droplet dance and fall. The swamp-smell of the marsh had blown away, leaving only dirt and pine in his nose.*

Same details, different voice. Now we're seeing the surroundings from Jake's perspective. He's smart but not a word-nerd; he's a kid who loves the outdoors.

Reading on in the original text:

> *Already out the back gate and turning for the trail, Jake's older sister Caroline jogged into view. "Hold up, Jake! I thought I'd go crawdad hunting down by that flat rock where the creek becomes marshy," she explained, lifting her bucket. "I saw some monster claws in there the other day, plus, I may catch some bullfrogs and finally talk Ma into cooking their legs for your supper tonight," she teased, giving him a playful shove.*

Remember "sequence of actions" a few pages ago? Here's a sequencing issue! Caroline is "already out," "turning," and she "jogged"—but we're in Jake's POV. If Caroline is following Jake, he's facing away from her. He would hear her voice or footsteps before seeing her.

Watch for in your own work: Sentence-starting clauses showing continuous or prior action. When you find one, put yourself in the protagonist's POV. Can you see or hear that action? How much of it? How soon relative to your action/location?

The fix: Arrange the sequence of actions in their real-life order and keep within the limits of Jake's POV.

It's possible that the writer means *Jake* was "already out the back gate and turning for the trail" when Caroline jogged into view, but that's not how the sentence works as written. While we could edit to:

> *Jake was already out the back gate and turning for the trail when his older sister Caroline jogged into view.*

...we'd lose the feeling of Caroline interrupting Jake's forward motion. Plus, "Jake was" gives us a state of being instead of an action (the bad kind of passive voice) and slows him down. Let's keep the focus on Caroline popping in suddenly:

> *"Hold up, Jake!" His older sister Caroline jogged into view and lifted her bucket. "I thought I'd go crawdad hunting. I saw some monster claws down by that flat rock the other day."*

Now her dialogue interrupts his movement. Here we've cut "teased," because Caroline's dialogue is about to show she's teasing. We've also cut "explained," which is pretty clinical for a young girl unless the point is that she's pompous for her age or being solemn. Instead, Caroline's actions serve as her dialogue tag.

If the writer really wants the "playful shove," Caroline could shove Jake with the bucket, or shove it at him to carry. The action shows the nature of their sibling relationship. Perhaps she's habitually mean to him:

> *"Hold up, Jake!" His older sister Caroline jogged into view. "I thought I'd go crawdad hunting. I saw some monster claws down by that flat rock the other day." She shoved her bucket into Jake's arms. "You carry it, Jake-flake."*

Caroline's also got a case of Special Writer Voice. Her dialogue can sound more in keeping with her age and location. If they're meant to be close siblings, she could still tease, but with less big-sister-lording-it-over-little-brother by changing her dialogue:

> *"Hold up, Jake!" His older sister Caroline jogged into view. "I wanna go crawdad hunting. I saw some monster claws down by that flat rock. Could be I'll catch some bullfrogs and Ma'll cook 'em for your supper tonight!" She shoved her bucket into Jake's arms. "Ma says be a gentleman. You carry it."*

Now we have a clear action, single verb tense, unified POV and more relaxed dialogue. There's just one more thing to fix:

> *His older sister Caroline jogged into view.*

The writer needs the reader to know this is Jake's sister. But the relationship is told through low-context communication/ As-You-Know-Bob phrasing.

Jake probably doesn't think, *Oh look, it's my older sister Caroline.* He might think, *Oh crap, it's my sister,* or *Caroline always pushes in everywhere,* or maybe he feels special that his older sister is joining his adventure. Instead of spelling out the literal relationship, use the narrative to show their emotional relationship and let the reader discover they're siblings.

In the rewrite on the previous page, "Ma says…" shows that they share the same mother. Let's show how Jake feels about Caroline coming along.

> *"Hold up, Jake!"*
>
> *Jake rolled his eyes. Caroline always pushed in everywhere.*
>
> *"I wanna go crawdad hunting. I saw some monster claws down by that flat rock. Could be I'll catch some bullfrogs and Ma'll cook 'em for your supper tonight!" She shoved her bucket into Jake's arms. "Ma says be a gentleman. You carry it."*

Or what about:

> *"Hold up, Jake!" Caroline jogged up, swinging her dumb plastic pail. "I wanna go crawdad hunting. I saw some monster claws down by that flat rock. Could be I'll catch some bullfrogs and Ma'll cook 'em for your supper*

195

tonight!" She shoved her bucket into Jake's arms. "Ma says be a gentleman. You carry it."

Notice that now Jake has a judgment about Caroline, and we get it from how he characterizes the pail.

We've line edited the original passage to fix and clarify:

- the sequence of actions
- physically possible actions
- mixed verb tenses
- speedy, continuous action
- summary/details combinations
- showing instead of telling
- Special Writer Voice
- Point of View
- low-context communication

Pretty intense editing for 237 words. But that's line editing: making every sentence as effective and clear as possible at carrying out your intention. Showing the reader the action, the world, the characters, their relationships, and the sensory experience in every word.

STRONGER SENTENCES

Your line editing will reflect your understanding of not only your characters' speech and thoughts, but also the mechanics of language. Don't freak out—we're not doing sentence diagrams. But understanding the way words and sentences function as building blocks will show you the reasons behind many "rules" of good writing, so you can make informed choices about which ones you want to follow.

WORD ORDER

My pre-writing circus career included performing at street festivals around the world. When I worked in English, I had to be funny. The scripted lines had to be funny. The improvised lines had to be funny. If an improvised line got a good laugh, we revised it, polished it, and put it in the show.

We often did four shows a day, 15-20 shows a week, which is a lot of chances to try out different phrasing. A punchline is funnier if the dialogue tag comes first:

> *Bada-boom is what he said!*
>
> *And then he said, bada-boom!*

Individual words are funnier if they end in hard sounds like *splat* or *smack,* rather than soft ones like *orange* or *cushion.* Anything with a letter K is funnier: *pickle, jackpot.*

Now that I write down my words and trust the reader's brain for the delivery, comedy techniques serve me well. Even writing "serious" scenes, the right word order sells a punch or a sob the same way it sells a laugh.

Unless you're using another deliberate choice for dialect or character voice, start and finish most sentences with strong words. When possible, begin and end with nouns, verbs, or adjectives rather than prepositions, pronouns, or filler words.

> *She was mean, kind of.*
>
> *Pat was kind of mean.*

Locating images in the middle of sentences can make them less important. This sentence has that problem, along with boring verbs, and a word order that isn't helping deliver the images.

> *The corpses were bloated and covered in maggots and blowflies, which crawled in and out of the corpses as Terzic approached them.*
>
> *The corpses were bloated and covered (passive voice)*
>
> *in maggots and blowflies (strong image buried in the middle of the sentence)*
>
> *which crawled in and out (which is a boring, indeterminate word)*
>
> *of the corpses (another buried image)*
>
> *as Terzic approached them. (The sentence ends weakly with a preposition and a boring verb, and the reader is zoomed out to watch someone else watching the gross thing.)*

As you edit, note that we are NOT heading for jazzy, my-English-teacher-said-use-my-whole-vocabulary verbs.

> *Terzic perambulated toward the bloated corpses.*

...and then he went to tea with the Queen.

Nor are we goosing a boring verb with an extra adverb, when there's a perfectly good verb right there.

> *Maggots and blowflies crawled slimily in and out of the bloated corpses.*

...unlike the maggots that crawl briskly or airily.

Instead, shift the strongest images to the beginning of the sentence, where they initiate the thought, and the end, where they stick in the reader's head. Stay in the character's POV by looking through his eyes instead of at him.

> *Maggots and blowflies crawled in and out of the bloated corpses.*

Maggots and blowflies (vivid subject)

crawled (strong but appropriate verb)

in and out of the bloated corpses. (The sentence ends with a strong image, and the reader is looking at the gross thing through Terzic's eyes.)

When you're comfortable putting strong words in the anchor positions, start paying attention to the sounds. Sharp consonant sounds (*d, g, k, p,* etc.) make good emphatic sentences:

Pat was kind of a dick. On Wednesdays, she threw rocks at her dog.

For more flow, choose sounds that slide into the next sentence, like *m, n* and *s:*

Pat was mean. Everyone knew about the poor dog, and what happened on Wednesdays.

Be aware of repetition. Using the same distinct word in a sentence, paragraph, or even chapter can catch the reader's eye[75] and bring them out of the story, pointing out the writing itself in a negative way.

They crept down the street, watching for deep shadows. A-Yeong turned to Jiwoo. "What about that shadow over there?"

Use variety but don't get vocabulary-crazy; find your own voice but make it precise. Yes, it's hard. You can do it, and it will be easier with every sentence.

SENTENCE LENGTH

I love long sentences, and it needled me when my fellow MFA students would correct them as run-on sentences. Those sentences were long on purpose!

The key differences between a clumsy run-on and a functional long sentence are the number of clauses and the number of prepositional phrases.

---

75 In each of P. D. James's mysteries, a character has exophthalmic eyes. Once per book and someone different every time...but once you know it's there, waiting for the bug-eyed person to show up is almost as suspenseful as finding the killer.

Clauses

A clause is a chunk of words with a subject and a verb, that have a unified meaning or concept.

One clause:

A sentence has parts.

Two clauses:

A sentence has parts that are made up of words.

The first clause is **independent** because it would still be a sentence all by itself. The second clause is **dependent** because "that are made up of words" has a subject and a verb, but it doesn't stand alone. Dependent clauses are sometimes called "fragments".

Two independent clauses, connected with a conjunction (and):

A sentence has parts, and each part is made up of words.

Two independent clauses can also connect with a semicolon:

A sentence has parts; each part is made up of words.

A "comma splice" is when a comma is pretending it's a conjunction, colon or semicolon; this splice is both technically incorrect and not serving as a choice:

A sentence has parts, each part is made up of words.

These five independent clauses joined by comma splices are technically neither correct nor incorrect, but they are working as a choice to emphasize the content and meaning of the sentence:

A sentence has parts, each part is made up of words, each word has letters, each letter has pixels—Bob's brain was spinning!

Prepositional Phrases

Sometimes a sentence runs on because it contains too many prepositional phrases.

We walked down the hall on that afternoon, the birds diving into the water beneath the windows, where we'd sat last week pledging our love for one another.

Prepositional phrases navigate time and space. Each new phrase relocates the reader: *down the hall, on that afternoon, into the water, beneath the window, where we'd sat, last week, for one another.* It's not just that the sentence is long—it's that the reader mentally visits seven different locations.

Many prepositional phrases can be tightened up:

The car of my neighbor.

My neighbor's car.

In many ways, my time with John was somewhat idyllic for me.

In many ways, my time with John was idyllic.

My time with John was idyllic.

I heard him take a breath in and out.

He took a deep breath.

He took a deep breath and let it out slowly.

He sighed.

Watch out for excess nested prepositional phrases. Stick with the most important movement or location.

Walked across the room to the window

Walked to the window

Long, Complex Sentences on Purpose

Too many clauses or prepositional phrases make run-on sentences. From an early draft of an issue of Erin Clark's *Sex Icon* magazine:

Even when we put our moments into stone, and the stone lasts thousands of years, eventually all that meaning that was so evident and essential and worth the immense effort to concretize, becomes just a series of Jewish

tombstones in the courtyard of a synagogue-turned-mu-
seum that some girl is looking at while sitting on a bench,
close enough to a babe that she can smell his skin, but not
any closer.

Independent clauses:

the stone lasts thousands of years

Dependent clauses:

even when we put our moments into stone

that was so evident and essential

and worth the immense effort to concretize

becomes just a series of Jewish tombstones

that some girl is looking at

while sitting on a bench

that she can smell his skin

Prepositional Phrases:

into stone

so evident and essential

eventually all that meaning

to concretize

of Jewish tombstones

of a synagogue-turned museum

in the courtyard

that some girl

sitting on a bench

close enough to a babe

but not any closer

So many parts! Five locations! Five deep thoughts!

The more clauses, the more complicated the sentence. The more *dependent* clauses and prepositional phrases, the more the reader must retain and then correctly assign descriptive clauses and phrases to a subject earlier in the sentence.

Yet Erin's voice is lavish and full of imagery and deep ideas (watch her sustain this through a whole memoir in *If you really love me, throw me off the mountain).* How do we take a big, complex idea into multiple sentences while keeping the flow?

We want the *structure* of the sentence to take us into both Erin's mind and her physical location, while the sentence's *content* sustains the tension of sitting next to a person she's attracted to:

> *Even when we put our moments into stone, eventually all that was so essential and worth the immense effort to concretize becomes just a series of Jewish tombstones in the courtyard of a synagogue-turned-museum, where some girl is sitting on a bench—close enough to a babe that she can smell his skin, but not any closer.*

Still quite a long sentence, still lots of parts. Still demanding of the reader's attention. Still stream-of-consciousness. But by reducing the amount of processing the reader must do to understand the structure, we let them focus on the content.

The longer and more complex your sentences, the more specific your images, clauses, and phrases need to be. The shorter and simpler your sentence structure, the more thought the content can demand from the reader.

FILTERING

> *I looked at Nisreen as she strutted over.*
>
> *I knew her Louboutin spikes meant trouble, and I felt nervous.*
>
> *I heard her speak my name.*

Looked, felt, and *heard* all filter the reader's experience. They remind the reader, "There's a narrator seeing and feeling and hearing these things. You're reading a book."

In a first-person POV, skip *I heard* and *I saw* unless it's significant that something was heard or seen. First person already establishes that the narrative is seen and heard by the person whose head we're inside.

> *Nisreen strutted over, her Louboutin spikes ready for trouble. "Caroline!"*

Removing filtering language lets the reader imagine themselves more strongly in the narrator's shoes. They feel the character's reactions to events alongside their own reaction.

Filtering is easiest to do without in first-person POV, but you can remove much of it in third person/omniscient by showing instead of telling.

In third-person POV, this narrator is telling the reader, "Step back and watch."

The seaweed felt cold and wet on Lisette's arm.

vs.

Cold, wet seaweed draped Lisette's arm.

We're still on the outside, but removing the filter brings the sensation subtly closer to the reader.

Make a choice about how close you want the reader to be to your protagonist's POV. Remove filtering language or use it by choice.

PASSIVE VOICE

In active voice, the sentence's subject is performing the action:

Jaxon grabbed the rope.

In passive voice, the action's object becomes the subject:

The rope was grabbed by Jaxon.

Active voice tends to be sharper and clearer. Passive voice hedges and avoids responsibility:

Mistakes were made.

However, when it's the object that's important, use the passive voice:

Six arsons were reported.

The arsons are the exciting part of the sentence. But:

The lottery was won by Ron Smoth.

only works if the focus here is on the corrupt lottery official, and Ron's the patsy. But if you're writing a family torn apart by sudden wealth, use:

Ron Smoth won the lottery.

While they aren't always technically in passive voice, sentences that start with: *It was; They were; There is; There are* feel passive and vague. Whenever you can, reframe those constructions for a specific noun and a stronger verb:

> *There were six cats on the fence.*
>
> *Six cats sat on the fence.*

WHAT'S HAPPENING

When I coach circus students, I'm constantly correcting their form. Sloppy form leads to injuries as well as looking unattractive. But rather than saying what *not* to do, like "Don't shrug your shoulders, it hides your neck," I replace the negative construction with a positive one: "Imagine you're wearing a necklace, and show us your pretty necklace!" and students joyfully lift their collarbones and roll their shoulders back and down.

It's much easier for students to remember the replacement behavior of "do this thing" than "don't do that...do this other thing." It's one less step.

Same goes for writing. Tell the reader what's happening instead of what's not happening.

> *"What took you so long?" Tomas asked, barely able to hide his frustration.*

Here, the reader goes back and forth. Tomas is...not showing his frustration?

> *"What took you so long?" Tomas asked, his voice smooth over his frustration.*

Here, we see what Tomas is doing, instead of what he's not doing.

> *"But you don't understand," Sami almost yelled at her.*

Sami is...not quite yelling? We've only been told what *isn't* her tone of voice. What's she actually doing? Shouting, snapping, hollering, hissing?[76]

---

76 Remember that for your characters to hiss at each other, they need sibilant sounds. "Get back" is hard to hiss without the letter s; "Stay silent" can be hissed.

It was not so much a wing as a separate room.

OK? It's a room?

The duchess held back a frown.

If she succeeded, we have no idea what she wasn't doing.

Not, almost, nearly, barely, and negative "not this but that" constructions are often noncommittal and convoluted. Remove most of them.

METAPHORS

Metaphors are when something *is* something else.

> *He will remember his first sight of the open sea: a gray wrinkled vastness...* (Wolf Hall)

> *A hush falls over the crowd at the sight of this magical wisp of a tribute.* (The Hunger Games)

Similes are when something is *like* or *as* something else.

> *The strange stones flicker in the light, showing their depths: a garnet like a blood bubble; a turquoise with a silver sheen; a diamond with a yellow-gray blink, like the eye of a cat.* (Wolf Hall)

> *Little lungs, like dragonfly wings failing to inflate in the foreign atmosphere.* (Life After Life)

Usually, metaphors are more powerful, bringing us into the emotional sense that this thing is, in this moment, another thing. Similes require the reader to weigh the comparison themselves.

> *I am like a child, he thinks, who cannot be consoled.*

> *I am a child, he thinks, who cannot be consoled.* (Hilary Mantel used this version in *Wolf Hall)*

> *Exposed to the elements. Like a peeled prawn or a shelled nut.*

> *Exposed to the elements. A prawn peeled, a nut shelled.* (Kate Atkinson used this version in *Life After Life)*

Search for *like* and *as if* in your manuscript, and see if you're happy with all of your similes. Can any be transformed into metaphors?

DIALOGUE TAGS

That comma wants to be warm and safe inside the quotes. Where bad writing will never hurt it ever again.

Chuck Wendig

No matter what your English teacher expostulated, don't worry about using a variety of dialogue-tag verbs. *Said* is a plain verb that blends in as a structural element, letting the reader focus on the dialogue itself. If your character has *exclaimed, babbled, shouted, yelled, interjected* or (please no!) *ejaculated,* the reader thinks, "Goodness that's a word!" instead of focusing on the dialogue. Use *said* unless you have a strong reason to pick another word.

Dialogue tags are always verbs that make sound.

"I'm going home," he glared.

Glared doesn't work as a dialogue tag, because a glare doesn't make sound.

If glaring is important, get the action in without making it the dialogue tag.

"I'm going home," he said, glaring.

"I'm going home." He glared.

He glared. "I'm going home."

Or *glared* could be swapped for a sound-making verb like *shouted,* or a verb-adverb combination like *said coldly.* The verb-adverb combination is the least-good choice. The best dialogue shows how it's said in the words chosen, as if we're listening instead of reading.

Action Tags

Action tags show who's speaking while filling in characters' physical movement or appearance. In this made-up example, tags reveal details without dumping information in the narrative:

"Hi, I'm Devin." They took a desk in the third row, although the lecture hall was empty.

"Any questions?"

"I don't understand this problem." My student ran a hand through their short, blonde hair, then twitched their lip piercing. "Are you sure this is Algebra I?"

I met their guileless grey eyes. "Are you sure you studied?"

"Whatever." Devin blew their bangs upward and shifted in the wooden seat.

We get a sense of what Devin and the room look like through the details used as dialogue tags.

Dialogue Tag Locations

Dialogue tags can go before or after what's spoken. For the order, imagine the dialogue happening in a movie:

"What are you doing with that puppy?" She looked at me.

This order feels off, because it's odd to imagine the speaker looking somewhere else while asking an important question. Action tags should flow in the order they'd occur in life:

She looked at me. "What are you doing with that puppy?"[77]

Dialogue tags that aren't actions are usually part of the same sentence:

No: *"I went to the store today." He yelled.*

Yes: *"I went to the store today," he yelled.*

Whether the punctuation inside the quotation marks is a comma, a question mark, or an exclamation mark, it's still part of the sentence with the dialogue tag:

"I went to the store today!" he yelled.

The exception is if the tag starts a new sentence:

"I went to the store today!" He yelled, thinking I wouldn't hear him.

---

77 The puppy is having a lovely belly rub. Nothing bad happens to the puppy.

When arranging text on the page, a character's action goes next to her speech:

> *Kaja smiled and said hello. Bronwyn nodded.*
>
> *"It's an honor to meet my chieftess's daughter," announced the giant woman.*

Um...which lady is powerfully built? Instead:

> *Kaja smiled and said hello.*
>
> *Bronwyn nodded. "It's an honor to meet my chieftess's daughter," announced the giant woman.*

To increase a line of dialogue's impact, end with the dialogue, not the tag:

> *Kaja grabbed her armor and headed for the door. "I wish I'd slashed your throat when I had the chance," she yelled over her shoulder.*

Instead:

> *Kaja grabbed her armor. Heading for the door, she yelled over her shoulder, "I wish I'd slashed your throat when I had the chance!"*

Here, ending with Kaja's angry speech is stronger than ending with her physical action. Think about the image you want to resonate in the reader's head. It's like saving a bite of your favorite food on the plate to eat last.

Skipping Some Tags

If your dialogue is clear and character-specific, you don't need as many tags. In a two-person conversation, tagging every third or fourth speech, or using action or the dialogue itself to indicate who's talking, flows better than using *said* after every speech.

- Use the listener's name: "Hello, Marta," shows it's not Marta speaking, so it's gotta be the other person in the room.
- Speaker can do something: "Hello, Peter." She flipped her towel and spread it on the sand.
- Speaker can take an action toward the listener: "I thought you'd want these." Peter handed Marta the snapshots.
- Use the location: She rolled over in the sand. "What did you ask?"

- Use a physical condition: His sunburn glowed. "Can I please have the aloe?"
- Show the character's attributes: "I didn't bring it." Marta tossed her long black hair.

EXERCISE: Dialogue Tags

Go through every dialogue tag. If it's not *said,* should it be?

Do you need this tag at all, or is there an action or detail that could serve as the dialogue tag?

Is there redundant or improperly placed punctuation?

TEXTS & THOUGHTS

When writing a character's texts, think about using a distinctive format and actual text-speak. If the texts are italicized and indented, and you've got phrases like:

> *Woke up frm weird dream u were in it*

Then it's clear it's a text, and characters can just check their phones without having to announce, "I had a text from Rania," in their dialogue or narrative.

When writing thoughts, consider how close your POV is. If you're writing in first person, the entire narrative is already the protagonist's thoughts. You may only need italics to signal something the person isn't saying out loud, but that is otherwise functioning as dialogue:

> *Jeanne said, "You should have asked him out, he'd probably have said yes."*
>
> *That's what you think. "Maybe. I just didn't feel like it."*

Indirect thoughts don't need italics:

> *Jeanne said, "You should have asked him out, he'd probably have said yes."*
>
> *She hadn't seen the look on his face. "Maybe. I just didn't feel like it."*

Thoughts with tags (like a dialogue tag, but silent) don't need italics:

Jeanne said, "You should have asked him out, he'd probably have said yes."

She still thought I had a chance, I guess. "Maybe. I just didn't feel like it."

That's also true in third-person POV:

Jeanne said, "You should have asked him out, he'd probably have said yes."

Susanne wondered if she really had a chance. "Maybe. I just didn't feel like it."

"I guess" and "Susanne wondered" are functioning as if they are dialogue tags for the narrator's thoughts.

WORDS & HOW TO LOVE THEM

I love words. (You may have noticed.)

You can be a good writer and sell books if you have moderate-to-OK craft and tell a great story. You cannot be a great writer without a respect for words that involves learning to use them properly.

Language is a powerful tool. Maintain it and oil it and use it with care. And take a playwriting class—everyone gets better at structure when writing scripts, and you can really understand what's not working when you hear it out loud.

In the Technical Draft, examine your sentences word-by-word. Look for places you can use more vivid language, remove distracting repetitions, and sharpen details.

This is not about what's "correct"—you can fix incorrect usage by rote[78]. But understanding how certain types of words and grammatical structures convey meaning and voice affects every sentence you craft.

VERB TENSES

Verb tenses indicate *when* something happens. English has quite a few tenses, but for the purpose of your book, you'll likely rely on past, present, future, and past perfect.

It's tempting to write in the present tense, which can get tiresome to read. If you're not truly committed, try revising a few pages into past tense and seeing what you prefer. Think about your reason for present tense. For example, if your narrator might die by the end of the book, present tense leaves doubt; past tense would signal that they've survived to tell the tale.

---

78 Lie or lay? Just look it up! If "grammarian" isn't your life goal there's no shame in googling every time.

In past tense, use past perfect for flashbacks and events before the "current" past-tense narrative. To navigate the reader clearly, cue the flashback with a past-perfect verb, tell the flashback in past tense, then use another past-perfect verb to signal returning to the main narrative.

> *I went to the store.* (Past tense of the story as a whole.)
>
> *It was the store I'd met Steve at—he'd been looking at the candy bars.* (Past perfect cues the beginning of the flashback.)
>
> *Steve told me I was pretty and patted me on the head. It was a shame I had to stab him with a spork. I stabbed him seventeen times.* (Past within the flashback.)
>
> *But nobody'd called me pretty since.* (Past perfect signals the end of the flashback.)
>
> *Today was the first time they let me back in the store.* (Past tense of the story as a whole and the time cue "today" returns us to the present.)

MODAL VERBS

Watch out for modal verbs like *would* and *could*. Modal verbs are the "maybe" tense used for possible future events or things that happened more than once in the past. Modal verbs make concepts and events hazy or indefinite.

> *It was 1994 and for the next thirteen years, I would wake up every morning....*

Would indicates that something happened a lot, or it might have happened a lot.[79]

> *I would go to the beach every morning. I would think about my life.*

But *would* is weaker than just the straight past-tense verb. *Would* softens the verb and makes it sound nonspecific, instead of: This. Definitely. Happened.

---

79 Technically, this verb tense is past recurring or past recurring conditional. You don't need to remember that, but why not whip it out at a party sometime to impress people? (It's possible your parties are more exciting than mine.)

It was 1994 and for the next thirteen years, I woke up every morning....

This tiny change takes us more to the narrator's definite misery rather than a hazy, possibly exaggerated state.

Indefinite repetition can also be shown through words like *whenever, however,* or *every so often*—phrases that indicate, "We didn't always do X, but when we did, we also did Y."

Whenever I went to the beach in the morning I thought about my life.

When you want indefinite repetition on purpose, grab a modal verb!

When I didn't have school, I could go to the beach and think about my life every day.

ADVERBS

Everyone hates on adverbs.

I believe the road to hell is paved with adverbs, and I will shout it from the rooftops. (Stephen King, *On Writing*)

Again and again in careless writing, strong verbs are weakened by redundant adverbs. (William Zinsser, *On Writing Well*)

But adverbs are still needed in your writing. When to use them, and when to throw them out?

Adverbs are dreadful when they are redundant, or when the sentence itself should show what the adverb is telling.

She was slightly annoyed.

But *annoyed* is already a smaller version of anger. *Slightly* isn't further illustrating her state of mind.

Skip the "duh" adverbs. If something happens *suddenly* or *obviously,* write the sentence so it's sudden or obvious to the reader. *Strangely* often means, "I-the-writer know this is not logical, so I'll skirt around justifying it by saying it's strange."

Currently isn't needed unless you're being ironic:[80]

---

80 Why yes, I am aware that "ironic" is not strictly defined as "humorously contradictory," because I'm a playwright and "irony"

~~Currently,~~ he was eating gumdrops.

Copies of his bestselling diet cookbook, ready for signing, were piled on the kitchen counter. Currently, he was eating gumdrops.

Use the dialogue itself plus punctuation to show how a line is said:

"Tell me right now!" she said ~~quickly.~~

Right now + exclamation point = quickly. No extra adverb needed.

In dialogue, let the words show the reader how they're said instead of slapping an adverb on dialogue that isn't pulling its weight:

"She did it," he said accusingly.

Instead:

"She ripped me off, I know it!" he shouted.

"Yeah, she's the freakin' thief," he said.

"That's the beeyotch who crashed my motorcycle."

With adverbs that modify verbs, look at adjusting the action:

He turned angrily and raised his fist.

He whipped around, his fist raised.

He spun, his fist raised.

Sooooo...when are adverbs good?

When they contradict or add another layer to what they're modifying:

He smiled bitterly.

They ran haltingly.

She danced jerkily.

Each of those adverbs suggests "the way you normally see this verb is not the way it's happening right now."

---

derives from the Greek *eirōneia*, in which the significance of a tragic character's words or actions is seen by the audience while the character remains unaware. But I'm a linguistic descriptivist, so don't @ me. Or Alanis Morissette.

In P. D. James' *A Certain Justice,* adverbs suggest a contrast with how memory is normally perceived and experienced:

> *Memory was like a film of sharply focused images, the set arranged and brightly lit, the characters formally disposed, the dialogue learnt and unchangeable, but with no linking passages.*

The memories aren't soft and blurry as we might expect, and they miss connections from image to image.

EXERCISE: Necessary Adverbs

1) Search in your manuscript for "ly"—if you put a space after the ly, you'll get only word endings (not all adverbs end in ly, but it's a start). Ask two questions of each adverb:

Is it already shown in the dialogue or action it describes?

Can you strengthen the dialogue or verb to make the adverb unnecessary?

2) Look up a list of common non-ly adverbs and repeat the process.

3) Read a play—I always recommend Patrick Marber's *Closer,* but any good play will do—and notice how dialogue can show how it's said without many adverbs.

ADJECTIVES

Don't use too many, duh.

The next level of adjective wrangling is how and when to deploy compound adjectives, and the delightful Royal Order of Adjectives.

A compound adjective is two or more words acting as one adjective. When a compound adjective appears before the noun it modifies, hyphenate:

> *dark-red sea*

That hyphen signals the reader, "These aren't the nouns you're looking for"—*dark* modifies *red*, then their unit modifies *sea*. The reader absorbs the description and brings it to the noun.

No hyphen for compound adjectives after the noun:

> *the sea was dark red*

We've got the noun, so we know the adjectives coming up are a description of the noun and not of each other.

No hyphen for adverbs ending in -ly. The -ly shows that the adverb modifies the very next word:

> *the darkly shadowed sea*

Hyphens and commas sort out meaning:

> *dark dirty blood red sea*

Is the blood dark and dirty? Or is the red a dark and dirty blood color?

> *dark, dirty, blood-red sea*

The sea is dark, dirty, and blood red. The commas signal "Not yet!" and the hyphen says, "Noun coming up!" These subtle cues to the reader help them read immersively—and they won't even know why.

The Royal Order of Adjectives

The Royal Order of Adjectives is beautifully summed up by Mark Forsyth in *The Elements of Eloquence: How to Turn the Perfect English Phrase*:

> *Things native English speakers know without knowing we know them—adjectives in English go in this order:*
>
> *Opinion-Size-Age-Shape-Color-Origin-Material-Purpose Noun.*
>
> *So you can have a lovely little old rectangular green French silver whittling knife. But if you mess with that word order in the slightest, you'll sound like a maniac. It's an odd thing that every English speaker uses that list, but almost none of us could write it out. And as size comes before color, green great dragons can't exist.*

If you're writing in English as your second or third language, adjective order and prepositions are the two trickiest elements for nonnative speakers. In your early drafts, write in whatever order lets you keep writing smoothly. Here in the Technical Draft, revise adjective order as least-integral thing to most-integral thing.

brick wall

The wall is made of bricks.

red brick wall

The wall is made of bricks; the color of the bricks is red.

crumbling red-brick wall

The wall is brick, the bricks are red, the condition is crumbling.

crumbling old red-brick wall

Old is the constant condition of the wall, crumbling is the current condition. The thing it is all the time (old) is placed closer to the noun than the thing it is right now (crumbling).

Asian woman

The woman is inherently Asian.

young Asian woman

The woman is inherently Asian and her current state is young.

young, mermaid-haired, Asian woman

The woman is inherently Asian, and her bodily attribute of colored hair is closer-in than her current state of young.

stylish, young, mermaid-haired Asian woman

An outside judgment goes farther from the noun than the current state, the bodily attribute, and her inherent ethnicity.

REPETITIVE MODIFIERS

Many modifiers are redundant.

When using words like *began, started to, became, slightly, a little, very, really* it's usually stronger to get to the verb or state of being.

> *I began to comfort her.*
> *I comforted her.*

> *He was a little irritated.*
> *He was irritated.*

> *He was very irritated.*
> *He was pissed.*

Being and doing verbs sometimes modify actions. Get to the verb.

> *She was doing her knitting.*
> *She was knitting.*

> *He was running down the street.*
> *He ran down the street.*

> *I was following their lead.*
> *I followed their lead.*

Watch out for self-evident or redundant prepositional phrases:

Nod of the head: it's only significant if a nod isn't a head movement.

Sat down on the floor: sat down, or sat on the floor.

EXERCISE: VERBS

Check for "was verb-ing" constructions with a wildcard search in Microsoft Word:

1) Open Advanced Find and Replace and click the down arrow that shows all the options.

2) Check the box for Wildcards On.

3) Enter in Find, including the < > part: **<was [a-z]@ing>**

4) Repeat with **<were [a-z]@ing>**

Each time a "being verb-ing" construction pops up, ask "Is my intention here to communicate an ongoing state or continuing action? Would simple past tense serve better?"

THAT

Many writers use *that* as a tic rather than for deliberate emphasis or grammatical need. Too many *that*s add stiltedness to your natural writing voice. Use your trusty Find and Replace. Keep only the *that*s you need for sense.

Here, *that* serves as an unnecessary conjunction:

> *I never expected that he would run away.*
>
> *I never expected he would run away.*

That functions best in its day job as a pronoun:

> *He's on the roof? That's bizarre.*

That substitutes for the situation or concept just mentioned.

That also moonlights as a determiner:

> *Give me that necklace.*

Not the other one.

This is a losing prescriptivist battle, but generally, people are *who* and things are *that*:

She was the one who...
This was the house that...

That or Which?

If you can take out the information afterwards and the sentence still makes sense, use *which*.

My books, which are many, are in boxes.

"Which are many" is optional—we still get the main point of the sentence without it. If the information must be included for the sentence to say what it should, use *that*.

My books that are red are in boxes.

Only my red books are in boxes. Without "that are red," the sentence doesn't say the same thing.

AWHILE, ANYMORE & ALL RIGHT

A while is a noun, meaning "an indefinite amount of time."

Awhile is an adverb. *Awhile* modifies verbs to show the action occurred for an indefinite amount of time.

I say this with love in my heart: in most manuscripts I see, *awhile* is the wrong one 90% of the time.

My shortcut is to swap in another adverb, or another amount of time, and see which one works.

He sat on the terrace for a while.
He sat on the terrace for quietly.
He sat on the terrace for a day.

The replacements make it clear we need two words.

She jogged awhile.
She jogged quickly.
She jogged a minute.

This time the replacement shows we need a one-word adverb showing how long she jogged, just as "quickly" is an adverb showing how fast she jogged.

Anymore and *any more* are much easier. Two words are a quantity, one word is an amount of time.

> *Are there any more chocolates?*
>
> *I don't eat chocolate anymore.*

Whether to use *all right* or *alright* is a face-off between prescriptivists and descriptivists. Prescriptivists believe that usage is dictated by absolute rules, kept sacred by grammarians against the tweeting barbarians of nonstandard language. Descriptivists believe language rules and vocabulary are determined by usage. Their job is not to enforce, but to record and report. You may have seen the July 2020 *irregardless* dustup,[81] which started with a Merriam-Webster's Words of the Week roundup:

> *Irregardless is included in our dictionary because it has been in widespread and near-constant use since 1795. We do not make the English language, we merely record it.*

The dictionary followed up with a brilliant blog, including,

> *The fact that the word is generally viewed as nonstandard, or as illustrative of poor education, is likewise not important; dictionaries define the breadth of the language, and not simply the elegant parts at the top.*

Which brings us to *alright.*

On a purely technical, prescriptivist level, *alright* is always wrong. Use *all right* to mean both "fine" and "barely acceptable."

Descriptivists see *alright* looming ever-closer on the horizon of standard usage.

I suggest a compromise: use *alright* as a deliberate choice in dialogue or narrative when it reflects how your narrator tells the story. Use *all right* the rest of the time.

All right?

---

81 Google it when you need cheering up. One of the great pleasures of editorial life is watching the dictionary deal out burns like *Fahrenheit 451.*

PHYSICAL EDITING (AGAIN)

After all that line editing, print your manuscript and grab a pen. It's physical editing time again! Mistakes, extra words, and weird sentences that blended in on the screen will stand out like overalls at a wedding. For a bonus power-up, print your manuscript in a different font or as two columns on each page—the new look will make your words fresh and different. Go through the manuscript and edit on paper, including any further scissoring-and-pasting to fix timeline or plot issues.

The next step is perhaps **the greatest secret editing weapon ever**. This step will make your book a minimum of 25% better. This step will tell you which scenes are missing and which don't belong; smooth your narrative; point out dialogue problems; and let you know which parts of the story aren't working.

Retype the entire draft into a new document.

Not cutting and pasting, not adding to and editing the previous document.

Retyping.

From a blank page.

I can feel your look of horror right through the ether. Retype every word? When there's a perfectly good Save as New File option?

Trust me.

Retyping lights up a new part of the brain. Reading words on paper and copying them is different than mentally agonizing over the same screen.

Retype the entire thing and you'll know what words to leave out because *you won't want to type them.* Pay attention to your instincts. Feeling resistance at the keyboard to a paragraph or moment? Does the book really need it?

Retyping instead of copy-pasting also re-immerses you in the flow of the story—sometimes new memories or scenes show up as you go. And it doesn't take nearly as long as writing the story the first time. For me, the word-count-per-hour is about four times faster, and a solid two hours of retyping feels like an honest day's work.

I've edited this way since I first started writing terrible middle-school poetry. Only final drafts belonged in my hardcover unicorn journal, thought Seventh-Grade Me. I didn't want to waste a page. Every poem was written first on notebook paper, then rewritten five, six, ten times, each time removing any word that could be left out. I didn't know why, but I knew this process made better poems.[82]

Seventh-Grade Me was right. Strip away the excess to reveal the heart of the work. Yes, there are voices and styles that require more words—make sure that's the strongest choice. Even then, ask of every word, *Do you belong here? Are you doing a job no other word can do? Are you earning your place in this line?*

Physical rewriting is just enough effort to truly question every line. To find the clarity in your natural voice.

When you're ready, print your draft. Mark it up. Cut it apart. And then retype. Your fingers will tell you what belongs.

If you can't face that prospect, something may be wrong with the book. To figure out what, just retype the whole manuscript.

If you're not feeling it, or you're in a rush, that's OK—just retype the whole manuscript quickly.

If you need support, tweet me @guerillamemoir and I'll cheer you on. I know this process is daunting, but it will make your book better.

A lot better.

I promise.

---

82 "Better" in that they now read like terrible high-school poetry.

FINAL CHECK OF TECHNICAL DRAFT

Finish your Technical Draft with one more check.

* If you're using an editing app like PerfectIt!, run it again.

Plot

* Does each chapter start with a compelling action or image?
* Does each chapter end with both satisfaction and forward motion?
* In each scene, have you gotten in as late as you can and still set the scene? Have you ended as early as you can and still have the scene feel complete?

Line editing

* Check sentence structure—have you carefully placed the strongest words? Do sentences end with strong words and images?
* Do paragraphs end with strong sentences?
* Do chapters end with strong paragraphs?

Voice

* Does the overall narrative have a strong voice and a consistent tone?

Story & Structure

* Zoom back out for another look at the overall story. Are there long stretches of sadness or anger that need a break for humor or tenderness?
* Is there a sense of build and tension throughout the book? Within scenes?
* Is the climax the most exciting part of the book?
* Do the clues you set up through the rest of the book pay off in the climax?
* Are there loose ends or nagging unanswered questions?

THE PERSONAL COPYEDIT

The Personal Copyedit is where you make your physical pages as inviting and wonderful as your story. This draft creates a clean, easy-to-read experience.

You'll put your manuscript into standard format, check your spelling and grammar, and seriously consider your punctuation. You'll start building a "style sheet" to assist your copyeditor when the time comes. And you'll be able to hand off your precise prose to your upcoming Friend Readers, confident they can focus on your story, plot, and characters without distraction.

FORMAT & STYLE

You can write in any font, style, or layout you wish. But when it comes time to share your work with others, format your manuscript professionally. Some agents and publishers specify a format for submitted manuscripts. Otherwise, follow these guidelines.

Format

If any of these steps are new to you, search "Word+[thing]" to find instructions. And yes—most editors, agents and publishers (for now) use Word. If you're working in another application, save your final file as a .doc or .docx.

- Set one-inch margins all around.

- Justify text left.[83]

- Use 12-point Times New Roman font.

- Delete any manually added headers and use the Header and Footer tool to put your last name and book title in the header.

- Add automatic page numbers in the header or footer.

- Double-space the lines, no spaces between paragraphs, indent first lines of paragraphs except the first paragraph in each chapter.

- Remove double spaces after periods in Advanced Find and Replace: enter two spaces in Find and one space in Replace, then hit Replace All until it comes up clean.[84]

- Add a title page with the book title, your name, and your email address.[85]

- Use page breaks (not multiple returns!) to start new chapters on new pages.

- Use * * * centered between sections that are divided but are not new chapters, or hit return for an extra blank line.

Style

"Style" is a set of agreed-upon rules for hyphenation, capitalization, abbreviations, etc., but also for correct terminology for specific groups and communities. Most novelists and memoirists use the *Chicago Manual of Style* (referred to as CMOS or Chicago). Journalists usually use Associated Press (AP) style. There are style guides for medical and scientific writing, and for cultural groups, like GLAAD's Media Reference Guide (free on their website) for writing about the LGBTQ+ community, and Gregory Younging's *Elements of Indigenous Style: A Guide for Writing By and About Indigenous Peoples*.

---

83 Justifying on both sides looks pretty, but as soon as an agent or editor starts making notes in your manuscript, words start physically moving around on the page. It's distracting.

84 There is debate about whether double-spacing after a period is an archaic holdout or an aid to the reader's eye. If you want to submit your work professionally, single-space. It may not be the way you think is right, but manuscripts that go to agents and publishers go with single spaces, and it's a subtle tick mark in the "professional" column if yours does, too.

85 No one needs your mailing address or phone number at this stage. Eventually, your agent's contact information will also go here.

Styles help determine how we use language. For example, most people no longer hyphenate "e-mail"; for writers, that choice is dictated by the publisher's style. Styles also reflect changing attitudes: in 2019, AP style changed to no longer hyphenating dual heritage like Asian American and African American. How we read these words can influence how we think about people who identify with these designations or are identified by them.

Choosing a specific style makes your choices faster: if one website says use a comma this way and another website says that way, or if two dictionaries hyphenate a pair of words differently, don't agonize. Go with the style and dictionary you chose, and let that rule resolve your issue without sucking away your creative time. The most important thing is consistency.

Style Sheets

If you're publishing traditionally, your publisher may send you a "style sheet." The style sheet defines how that particular publishing house formats their manuscripts, and which style guide and grammar conventions they use. For example, how to format bullet points, or their policy for italicizing foreign words.

Even before that stage—and if you're publishing independently—a personal style sheet will help you stay consistent. Note character names, especially those with unusual spellings, and a brief physical description. Note any made-up language words or technical terms. If you look up a fact that seems counterintuitive, make a note and list your source. Recording your clear intentions will help your copyeditor and help you avoid continuity errors.

PUNCTUATING FOR POWER

Punctuation is not merely "correct" or "incorrect." Commas, periods, and other marks convey emotion and meaning. You can't read your work to everyone who buys the book, but your punctuation shows the reader how to hear the words. You are scoring the text like music on the page.

For straight-up correctness, refer to the Grammar Girl or Purdue OWL websites; for how to stylishly follow and violate punctuation "rules," Benjamin Dreyer's *Dreyer's English* goes into much more depth. Here, we'll skim like water striders across the surface, looking only at key ways to use the most common punctuation.

EXCLAMATION POINTS

Watch out for too many exclamation points!!! Write sentences to convey excitement, anger, or whatever powerful emotion. Save the exclamations for where they're really needed.

Skip double exclamation points unless someone's texting.

ELLIPSES

Ellipses are the cargo shorts of punctuation marks. Overused, over-worn and rarely appropriate.

In quotations, ellipses show that words have been removed. In fiction and memoir, think of an ellipsis as a trailing off or a sigh. Some styles call for an ellipsis to be made of three spaced periods with spaces before and after. I prefer the ellipsis character (Word makes it automatically), and I put it next to the word to show the thought "fading." I don't space after the ellipses unless a new sentence begins. However you compose your ellipses, be consistent with your spacing choice.

In dialogue, ellipses are often misused as interruptions:

> *Jana said, "I'm not sure what you mean by..."*
>
> *"I mean you're cruel!" Nikolai interrupted.*

But the ellipsis shows Jana running out of steam, not Nikolai jumping in. Instead:

> *Jana said, "I'm not sure what you mean by—"*
>
> *"I mean you're cruel!" Nikolai interrupted.*

The "interrupted" dialogue tag is a little obvious. An action might be better:

> *Jana said, "I'm not sure what you mean by—"*
>
> *Nikolai slammed down his fork. "I mean you're cruel!"*

Too many ellipses slow down the narrative:

> *Raj ran down the street...hung a sharp left...dodged around the corner*

The quiet ellipses are fighting the action of the verbs. If someone is flashing from one thought or action to another, use periods or dashes. Here, em dashes give a sense of actions interrupting other actions:

> *Raj ran down the street—hung a sharp left—dodged around the corner.*

Commas show actions happening in sequence:

> *Raj ran down the street, hung a sharp left, and dodged around the corner.*

Chapter or section endings are often stronger if they end with a solid period:

> *Statement of dramatic fact.*

This leaves the action or thought to resonate with the reader. But ellipses can keep the reader wondering or feeling "lost" with the protagonist:

> *Something happened...maybe....*

Chapter-ending ellipses can look overdramatic, so use them sparingly.

This ellipsis signals a pause in thought:

> *Naoko considered a nap...it would be pleasant to lie here with her eyes closed.*

The following phrase continues the previous sentence, so it starts lowercase. If an ellipsis signals trailing off before a new thought initiates, the next sentence has a space after the ellipsis and starts with a capital letter:

> *Naoko considered a nap... No! She had to be in the grand hall at two.*

When using ellipses, read the sentence aloud and take a big sigh at each ellipsis. If it feels right like that, go for it. If it's weird, use a different punctuation mark.

DASHES

The em dash is your friend![86]

Em dashes are the longest dashes, and they are terrific for interruptions, jumps in thought, and asides that are more abrupt than a parenthetical explanation. Dashes are a nicely casual element in dialogue, where semicolons sometimes look too formal for more relaxed speakers.

> *Jenna, I wanna go to the club tonight; I need to party!*

is technically correct, but an equally correct em dash keeps the feeling of casual speech:

> *Jenna, I wanna go to the club tonight—I need to party!*

Em dashes go *outside* the quotation marks when an action interrupts a line of continuous dialogue:

> *"Oh, by the way"—he opened his desk drawer—"we found your purse."*

Em dashes go *inside* the quotation marks when a speaker is interrupted, or when they cut themselves off with an action:

> *"Oh, by the way—"*

---

86 Also my favorite punctuation mark.

"Where's my freaking purse?"

"Oh, by the way—" He opened his desk drawer, but stopped speaking for the purpose of this example.

Create em dashes in many word processors by typing:

word[hyphen][hyphen]word[space]

The space after the second word triggers the two hyphens in the middle to convert to an em dash.

COMMAS

Commas are pauses. If you have more than two in a sentence and they aren't in a list of things, consider breaking the sentence into multiple sentences. (See the Stronger Sentences section in Chapter 4 for more on comma overuse.)

Watch for "comma splices"—run-on sentences[87] made of two or more independent clauses connected by commas:

We danced all night, our feet were sore.

The car is broken, the ignition is stuck.

Six ways to correct a comma splice:

1) Make one of the independent clauses a dependent clause.

Because we danced all night, our feet were sore.

2) Break it into two sentences.

We danced all night. Our feet were sore.

3) Connect the two clauses with a conjunction.

We danced all night, so our feet were sore.

4) Use a semicolon instead of a comma.

We danced all night; our feet were sore.

---

87 Notice it's possible to have a very short run-on sentence, and, as per our examples earlier from *Wolf Hall,* being very long doesn't make a sentence a run-on. True run-on sentences usually have too many prepositional phrases or multiple comma splices, or cover too much content at once.

5) Use a semicolon plus a conjunctive adverb.[88]

We danced all night; hence, our feet were sore.

6) Use an em dash.

We danced all night—our feet were sore.

COLONS & SEMICOLONS

Colons and semicolons are less common than other punctuation but have their places.

Colons

Colons introduce lists when a list is "named."

The stationery store carried three items: pens, stickers, and notebooks.

The name of the list is "three items."

These are my friends: Sky, Chris, and Aaron.

The name of the list is "my friends."

Skip the colon if the list isn't named (the items come right after the verb).

The stationery store carried pens, stickers, and notebooks.

My friends are Sky, Chris, and Aaron.

If the list is made of multiple sentences, capitalize the first one after the colon, too.

Sara hated lamb chops: First, animal cruelty. Second, too greasy. Third, somehow in Dubai they were always overdone to charcoal.

No need to capitalize if they aren't full sentences, or if there's only one sentence after the colon. You can separate list items with semicolons or commas. Semicolons feel more formal and are better with lists of "separate" items.

---

88 Or don't. Conjunctive adverbs are a bit stiff.

We have a strict protocol: bows to the Queen; the knights proceed to the garden; the parade begins at two.

Commas keep the list items flowing as a continuation of the same thought.

I think you'd like Wild: you also love hiking, you want to hike the Pacific Coast Trail, and it's well-written.

A colon can also separate two independent clauses where the second one is an explanation or an illustration. If you could stick "because" or "such as" or "for example" in there, that's a colon.

Eman didn't want to be a cashier at the cafe: she'd only read bad reviews online.

Sasha's girlfriends came in two types: those unwilling to support her, and those unable.

A colon also emphasizes a final revelation, though if you're writing in a less-formal voice, an em dash can flow better.

The dream had come true: she was in Nepal.

The dream had come true—she was in Nepal!

Semicolons

You'll occasionally sight the rare and elusive semicolon. So seldom used correctly; so necessary to connect two clauses, yet separate their meanings.

Semicolons can replace conjunctions:

I went to Bombay and Chennai, but Patna was my favorite.

I went to Bombay and Chennai; Patna was my favorite.

Or connect clauses that build on each other:

The Andaman Islands were paradise; the blue of sea and sky joining at the horizon.

Or show an emotion-driven change of thought:

The Andaman Islands were paradise; she could forget everything that had happened in Bombay.

Colon or Semicolon?

When you're not using them strictly grammatically to punctuate a list or connect clauses, colons and semicolons can add subtle emotion to your text.

Colons are pauses with consideration. The character is in their thinking place, rather than acting on impulse or rushing out an unformed idea.

It was true: he'd been unfaithful.

They're considering a deep betrayal and letting it sink in.

She'd always known it: Jackson was her brother.

She's processing information that she intellectually knows.

Semicolons are a little hitch in certainty. The semicolon is a thought-breath. A place where the reader picks up a half-inhale before slipping into the next idea, but not too quickly or harshly like a stabby dash.

It was true; he'd been unfaithful.

The thinker is pausing, but that betrayal hits them anyway.

She'd always known it; Jackson was her brother.

She's experiencing an emotional change in her relationship to Jackson.

Here we leave the world of widely accepted grammar and dive into Allison's Long Experience with Shakespeare as an Actor and Director. (Stay with me!) When learning a Shakespearean speech, the punctuation of the lines can help actors make choices:

- periods are stops
- commas are pauses
- colons show decisions and conclusions
- semicolons connect emotions

Here, in *Measure for Measure*, Isabella, a nun, has just been informed by Duke Angelo that she has one chance to save her brother from execution: have sex with Angelo.

Isabella's about to go see her brother in jail, and she's considering what to tell him. Read this out loud, if you're feeling it.

> *...I'll to my brother:*
> *Though he hath fallen by prompture of the blood,*
> *Yet hath he in him such a mind of honour.*
> *That, had he twenty heads to tender down*
> *On twenty bloody blocks, he'd yield them up,*
> *Before his sister should her body stoop*
> *To such abhorr'd pollution.*
> *Then, Isabel, live chaste, and, brother, die:*
> *More than our brother is our chastity.*

Notice how the first colon at the end of the first line shows a decision: she's going to trust her brother's honor that he'd never want her to break her vows.[89] To paraphrase the first seven lines:

> *...Gonna go see Claudio:*
> *even though this is his own darn fault,*
> *he's still basically a good guy.*

The second colon, in the second-last line, is another decision, and it comes after *five* commas in seven words.

> *Then, Isabel, live chaste, and, brother, die:*

Isabella does not want to get to the end of that sentence. She doesn't want to say aloud the choice she knows she must make. The clause after the colon is all one breath: she's made her decision, and she's OK with it.

> *More than our brother is our chastity.*

In modern language: My vows to God are more important than my brother's life.

Actors working with Shakespearean text can use this way of interpreting punctuation to make acting choices. Writers can use it to score their text, showing the reader how words might sound, and influencing how quickly their eyes move down the page.

---

89 In the next scene, Isabella visits Claudio in jail and tells him of Angelo's bargain. Claudio responds (more or less), "You're gonna do it, right?"

Should your punctuation be as good as Shakespeare's? Absolutely.[90] Even if you're writing sweet romance novels or cozy mysteries or lighthearted beach reads. Remember: Shakespeare wrote popular entertainment to make money. If he lived today, he'd be writing the next installment in *Saw*.[91]

---

90 It's entirely possible Shakespeare didn't finalize that punctuation himself, but the actors who reconstructed his scripts for publication in the First Folio had a strong sense of how the text should sound.

91 Go read Titus Andronicus and tell me I'm wrong. I'll wait until you get to the "served a lady her own sons baked in a pie and told her after she ate them" scene.

INTERMISSION

You've got a manuscript. You've thought carefully through your story, you've revised and restructured, and you maybe even typed "The End" in a deeply satisfying way.

You're not done.

You're not ready to hire a professional editor yet. You're not even ready to have someone else read it.

There's still quite a bit of work to do—and I'm not sorry to tell you that, because if you do the work, your writing will be better.

But first, breathe. Get some Raisinets. Enjoy that you made a thing—you made a whole thing! In a little more time, you're going to make it better, and someone who reads it will love it. You will change their life.

Don't dive right back into your next draft—let the manuscript breathe, too. Time away will help you see challenges you missed when you were up to your ears in words. In six to eight weeks (or at least a couple of weeks if you *just can't wait)* you'll be back.

What to do while you're waiting?

Learn about publishing. Many agents write blogs or produce podcasts. Pick five or six to be your main sources of information and start reading/listening regularly. Go back through their archives a few posts at a time and notice what issues recur, and how publishing has evolved through the last ten years. Even if you're planning to self-publish, this will teach you common issues that stop books from selling.

Read Query Shark. This blog, run by (my) literary agent Janet Reid, critiques fiction queries. Authors often revise their query several times, evolving from "meh" to "send your book!" and seeing those revisions is an eye-opener. Not writing a novel? Read it anyway. Seeing mistakes writers make when summarizing their stories to pique an agent's interest is valuable for memoirists and narrative nonfiction writers, too. You'll also absorb the format and flow of a typical query.

Read the Writer Beware! Blog, which covers common publishing scams and shady contracts, and names and shames predatory publishers and fake agents. You'll learn the telltale signs of suspicious offers and bad publishing deals.

Follow agents on Twitter. If you don't already have Twitter, start an account just for this. Agents often post their pet peeves and manuscript wishlists, or evaluate queries as they come in. Don't worry about tweeting much or racking up followers; just get used to the platform, see if you like it, and get the information.

Sign up for the Publisher's Marketplace mailing list—there's a paid version and a free version, and each comes with a newsletter. It's not the Rosetta Stone, but a casual scan lets you know what's selling right now and who's selling it. When you start serious agent research, this will be one of your key sources.

Read (and reread!) books in your genre. Spot specific tools and technical elements you've been working on and identify craft issues. How do they use dialogue with or without adverbs? What words make actions clear without telling? How is mood clear from what a character sees?

Read some bad books. Or stories posted online from beginners. You can learn as much or more from looking at bad writing as you can from looking at good writing—it's easier to spot someone's mistakes when you aren't intimidated by the quality of their prose.[92]

Start building platform (for nonfiction). Novelists don't need a public platform to sign with an agent or get a book deal. But if you're writing memoir, narrative nonfiction, or self-help/business, start establishing yourself as a resource and/ or an expert. Discover who shares the problem or relates to the issues your book addresses, figure out what they already read and where they already gather, and become a generous, trusted source of information in those spaces. Use your blog, newsletter, and/or social media to establish that your story is compelling and your voice engaging.

---

92 If commenting is an option, pick out one thing they did well and praise it. Early-career writers need encouragement, and your (honest but kind) words will mean a lot.

Start building bridges (for everyone). You need *evangelists.* People who may not read your book themselves but will write a review anyway *(shhh!).* People who will tell their friends about your book, blog about it, retweet your presales links and publicly applaud your milestones. Social media is not the only way to build your fan base, but it's the easiest and most accessible. Start creating public Author-You's presence and connecting to readers, however you are comfortable reaching out.

When you've had a break, come back to your manuscript.

KNOW WHEN TO QUIT

What do you do when you have a raw, exciting piece, and then several drafts in, it's gone flat—you've lost the spark?

Inspiration must come twice: in the initial draft, to get the idea down; and in revisions, to allow your story to change and reshape with new ideas that arise as you work. This is why "second draft" does not mean "fix the spelling."

Buckling down to another draft despite being bored with your own book feels like working a job you don't like, but also not getting paid and with no penalty for not showing up. Fight for it. Plow through boredom/disinterest/horror: grasp moments of re-inspiration. Make a new playlist an hour long, put your headphones in, and work for the length of the playlist. Make a coworking date with a writing buddy. Bribe yourself—one page, one very nice chocolate. Whatever it takes. This stage will almost always pass, as long as you actively fight to sustain your interest.

It is possible to never regain your interest.

An editing client emailed me:

> I made a decision that was most difficult, that I thought about long and hard. I decided to put [the characters] away, to relegate them to my first experience writing a novel, to allow them to have the run of their life without my interference. Or, in other words, I have ceased all work and will not be doing anything else with that story again. Ever.
>
> I really feel/felt like the story needed to be rewritten to make it what I wanted it to be and I just didn't have what it would have taken to go that distance. I have learned so much from making it through

one book, but I want to use that energy on a new story, not that I know what it is yet, but it will come.

Have you done this? Do you have regrets?

It is hard, or can be, to stop. The guilt can be really black.

It's totally possible to put in a great deal of time and effort, go through seven drafts, make giant strides as a storyteller, improve your craft, and still not have a book. This happens enough that there's a catchphrase—"drawer book." As in, you're going to stick this manuscript in a drawer and not look at it again for a long, long time.

Some years ago, I finished a memoir that took ten years to write, revise, workshop, and have edited. My then-agent sent it to publishers. After a year on submission, nobody bought it.

But the first page was really, really good.

Good enough that when I did that "Writer Idol" thing at a conference, where someone's first page is read aloud anonymously and the panel of agents raise their hands when they'd stop reading if it came to their inbox, the reader got through my whole page. The room paused for a moment and then applauded. What a stroke to the writer ego!

I thought, hey, there's a student reading tonight, why not capitalize on this momentum? and looked for a section to read. What I saw was

boring,

boring,

porn,

boring,

I am no way reading that,

awful,

porn,

boring.

A year's worth of publisher rejections suddenly made sense.

I stopped feeling like maybe the world wasn't ready or we'd been submitting to the wrong people or I'd ended up with the wrong agent, because clearly the problem was my book.

It wasn't good enough.

It sucked that ten years of work wasn't enough. That I may have burned through the chance of ever publishing this book, because once it's been shopped around, you don't get to shop the same book again even if you make it a whole lot better.

It might sell one day after I publish another book. Or if I drastically rewrite, then find a publisher who hasn't seen the previous version.

But my better choice was to let it go.

My drawer book was worth it. I learned I could write a whole book. I spent three years reading agent blogs, going to conferences, learning how the publishing world works and meeting writers I could help and who could help me. I learned how to write a query. I built the habit of sitting down every day alone or with a writer friend and doing my work. I learned to step back, look at my manuscript with a critical eye, and say, "close but no cigar."[93]

Next time I'll know it faster.

My unsellable memoir functions a lot like my MFA. The piece of paper is not the path to fame and success. But everything I did to earn it is.

If you really believe this project has gone as far as you can take it, it's OK to quit. Truly. Writing your next book will start at a higher level because you did your best with this one—and next time, your best will be even better.

ENVY

Some years ago, I opened up Facebook and spotted two status updates, one right after the other:

> *Friend Horror Writer: Second book tour starts Feb 1 in NYC!*

> *Friend Urban Fantasy: Can finally tell my great news!!!! MS sold in a four-book deal with Noted Publisher!!!! First one out next year!!!*

That heavy feeling in my stomach? That's *vicarious joy.* That's *pride in my friends' accomplishments.* Of course I was happy for my fellow writers, it would be mean to be jealous, *screw them.*

---

93 If your unfinished projects are filling your mental creative space, check out Jessica Abel's work on Idea Debt at **http://jessicaabel. com/2016/01/27/idea-debt/** She's got a great plan for escaping the list of undone projects.

My business brain reminded me, "Hey, them getting a book deal means they'll blurb for me when the time comes, we can do readings together when their fourth book comes out the same time as my first, right? This could do a lot for me!"

But I was still sick about it, my insides burning with acid. *What do they have that I don't?*

Buddhism says all anger comes from "should" thoughts, and the biggest one is *that should be mine.*

Friend Authors both wrote for years, on top of their full-time jobs. I read multiple drafts of their work, and I wasn't the only one scribbling notes on their manuscripts. They changed settings and killed main characters and deliberately got critique from people they knew wouldn't just say "It's so good!" but would give them stuff—big stuff—to work on.

They earned it.

And if I wanted that, it was up to me to put in the time to make it happen.

That's the power of envy—it's fuel. Every time you look at someone else's accomplishment and get that sick, hollow feeling of *that should be mine,* that's the universe saying, *You're right. They aren't any more special than you are.* It means you're getting closer.

We don't envy people whose success we'll never have; we envy those only a few rungs above us on the ladder. Work harder. Make a plan. Get better feedback and become a better writer. You'll know it's better feedback, because under the initial flash of pain and defensiveness, you'll feel caught—*crap, I thought I could get away with that*—and know in your heart that if you address the issue, your work will be better.

"Excuse me, sir, how do I get to Carnegie Hall?"

"Practice."

Whose success is making you sick, and what are you doing about it?

THE FRIEND READ

This is your first non-you reader who will read the whole book. You may have multiple Friend Reads if you've got good critique partners and needed eyes on earlier drafts. But after the Technical Draft and the Personal Copyedit, it's time to send your cleanest draft to your best feedback person. Your friend, or "beta reader," doesn't have be a writer, but should be someone who reads your genre, and whom you know to be thoughtful and intelligent.

Sometimes beta reader feedback is awesome—you get great insights from someone who doesn't know your story yet; you learn, "Hmmmm...maybe that reference isn't as widespread as I thought it was," or "Funny? I didn't mean to be..."

Sometimes the feedback is less helpful. Like early-stage dating, writers employ polite euphemisms.

"Great concept!"

Too bad you couldn't write it.

"This has so much passion!"

WTF are you talking about?

"I loved your structure!"

At least it had a beginning, middle and end. Thank goodness it had an end.

"Can't wait to see what happens next!"

Nothing happened.

":)"

:\

What is good feedback? How do you develop a critique relationship and build mutual trust?

Treat critique like sex. Give as much as you can, paying attention to what the writer needs. Ask specifically for what you want and remember that some people are lousy at it. If you're hurt, speak up. If you're not in the mood, it's OK to politely decline.

Now let's put on some soft music...and get feedback.

CRITICISM IS RESPECT

Praise makes you feel good. Criticism makes your work better. When it comes from a trusted source, no matter how much it hurts: criticism is respect.

Before becoming a full-time writer and editor, I performed and trained around the world as an aerialist and acrobat. In a circus gym, the best performers get the most corrections, because coaches see, *You're worth my time. I can help you be great.*

As a writer, you must move past the stage of generic encouragement and into a realm where your trusted feedback partners or writing group give specific critique you can use to improve your manuscript. In order to get that feedback, you must be willing to receive it. You must actively challenge yourself to write better, because giving feedback to people who don't improve is discouraging. You must embrace useful criticism from people you trust as a loving act.

I have a friend who was a champion ice-skater into her teens. Then she fell in practice and tore up her ankle. She had surgery and came back to skating, but never reached her former level. I have never heard her so sad as when she said, "My coach stopped paying attention to me."

She knew it was over when no one was yelling at her. No criticism meant, "You're not worth my time."

Elite gymnastics runs on this same anger-is-beauty model. So does ballet. Elite coaches and high-level dance teachers don't waste their time on students who aren't going to make it. They want to focus on the ones who can take the harshest, pickiest criticism and use it to improve. The ones who show up day after day, who listen to adjustments that seem ridiculously small, and commit 100% to incorporating that feedback into their work. Those are the students who are going to be the best.

In this model, talent is only moderately relevant. Talent is the natural ease at a new skill that makes it fun to practice and enjoyable to challenge yourself with something more difficult. But a dedicated worker with a modicum of talent can go much farther than an early star who lacks work ethic.

If you cultivate the people who respect you enough to criticize your work, and genuinely use their feedback, you will get much better, much faster.

HOW TO GET USEFUL FEEDBACK

How can you find the right people to read your work, get the type of feedback you need, and make them feel good about helping you?

By building community, respecting readers' time, being specific about your needs, and writing better.

Your writing community often becomes your feedback community. I have a small group of writers I trust that has been built over many years. A couple have been my friends since high school; one was formerly my intern; some are people I've been in workshops with. I read their manuscripts and give detailed feedback. I connect them with opportunities and leverage my connections to promote their books.

I have context for my friends' feedback because I've read their work. I know where they're coming from and I respect their writing.[94]

I don't ask everyone to read everything, and I send manuscripts to people whose interests line up with what I've written. Often, I ask a question and say why they are the right person to answer it, to give them a vested interest beyond, "Oh, how nice, Allison wrote something." It's more appetizing to be solicited for special expertise than general services.

> *Computer Expert Friend, I'd love your thoughts on this manuscript, and can you tell me if I got the programming language right?*

> *Attorney Friend, I'd love your thoughts about the storyline, especially if the court case is logical?*

---

94 Make sure you have a sense of your readers' ability and credentials—Misty Copeland's feedback on your ballet sequence is going to be more important than comments from your neighbor, the die-hard *Dance Moms* fan.

Frankly, as writers, we are barely a half-step above the kid waving a crayon drawing calling, "Mommy, look!" Respect your readers' time by preparing for feedback. Make sure you've already cut as much unnecessary material as possible. Format your manuscript so it's easy to read, and deliver it in the medium in which your readers already read for pleasure. I've sent out docs, PDFs, ebooks, paper manuscripts, and bound copies that look like published books.

If you've got specific questions, ask them:

I'm just trying to get the plot down—would love some feedback on that.

Does my dialogue ring true?

Share your parameters in advance:

I'm so pleased you're interested in reading. If I send 200 pages, would you be able to respond by September 15th?

When responses come back, watch for comment patterns from multiple readers. Does everyone wonder what happens next? Did nobody comment about that big twist? If more than one person's asking what you meant, it's not on the page as strongly as it is in your head.

It's normal to resist and/or feel hurt by editorial feedback. Give it a few days to settle in. After a few rounds of feedback, you'll start to recognize how you receive it.

My personal process:

1. Write draft of new play.
2. Send the mewling infant of my work to my theatrical publisher (with whom I have a preexisting relationship).
3. Get feedback.
4. Sulk and whine about how she doesn't get it, it's *fine*, why can't she just publish it *now*.
5. Recognize that not everything in my head is on the page and rewrite, getting ideas from her feedback but solving the issues and answering the questions in my own way.
6. Send another draft.
7. Repeat.

It's easier to receive feedback when I already know I'm going to sulk about it before I can use it.

Sometimes, people won't read the whole thing, won't respond in time, or give feedback that isn't useful. How do you get people to go from "Oh, that sounds interesting!" to actually reading it?

Write better, and include them in the process.

Let your Friend Readers see you using feedback from them and others; let them see your work improve. Share your successes—text that you finally figured out that chapter, or Instagram how excited you are about your dialogue and Tagged Friend's comment was key. The more invested they become in your success, the more they feel part of your team, the better, prompter, and more helpful their critique will be.

HOW TO GIVE GREAT FEEDBACK

Give feedback whenever you can. The number-one thing that made me a better writer was critiquing other writers. Once you're able to identify specific things that are or aren't working, you'll see issues more readily in your own manuscript.

Thoughtful feedback is a golden gift. Praise makes us happy; criticism makes us write better. How can we give meaningful, positive, useful feedback?

If you're speaking to your workshop group, try the classic Critique Sandwich: a positive comment, a question, another positive comment.

> *Great setting. I love how you built the world through how the characters interacted with the technology. I didn't completely understand why Inara killed Meri—it seemed like there was backstory, maybe in another chapter? The death was so vivid, I'd love to know more about why.*

The sandwich filling is a specific question. This allows the author to take ownership by actively agreeing—or write off your question if it hurts their feelings (which may not make them write better, but is a legitimate emotional response).

If you're responding in writing, here's a framework to start with. As you get more experience giving feedback and get to know your critique partners, you'll develop your own way of responding.

1) Start by saluting the author and say what you received from the piece (literal plot and emotional impact).

Thanks for asking me to read! What I got was that this is literary fiction centering on Rahul boating with his dad, with a larger theme of re-negotiating the parent-child relationship. It felt reflective and lyrical.

2) Write a couple of paragraphs that show your understanding of the work. Summarize the major actions and what you received as the dramatic impact of those actions. Mention the tone (funny, sad) and how you felt as a reader throughout the book.

I loved the image of the oarlocks; I could see Dad's hands, and that made the power imbalance in the relationship clear. The lake felt like an intimidating and ominous place. Detouring into the dream at the end was really effective—I thought it conveyed the transient nature of parent-child bonding moments....

3) Talk about what's working and why.

On page 76 the description of the river is so detailed—I could clearly visualize the actual river and it felt like a strong metaphor for Rahul's journey stretching ahead of him.

Throughout the book, Aarti was shown sympathetically through her actions. When she visited the baker, I got a sense of her immense grief at the loss of her child, even though I didn't know yet why she was sad.

4) Mention what isn't working and why. I like to phrase this as, "As you keep working, here are some things you might focus on." Ask questions rather than dictating solutions.

The timeline confused me around page 28—I wasn't sure when they were in the present and when they were in the past. Is there a way to more clearly signal the flashbacks and how we know we're back in the present?

When Rahul slaps the girl on page 182, it was hard to still like him as a character. Is that the intention? Is there a way to either show his frustration through a different action, or to show more of how he feels about having slapped her, so that the reader still wants to spend time with him?

5) Give any more overall observations; whenever possible, in the form of a question.

Opinion:

The family dynamic is unclear and I don't understand how the mother thinks or why they stopped talking to each other to begin with.

Question:

Can you show more of the family dynamic in the early chapters? What's the cause of the original break between Rahul and his mother, and would that give us any insight into how the father-son relationship also deteriorated?

6) Sign off with something positive, whether that's restating things you liked about the book, saying how it affected you emotionally, or complimenting the writer on something done well. If you are familiar with their previous work and you have an ongoing critique relationship, identify an element of their craft that has strengthened since the last piece you read.

Notice that the overall tone is respectful, self-effacing, and grateful to have been entrusted with someone's precious work. Remember that non-specific praise and criticism are not useful. One of the greatest compliments you can pay another writer is to believe they are ready, willing, and able to accept constructive feedback.

WRITING WORKSHOPS

In the classic "Iowa-style"[95] writing workshop, the group reads a piece and discussion happens while the writer takes notes and doesn't talk. At the end of the conversation, the writer might ask a couple of questions for clarification or say something about their intention in writing the piece.

This can be useful—it's good for writers to learn to listen to critique without pushing back with, "What I meant to say was..." because if it's not on the page, we didn't say it. Defensiveness also reduces the quality of the feedback, because the responders think, "If she doesn't want to hear what I thought, why did she bother to ask?"

This workshop style can also be traumatic, especially if the class misinterprets a point in the story and spends the whole time arguing about a meaning that doesn't matter. This can be a

95 Developed at the University of Iowa's storied creative writing program by older white men with established literary careers, and funded by foundations associated with the CIA.

particularly terrible experience for underrepresented students, when cultural and/or racial context is missing between writers and readers. If you are a writing workshop teacher or participant, please seek out Matthew Salesses' revolutionary *Craft in the Real World: Rethinking Fiction Writing and Workshopping*, which explores new ways of looking at both student writing and the canon.

Recently, the trend is toward workshops in which the author engages more in the discussion. They might introduce their piece by discussing why they're writing this story and how it developed, or what kind of feedback they need: "I know the setting is a mess and I need more research there, so can you focus your feedback on whether the dialogue is working?"

A speaking author can help the readers "prescribe" less (comments like "I wanted to see this happen" or "I didn't like that character") and engage the writer with a question like, "Do you want readers to like this character?" The discussion often reveals information in the writer's head that should be in the story.

In both types of workshop, good leaders guide the discussion, cut off unhelpful feedback, ask follow-up questions and keep everyone on track. But their job is guiding the workshop as a whole, rather than serving as an individual writer's advocate. Sometimes, workshops go off the rails or turn into a pile-on, leaving the writer bruised and defensive, or questioning their writing ability rather than the impact of today's pages. Without an active mediator, it's up to the writer to weed out what's helpful from irrelevant tangents.

Always write down the comments, or you won't remember the comment, you'll only remember how you felt when you heard the comment.

If you're in a writer-doesn't-talk workshop, write down every comment. Even if you write "said stupidhead" after some of them.

If you participate in the discussion, you should still listen and take notes more than talking. If a reader has a question or raises an issue, do not explain "what I meant" or point out why the reader is wrong. Often, another participant will answer that question for you, and their interpretation teaches you more about your own work. Even in writer-talks workshops, I sometimes don't answer direct questions. Instead, I smile and say, "That's an interesting question to address," and make a note.

I'd rather write the new version than process verbally what it's going to be.

Pay attention to the critiques of other manuscripts. When someone opens their mouth about another writer's work, and I think "Dude, did you *read* it?" then I know to take them less seriously when they talk about mine.

Consider your notes later, after the heat of the moment. Look for patterns in the feedback: your responders may be wrong about *what* the problem is, but they're usually right about *where* it is. Rewrite in a way that solves the problem, which may or may not involve addressing the original question.

For example, a reader might say, "I don't understand why Juliet kills herself, since her monologue is so hopeful in Act V."

Shakespeare doesn't answer the question in the workshop or explain why the monologue is, in fact, hopeless—he just writes down the comment.

Back at his desk, he may

- rewrite the monologue to be more hopeless
- cut the monologue
- have Romeo leave a note that sounds like he's dumping Juliet instead of coming back
- have Juliet's father lock her in a room with no escape
- decide that the dumbass who asked this question just didn't get it, and change nothing, because two other readers said it worked just fine

If you're in a workshop where writers respond, ask for clarification rather than explaining or defending.

Instead of snapping, "I think she sounds plenty hopeless," Shakespeare might ask:

"Can you point out some words you feel are hopeful?"

"Is it the structure or the words that feel hopeful here?"

"What if the monologue took place in her bedroom instead of in the garden?"

Good workshops

- talk about "working" and "not working" rather than "good" or "bad."
- are willing to engage a piece on its own terms. They don't expect genre to be literary, or literary to be genre. They

might say, "The mood in this scene is really intense, especially in these lines. Should that be eased up a little or is it working for the 'horror' feeling?" instead of "I think it's too overwrought."

- ask questions and discuss the answers using specific details. They might ask, "Did anyone understand what she became at the end of the story? From the horns, I got demon." Another reader might respond, "Huh—it says her cloak swirled, so I got vampire. Did anyone else get that?"

For memoirists and essayists, critique always includes talking about the author on some level. The best practice here is to say "she" or "the narrator" or "Shonda in the essay" rather than "you." That way, the writer can remove themselves a tiny bit from having their thoughts or behavior discussed in ways that can be personally hurtful.

Find and develop readers you trust, so you can spend time fixing instead of saying, "They're dumb and didn't get it." I may not always agree with my feedback partners, but I know they have my best writing at heart.

THE TIME IT TAKES

Allow yourself patience with Friend-Reader feedback.

You may receive a lot of critique. Enough to make you question whether you're really meant to do this writing thing, or if a better career choice would be megastore greeter. But copious notes are a good sign. Writers and readers are more likely to give detailed critique on something they loved with little flaws, or liked with great potential. If it's boring or terrible, they'll probably just say something nice and move on.

The more involved we are in a particular project, the more meaningful it is to our writer-self, the longer we spent writing, the more time it takes to let serious feedback sink in.

I've been writing a Young Adult novel for ten years. I wrote and published other things in that time, but from pre-first draft ideas to querying agents took ten years. I had a devastating rejection from an agent who'd been excited to read the full manuscript. She told me, "Great opening, you write well, but nothing happens in the middle."

It took a week to become un-devastated. I mean, hadn't five beta readers, all excellent writers themselves, loved it? What about the high-school student readers who agreed to give feedback before school and were already deep in discussion when I arrived at 6:50 AM?

Another agent rejected the full: "It slows down in the middle."

Then a writer contacted me about editing her Young Adult novel. I looked at the first twenty-five pages and emailed her, "You write very well, but the story hasn't started yet."

A bolt of lightning. I dragged out my own book and flipped through.

Chapter One: Girl with gun ready to shoot.

Chapter Two: Flashback...to a nap...in a library.

Chapter Three: Girl recaps everything we already know to another character.

Well, crap.

My Friend Readers were wrapped up in clever voice and interesting premise. They hadn't noticed what two merciless strangers found: nothing happened in the middle. And it took me six weeks to understand what that meant and another full draft to apply it to my manuscript.

You can be an incredible sentence-writer but lack dramatic structure. You can be a sharp structuralist without much voice. You can make characters live and breathe on the page, then find them staring at each other over a kitchen table while the agent flips ahead to see if it gets good anytime soon.

You won't know any of these things about your work until after you have invested as much time as it takes you to write a book, plus some more.

We all want to be done, to share our book with the world. An author I work with sent a third draft of a chapter. I sent it back with more notes. She wrote:

> *I love diving in deeper and hearing where things can get amped up. Am only worried it will take another year to edit the book if I do this for each scene.*

Polishing each element of our book—scene by scene, character by character, sentence by sentence—takes time. Time at the page. Time ruminating while walking, or gardening, or staring into space. Time working on another writing project. Time at our day job, where one day an overheard remark in the break room snaps a recalcitrant plotline into place.

Let your work blossom both from your tending and your absence.

That doesn't mean "don't write fast." But the biggest separation between writers who publish and those who don't is that **writers who publish keep working after they feel entitled to be done.** After feedback, they write yet another draft. They cut thousands of words that were painstakingly revised. They let time pass.

For my novel, I've done quite a few more than seven drafts. I've taken pages to workshops and paid for editorial feedback. "Not done yet" interferes with my sense of entitlement. I ticked all the boxes! Why aren't I finished? It's frustrating and annoying and makes it hard to want to work on the book. But now that I know it's not as good as I can make it, now that I understand the problem, I need to work some more.

Friend Readers give you their time. Give their feedback the time it takes.

EXERCISE: THE FRIEND READ

Choose a friend or friends whose feedback will be valuable to you. Ask them if they're willing to read, being specific about your book length and when you'd like to hear back. Ask what file format is easiest for them.

Send your readers your manuscript and some specific questions. You might ask:

How would you describe this book?

What story do you think the author is trying to tell?

Did they succeed in telling that story?

Is it a story worth telling?

Is the storyline believable?

Do the characters actions seem motivated and logical within their own worldview?

What didn't make sense?

Is anyone presented without a single redeeming quality, and are you OK with that as the reader?

Whose side were you on?

What scenes were the most interesting?

Where did you find yourself skimming or less involved?

What were any mysteries you wanted to know the answers to?

What was surprising or shocking?

What did you see coming a mile away?

Who is the ideal reader for this book?

What books would this be shelved next to, or where would it sit in a bookstore?

What would you enter in a search engine to find it, beyond the title or author?

When your feedback comes back, look it over and write down your initial reactions. Then give it 24-48 hours and read it again. Apply the feedback you agree with and revise as needed to resolve confusion, plot holes, and other issues.

THE EDITOR READ

When you've revised as much as you can on your own, but the book still isn't "done," or you're sick of getting rejections and you don't know why, you might find a professional editor—or an equivalent friend—useful.

Most authors get to a point where they can't make their book any better without some outside input. This is the draft where it's worth either calling in a big favor or spending money.[96]

Get a writer you trust, whose work you believe is more polished than yours, to give feedback. This should be someone who doesn't love everything you write—praise is not useful at this time. Later, you read their work, or buy them a nice present. It helps to ask for specific feedback, like "Does the main character's emotional journey make sense?" or "Can you please highlight everything you think I can cut?"

Outside input can also come from a professional editor. A good editor will help you make your book the best you possibly can, and much readier for submission to agents or self-publishing. Unlike your friend doing you a favor, you'll have a specific due date and a clear idea of the editor's scope of work.

For most of us, money is a factor, so do as much as you can before dropping cash on a pro. Go through the first six of the Seven Drafts, join a writing group, trade manuscripts with a writer buddy. Cleaner manuscripts generally cost less to edit; you'll also get more bang for your buck if the editor spends her time on issues you couldn't see or fix yourself.

---

96 You've been reading for other people as much as you can this whole time, right?

It's useful to start with professional feedback on a small section, usually your first 1-3 chapters. Any problems at the beginning are almost certainly problems through the whole book. Get your first pages edited and ask for a list of what to fix, then address those issues yourself in the rest of the book.

Before you send out pages or a manuscript, read through one more time. Knowing that feedback is imminent, more issues will stick out.

Editing is not a magic cure. Your book still may be unpublishable. Your writing may not be ready. But a good editor will not just polish this book—her feedback will teach you more about writing, and your next book will start at a higher level of craft.

WHAT WILL IT COST?

Editing prices vary wildly, with several factors influencing the cost:

* What shape your book is in. I've gotten manuscripts with barely a typo to be found, and work that's barely coherent. As discussed in the introduction to Line Editing back in Chapter 4, sloppy writing costs more to edit because it takes longer.

* Length. Editors may price by word count, by page count (a "standard" page is 250 words), or by the hour. Books with more words take longer to edit.

* Quality of writing. Not gonna lie—I've cut a better deal to writers whose work I adored and wanted to read to find out what happens. That said, plenty of editors charge the same whether they like your work or not, and you don't have any way to find that out.

* The editor's work schedule. Freelance editors are self-employed. If their calendar is full, they're not handing out any discounts. If they have open time or an unexpected household expense, they may set a more attractive price to get your business.

* The editor's training and experience. Early-career editors are building their client lists—someone with few books or client testimonials on their site will be less expensive. You'll pay more for someone who's previously worked for a traditional publisher or as a literary agent, because they presumably have more expertise on what sells.

As a freelance editor, I mostly bill by the word, charging anywhere from low-four to low-five figures depending on word count and the depth of the edit. A relatively quick manuscript evaluation will cost much less than multiple rounds of developmental, line and copyediting. You can find suggested editorial rates at the Editorial Freelancers Association's website—do note the listed rates are a median, not an average. Outside of North America, contact your local editors' society for more information about pay rates.

Yes, you could find an editor on a gig-labor site for much, much less. But you really do get what you pay for, and whole-manuscript editing quotes below $500 should come with strong references.

Why is editing often expensive?

Editing is time-consuming. I work pretty fast, about 1500-2000 words per hour for a full developmental edit. That's around 40 hours for an 80,000-word manuscript. If I note and explain every error in the first fifty pages—useful for writers improving their craft, or non-native speakers publishing in English—I'm much slower. A 15-20-page single-spaced editorial letter summarizing the notes, asking questions, and giving mini-lessons on craft takes another 2-3 hours.

Editing is highly skilled labor. Many editors have graduate degrees and have edited Big-Five published books. Some editors are indie specialists who can advise you on how best to package and market your self-published book as well as working on the text.

Good editors are strong analytical thinkers. They can say *why* your storyline isn't working and ask the right questions for you to realize how to fix it. They'll give you enough information that you can decide what notes you agree with (however painful) and what's a difference of opinion that you choose to ignore or solve differently. They'll identify when a problem is structural and when it only needs a minor rewrite. As well as annotations throughout the manuscript, they'll give you feedback on your major craft issues and thoughts on how to solve them.

A good edit is the equivalent of a personal MFA class (and costs about the same). But with a professional edit, someone reads your entire manuscript (most university writing courses don't workshop whole books), and you don't have to read or give feedback on anyone else's work. An edit takes 2-8 weeks, rather than an entire semester.

Get a sample edit and references. Be prepared to pay for quality editing, and be prepared to find out you need a massive rewrite. But now you'll be aware of craft issues you can fix with practice. Your next book will be better. That's where you really get your money's worth.

Paid editorial help is always optional. I say this as a professional editor, as a writing coach who has helped people write better and publish, and charged them money for those services. Does it help to spend money on your writing career? Sure. But it helps like a personal trainer helps you get fit. If you're focused and ready to work, money can help you over some speedbumps. But if you're focused and ready to work, you can get over them alone, too.

HIRING AN EDITOR

You need an editor on your wavelength, who enjoys your genre and gives critique you can receive. How do you find someone you can afford, and how do you know they are qualified and able to do the work you want?

Some editors hold certificates from formal training, others have extensive professional experience. Most editors will provide references from previous clients. Some provide pricing on their website, others only do custom quotes. If you have a small budget, a newer (often younger) editor who has insight and training, but not a ton of experience, can be a good match.

There are some lovely, well-read people who believe their lifetime of reading or experience teaching English has made them an editor. Those are valuable pursuits, but no substitute for specific, serious study of editing.

Your number-one way to evaluate an editor is through a sample edit. Make your top two or three choices, based on their websites and testimonials, or recommendations from other authors. Don't get more than three samples—it's confusing for you and mean to waste the time of people you have no intention of hiring.[97] How many pages and whether a sample is free or paid depends on the editor.

---

97 Sending different chapters to many editors for samples in hopes of compiling a free edit won't help you. Editors vary in style choices, and won't approach your book in the same way. Plus, we already know about the Frankenedit, and we out those authors to other editors in professional forums. Hilarity always ensues.

The editor determines what kind of edit to offer based on the sample pages, because authors are frequently wrong. Authors request "a quick proofread" when the book needs a developmental edit and a top-to-bottom rewrite, or "copyediting" when the dialogue is a mess. It's hard to hear that your manuscript isn't ready, but it's stealing from the writer if the editor doesn't tell them what's really needed—as if an auto shop agreed to paint your car a pretty color when your engine has a cracked head gasket.

The editor sends back the edited pages with their recommendations, a price quote, when they can start (good editors often book months in advance), and time needed (usually 2-8 weeks). If you look at their work and think, *Wow! They get me, and those fixes will make my book better!* you've found the right person.

The writer pays a deposit to hold their place in the editor's calendar. Editors have differing payment policies—most will work with installments, but you usually pay in full before receiving your edited manuscript.

A bad editor is a nightmare and a waste of money. How do you avoid scams, predators, and poor work?

Danger Signs

- An agent or publisher who suggests they're interested in your book...but only if you work with a specific editor. It's not always a scam, but it's unethical and the agent may be getting a kickback.

- An agent or publisher who accepts your work but wants you to pay for editing through them. This is a conflict of interest, and unethical according to the Association of Authors' Representatives (the primary professional association for literary agents).

- Editing services that employ multiple editors can deliver quality work. But make sure you know exactly who will work on your book...and that it's the same person who edited your sample.

- Pie-in-the-sky talk like "bestseller potential!" or "We'll get you on Oprah!" Solid professionals don't make big promises.

- An editor who edits "everything!" rather than specifying their expertise. Many editors work on a wide variety of books, but no one has time to be excellent in all genres.

- An editor who asks for a royalty or sales percentage on top of their fee. Editing is work-for-hire, and editors only get royalties in major ghostwriting contracts. If it's a big enough deal for anyone besides the author of record to earn royalties, it's a big enough deal that everyone's agents are working that out.

- An editor who agrees to work for a percentage of future royalties with no up-front payment. New authors with a healthy belief in themselves often suggest this. Only very inexperienced editors will accept this (terrible!) deal.[98]

The Pro Editor Checklist

- Review the types of editing in the Introduction and determine what will best serve you and your book right now. You may still be incorrect, but it's a starting point.

- Ask fellow writers for referrals to editors they like. Look at profiles on editing association websites. Membership indicates the editor is focused on their profession, but be aware that some associations require qualifications and others only a membership fee. Reputable professional organizations include the Editorial Freelancers Association[99] (US), the Society for Editors and Proofreaders (UK), the Institute of Professional Editors (Australia), and the Editors' Association of Canada.

- Read potential editors' credentials. Do you want someone who's worked for a big publisher? Someone with copyediting certification? Someone who's edited a book you've enjoyed?

- Look at past clients. Has the editor worked in your genre? Especially for romance, historical fiction, high fantasy, hard science fiction, erotica, or memoir, it's important the editor is familiar with genre conventions. She should be able to identify where you're wandering from the norms ("Hey, where's the happily-ever-after in your Amish romance?") and tell you if a broken "rule" is a bold decision that's working or needs another look.

---

98 "But I'm going to be a successssssssss!" At $2 profit per self-pubbed book, you'll sell 1500 books before the editor's 10% makes minimum wage. You'll sell 16,000 books before they approach reasonable editorial wages.

99 Links to organizations and software vendors mentioned in the print edition can be found at http://www.sevendrafts.com

- Look inside the editor's clients' books—do they seem well-written? Reasonably error-free? It's nearly impossible to reach zero typos, but more than a few could be carelessness. Be aware that in a self-published book, the author may have done post-edit revisions and introduced errors the editor is not responsible for.[100]

- Request a sample edit.

- Ask "Do you have a couple of previous clients I could contact?" References aren't required if you love your sample edit, but a good reference can support your choice. Prepare a short list of questions—was the editor timely, how did the edit help the writer improve, did the writer feel they got their money's worth?

- If you're in an online writers' group, ask if anyone's worked with this editor. Usually, good references will post publicly and dissatisfied authors will message you privately.

- Get the scope of work in writing. Your contract or email agreement should set the price and the basis (per word, per page, project fee, hourly) and spell out the payment plan. If you're paying hourly, there should be an estimated number of hours, and a notification process if they're going into overtime. You should have a delivery date when you send your manuscript, and a return date from the editor.

- If possible, pay through PayPal's "goods and services" option (not "friends and family"), or with a credit card.[101] Insist on accountability from people you pay. Missed deadlines or meetings should have a definite reschedule and a reason. If you sign up for a workshop or event, email the hotel and confirm the rooms have been booked before you purchase travel.

Most editors are honest businesspeople deeply invested in the quality of your work. Clear agreements help everyone know what's going on and reputable editors want clarity for you both, as they help you write your best.

---

100 The pain... the pain...

101 Some editors prefer checks or direct deposit to save on processing fees. International clients may need to pay by bank ... transfer. In those cases, double-check their references.

USING YOUR EDIT

So your editor got back to you with a letter and a manuscript full of comment bubbles. Track Changes appears to have bled copiously across your pages.

How do you tackle the next draft?

Start by reading the editorial letter, which may be called a critique or report. This should contain an overview of major issues, and probably covers things like timeline, story structure, setting, world-building, and the protagonist's overall journey. Notice if there are any trends—things your beta readers called out that the editor spotted, too.

Make some notes as you read. Your first reactions can be valuable, but they aren't always correct, so write them down to get the hurt feelings and defensiveness out of your head.[102] Ideally, you'll also have moments of realization: *That's how I'm going to fix it!* And, *Oh, now I see what the problem is.*

Next up is the manuscript. Save the draft the editor sent back, and save it again as a new file that you'll work in. You can check the original if you accidentally delete something useful. Spend a few moments with the Review Pane in Word, and experiment with showing and hiding different types of edits (comments, deletions, and so forth). That way, if you want to focus on just one element at a time, you can.

Working from the new file, deal with technical elements first. If you put "comma" for "coma" and the editor fixed that, it's not an opinion. Accept Change. Colored text goes back to your normal color and the bubble on the side (if she used bubbles) will disappear. As you move through the manuscript and accept purely technical fixes, this will reduce the amount of notes/bubbles/colored ink to look at, and you'll be able to better see your words and her feedback. Anything you're cool with, Accept Change and move on. It's deeply gratifying to clean the manuscript as you go, and it's a visible sign that you're making progress.

Next, read through the comments. If there's anything you can deal with right away ("Bob? I thought his name was Rob?") fix it and delete the comment.

If there's a comment you don't understand, write your question in the same place, as a new comment bubble, or in the same bubble with a Q: in front of it, or whatever makes your questions

---

102 Feel those feelings, and then move on to fixing your work, because you have just discovered you are capable of more.

easy to find again. If there's a comment you disagree with, feel for the itch underneath your defensiveness that says, "This might be right." Don't delete those yet—wait for the cumulative sense of all the comments, because one coming up later might put the one you disagree with in perspective.

If you have a post-edit meeting with your editor, write down any other questions, with references to specific page numbers if needed.

Start thinking about your rewrite. Will you deal with structural elements first, rebuilding big things before tweaking little things? Will you deal with character first because you need to know more about why they do what they do? Will you polish the dialogue, so you can build the habit of better dialogue before larger revisions? Do you want to fix grammar and punctuation so you can work from a cleaner draft?

If you have a follow-up call or meeting with your editor, share your work plan with her. Ask for suggestions about how to approach revisions as you move forward. Ask questions about comments you didn't understand. Kick around some ideas. It's best if you record this conversation (some editors do this for you). That way you can be 100% in the conversation without worrying about taking notes. If you don't have that option, take notes as you go and review them right after the call to make sure you got down all the important stuff.

Tackle one step at a time. Each time you make a substantial change, go back and read the still-active comments again. You may have solved the motivation problem on page 108 by revealing some backstory on page 60. Maybe once you changed a character's speech pattern, the comment about his dialect is no longer relevant.

If your edit includes any follow-up, see if you can send one revised scene or chapter to see if you're getting it right before tackling the entire draft. If your editor isn't available, show a writer buddy the new version and the original and get an outside eye.

When you've gotten to a place where this draft has as many improvements as you can make, revisit the Self-Edit Checklist in Chapter 10. Get another Friend Read. Talk to your editor about whether you need another round of deep revision or whether you're ready for a copyedit or proofread.

And feel good. You're getting better. You can do this.

SAMPLE EDITING WORKFLOW

If you're blessed with the finances to invest in professional editing throughout your writing process, here's how that might go:

1) Vomit Draft

2) Story Draft

3) Character Draft

The above drafts might include some editorial coaching, or feedback on a few chapters and/or a synopsis. For a memoir, a writing coach might help the author choose the most interesting parts of their story.

4) Developmental Edit

The editor provides plot/story/structure feedback and identifies major craft issues.

5) Story Draft 2 and/or Character Draft 2

The author fixes craft issues and adjusts the plot and characterization.

6) Friend Read

One or two trusted readers answer general questions.

7) Story Draft 3 and/or Character Draft 3

8) Small Line Edit

The editor line edits only the first 10-25 pages to show craft issues that the author can fix in the...

9) Technical Draft

The author carries out the editor's suggestions (that they agree with) from the opening pages and anything left over from the Developmental Edit, cleaning the whole manuscript at the sentence, paragraph, and chapter level.

10) Personal Copyedit

11) Full Line Edit

The editor line edits the entire manuscript, builds a style sheet, and runs PerfectIt! or similar editing software as a first-pass copyedit.

12) Review

The author accepts/rejects changes and addresses any editorial questions in the line-edited draft.

13) Personal Copyedit

14) Friend Read

Two to five trusted readers, including needed experts and members of the target reading audience. The editor and author compile and discuss reader feedback and how to implement it.

15) Final revisions based on reader feedback

16) Proofread

A new editor, often a subcontractor, reviews the final manuscript with fresh eyes, and any last corrections are incorporated.

From here, if publishing traditionally:

17) Query Prep

The author writes their synopsis and query for feedback and a couple of rounds of revisions. This process can be included in your editorial contract, or you might work with fellow writers, or a querying specialist.

18) Querying

Additional editing may happen if the first queries are unsuccessful.

19) Publishing

After signing with an agent, the author does additional manuscript revisions based on the agent's feedback. If the book sells, the author usually does more revisions from the acquiring editor's feedback.

If self-publishing:[103]

17) Design

The author chooses cover/interior designer(s) and begins the design process.

18) Paperwork

The author secures ISBNs, decides whether to set up a publishing business structure, plans where to sell the book, and sets the publication date.

19) Marketing Prep

The author approves writes blurb and cover copy which the editor reviews; updates their online presence and contacts bloggers and early reviewers.

20) Final Designs

---

103 Notice the plethora of extra steps for self-publishers? That's why royalties are lower with traditional publishers—they handle those elements.

The author approves the final cover and interior designs for ebook and print.

21) Advance Reader Copies

ARCs are sent to early reviewers and used for promotion.

22) Marketing the Launch[104]

Worthy of a book in itself.

23) Publication

The book is uploaded print-on-demand and ebook distributors, and printed copies are distributed.

If your finances are more limited, but you still want to hire an editor, a developmental edit and 25–50 pages of line editing are the most important. Developmental editing will highlight and help fix any story or character issues before you fine-tune everything else. A short line edit can be extrapolated throughout the entire manuscript to improve your writing craft.

---

104 Whether you are publishing traditionally or independently, building connections with your audience ideally starts about two years before publication, and serious marketing begins at least three months prior; six is better.

PUBLICATION

Every so often, a would-be author asks me, "How do I write a bestseller? Because if I'm putting the time in, I want it to be worthwhile."[105]

No one can guarantee any book will sell. If bestsellers had a formula, publishers would only print sure-fire hits and writers would write them every time. Even trends like "dystopian YA" or "vampires" aren't reliable indicators. Most books now on shelves started being written *at least* three years ago. By the time publishing identifies a trend, it's almost over.

For most of us, publication is not the road to money and fame. The average traditionally published book[106] sells fewer than 5000 copies.[107] Rather than chasing a "bestseller," keep your eyes on the larger purpose—to share a story your readers will love and that you're proud of creating. Publication, money, and fame may follow—but they follow good books.

If you're writing for money, pick a genre you love in which the stories are straightforward. YA spy novels. Category romance. Dinosaur porn. Learn the genre's structure and your craft so well you can write a reader-satisfying book in a month. Learn marketing so well you can sell at least a thousand copies each. Be a writing machine. Or build your public-

---

105 I usually take a couple of deep breaths with my eyes closed before answering.

106 Most self-published books sell fewer than 100 copies.

107 Imagine how many books sell in the low hundreds to balance out Stephen King and Nora Roberts.

speaking career until the tickets to your sold-out events include a copy of your latest memoir.

But you're just as likely to succeed writing the book of your heart. E. L. James didn't think, "I'm going to write a bestseller." She wrote what she loved, and what she loved was *Twilight* fan fiction. The combination of a straightforward story, transgressive-but-not-too-out-there erotica, and a huge fan base of *Twilight*-lovers made *Fifty Shades of Grey* a hit.[108] Jenny Lawson's comic musings made The Bloggess huge and then made a memoir. John Grisham fit writing in at 4 AM every day until he published *The Firm*—which wasn't his first completed manuscript.

Write what you love to write. Make it as amazing as you can. Let publication be the icing on the cake.

---

108 Another booster: the growing popularity of ebooks and the nonsexual cover art made it easier to read erotica without being embarrassed on the subway.

MEMOIR: PUBLICATION

Many memoirists worry about exposing loved ones or family members to ridicule or shame. You're still allowed to tell your story.

Roz Warren writes revealing personal essays for a living. When she found out her partner had been cheating on her, intensely, intimately, for ten years, she wrote about it. At *Broad Street Review*, she addressed the obvious question:

> *Why? I'm a writer. It's what I do. I write about everything that happens to me. It's how I cope and how I understand my life. For years, I've been writing about how wonderful Mike is. He's turned up over and over again in my essays. I told the world how funny and clever and loving he was. How I loved him. How much fun the two of us had together. I've even appeared on the* Today *show, where Savannah Guthrie interviewed me about an essay I'd written for the* New York Times *in which Mike was featured, being fabulous, loving, and supportive. When Mr. Wonderful turned out to have been Mr. Infidelity all along, why wouldn't I write about that too?*

Roz talks about the tiny voice she heard—a voice I've heard, too—when her partner admitted the affair:

> *This is awful. This is devastating. And unbelievable. And hateful. And...this is amazing material.*

At moments of horrifying emotional trauma, part of my brain steps back and starts jotting down metaphors. *No, I'll tell it like this—remember that detail, the cement bench under your butt, the weird lighting....*

Roz Warren's partner was unhappy about her new topic. Furious, in fact. She wrote it anyway. A writer's obligation is to the truth as they experience it. We should be fair, but we don't have to stay quiet for fear of hurting feelings. As Roz put it: "I wish with all my heart that Mike had been the loving, trustworthy man I thought he was, and that I didn't have this terrible betrayal to write about. But I do. So I am."

Memoirists' relationships can be affected by publication in a way that novelists' rarely are. Start thinking about where you hope to publish. Think about how much publicity may happen, and plan ahead.

If you're already estranged, you don't have to seek out people you've written about critically. You're writing about your world, not theirs. Even in strong relationships, not everyone wants to know if they're in your book. My husband has said, "There are a lot of books in the world, and that's one I won't be reading," about my memoir. I'm OK with that.

Respect boundaries. For example, I had limited consent to tell a story about a friend in a venue outside the friend's orbit. The story was republished by another outlet (beyond my control) with a bigger audience. Even though it was one of my bucket-list venues, I didn't promote it, because doing so would have brought it into my friend's line of sight and been hurtful. Try not to publish the essay about your horrible mother in the magazine all her friends read.

Sharing information is not asking for permission. If you choose to tell someone you've written about them, try, "I had some complicated feelings about X and I've written about them. Would you like to know anything about the content before I publish it, so that you're aware of what's out there?" You might add (if it's true), "I value our relationship, and I'm not mad at anyone, but I needed to process how I felt in the moment. This is a snapshot of a particular time and place." Based on their response, you could allow them to read the actual piece, summarize the content, or summarize just the part they're in.

It's not your job to protect the people who hurt you. Make sure you're representing your antagonist's own perceptions, and let the reader be the judge. For legal concerns, see the next section, What If I Get Sued? For moral concerns, review the Villains and Memoir: Character sections in Chapter 3.

WHAT IF I GET SUED?

You own everything that happened to you. Tell your stories. If people wanted you to write warmly about them, they should have behaved better.

Anne Lamott's maxim is oft-quoted in the memoirist world. Followed closely by: "Write the book first, worry about hurt feelings later."

That doesn't stop us from worrying our way through the final draft, fearing a family explosion, resentment, or even legal action.

If I tell that secret, will anyone talk to me at the family reunion?

My sister told me I better not write anything about her... what if I change her name?

If I write about my mom hitting me, can she sue me?

We can't control how our loved (or unloved!) ones will react to our memoir or thinly disguised fiction. We can only be as truthful as we can, allowing ourselves the distance to write from analysis as well as from emotion, showing why other people behaved as they did, as best we can tell from hindsight. It's our choice to brace for anger from a parent or sibling, or practice verbal judo with a smooth, "I can see how the story would be different from your perspective."

What if someone you write about, or upon whom you've based a fictional character, threatens to sue?

In the USA, anyone can sue anyone for any damn reason they want. Even if you signed a release, even a big scary release with ACCEPT ALL RISKS FOR INJURY AND/OR DEATH on it. In most American jurisdictions, no one can sign away their right to sue. Releases provide evidence that a suit is baseless, because the signer accepted responsibility, but they don't stop anyone from filing paperwork and demanding their day in court.

So why aren't alcoholic parents, angry ex-boyfriends, and pedophilic religious leaders stampeding into court to bankrupt and destroy the fragile writers telling their own stories?

Money.

It's expensive and time-consuming to pursue a civil case, and they aren't easy to win without a phalanx of top-notch attorneys laying out extensive documentation of the kind most non-writers rarely preserve. Unless the suit is against an insurance company with the potential for a huge payout (as in medical malpractice, accident, and wrongful-death cases), lawyers rarely take civil cases without an up-front retainer.

Say your poorly behaving former spouse has five figures to spare and a sense of vengeance strong enough to waste every dime. First, they must lawyer-shop until they hear, "Sure, you're not crazy at all and I'd love to take on a hard-to-prove case against a writer with no money." The lawyer must then find a judge who doesn't laugh them out of court and agrees to consider the plaintiff's hurt feelings as facts.

If the suit actually makes it to court, the person you wrote about must prove three things:

1) You lied

2) You lied on purpose to hurt them

3) Your story hurt them in terms of hard cash or public reputation

First, the truth is always a defense against libel. Police reports. Affidavits from your friends. Photos or videos. Your convincing presence on the witness stand.

Then, if you *accidentally* didn't tell the truth, that's still not actionable. A plaintiff has to prove you lied on purpose or were very careless, not just that you were mistaken or have a different opinion. Memoir is inherently the writer's opinion; it's also worth adding caveats like "As I remember it..." or "What it felt like was..." in your narrative, especially if you're truly concerned about legal action.

Finally, damages are meted out based on actual, provable harm. By portraying people's behavior in interpersonal relations rather than their ability to do their job, you are unlikely to damage their finances or their reputation enough for a judge to believe they need redress. You can say your doctor treated you cavalierly, that's your opinion. But criticizing his medical ability could do him financial harm and he's likely to have business records to prove it.

Our final protection against being sued?

Most of us aren't worth suing. We don't have enough assets for a long-shot winner to take. In most jurisdictions, a lawsuit can't take your homestead. Your homeowner's insurance is unlikely to cover libel, so your angry relative won't be suing that company. Generally, if you have enough money to be worth suing, you can already afford your own excellent lawyer to tell you all this. If you don't have that kind of cash, it's almost never worth the time and money for the plaintiff or their attorney.

I am not a lawyer. This is emotional, rather than legal, advice. But emotional fallout from a published memoir is far more likely than legal action. Instead of fearing a suit, spend that time being as honest as you can on the page, letting other people's actions show who they are and being clear about what you remember and what's your best guess. Read Tara Westover's *Educated* to see how she honors competing stories while insisting on her own truth.

Threatening to sue is easy. Actually suing, winning, and collecting damages are pretty darn hard.

Be fair, be kind, write the best book you can that tells your own true story. If someone threatens to sue, smile gently. Tell them, "I can see you're passionate about getting your story out there. I hope you write a book."

THE PUBLISHING TIMELINE

It often takes years to finish a book, get an agent, get a traditional publisher, and see the finished product in a store. In fast indie publishing, it's the author's ability to create a steady pipeline that makes money.

If you're hoping for a Big-Five publisher:

1-10 years to finish the book. Seriously. Especially if this is your first book, you're likely to pursue other writing and/or need months away from a draft before revising. Writers commonly move from their seventh draft into the Augh That Feedback Was Right Draft, the Augh Augh I Finally Realized What I Need to Change Draft, and the Auuugghhhh Dammit I Thought I Was DONE Draft.

1-3 years to sign with an agent. You may undergo multiple rounds of querying, revising the book based on feedback from a rejection or meeting an agent at a conference, and querying again.

1-3 years to hit the shelf. Your publisher will almost certainly want more revisions. Then they'll fit publication into the best time of year for your book—and those slots might already be filled with other authors for the next two years.

If you're going for a literary or small press:

1-10 years to finish, same as for the Big Five.

1-3 years to match with the right small press. You won't need an agent, though. Additional revisions based on your publisher's feedback are likely.

1-2 years to shelf. Small presses move faster, but they still have publication schedules.

If you're independent/self-publishing:

Allow 2-3 years for a first book. Self-publishing has fewer gatekeepers, but requires market research and an understanding of Amazon and online marketing to sell a meaningful number of copies.

Many indie authors turn out several books a year if they're writing a strong-selling genre they know well. Usually they have an editor, layout and cover designers, marketing help, and business practices in place to support this kind of speed.

SELF & HYBRID PUBLISHING

If you've truly "done the work," why wait for someone else's permission to live the dream?

Self-publishing gives the satisfaction of seeing your words in print. A calling card at conferences. Sweet, sweet profit.[109] Lots of people put their books on Amazon every day. How hard can it be?

Or perhaps a publisher has contacted you. They would love to publish your book! But due to "the difficulty in placing the books of new or untried authors, as well as the general increased competition in publishing today"—the publisher feels "that it may be necessary to ask for a contribution from you."[110] Maybe it's even right up front: We're a hybrid press. Our package costs $X,XXX, and you can add on additional services at $XXX, $X,XXX or $XX,XXX.

That's not a book deal. That's an ad for a publishing services package.

What are your options?

Vanity Presses

Old-school vanity publishers know their terrible reputations, and many have rebranded as "hybrid." Vanities charge authors a "contribution" that pays the publisher's costs and a healthy profit margin. They don't care if your book sells—they already made their money. In fact, they often require you to purchase a few hundred copies. You may end up with cartons of unsold books, edited badly or not at all, with a dreadful cover and crappy page design. Vanity presses are always overpriced and the services they deliver are often poor quality.

Hybrid Publishing

True hybrid presses offer a legitimate package of publishing services. Hybrids cost more than self-publishing—they still

---

109 Most self-published books sell fewer than 100 copies. Any profit made is likely to be substantially lower than what you paid for cover design alone.

110 Actual quote from actual vanity press email.

profit before selling your book—but you have professionals coordinating the work and steering you toward good design and editing choices. Genuine hybrids can provide a smoother publication process and some of the legitimacy of an imprint.

No matter what a hybrid press tells you about "their share of the publishing costs," they make their profit from the check you write.

Self-Publishing

This is truly going it alone. You find and hire your own editor and interior and cover designer(s) or learn to do those skills yourself. You buy an ISBN, write marketing and promotional copy, and upload files to Amazon and Ingram. You market the book, harangue your friends and family for reviews, and collect any profits.[111]

Should You Go Indie?

Indie publishing is an industry, not a consolation prize. The magic combination of quality and marketability that makes a book sellable to a traditional publisher is also the key to indie success. Self-published novels must fit one of the narrow genres that sell ebooks like mad. Self-published memoirs need a clear hook and a specific reader demographic.

Authors may self-publish because they believe "the establishment" is overlooking their vast talent or snobbishly gatekeeping the doors to success. But traditional publishing wants to make money. If a book is likely to make money, the establishment will buy it and try their best to sell it.

Meanwhile, presses large and small buy quite a few brilliantly written, medium-marketable books, hoping sales will surprise them as they enjoy the warm glow of nurturing new talent. Tremendously marketable books may not be great from a literary standpoint—but saying a popular, badly written book is a bad thing is like insisting everyone finish their broccoli before having ice cream. Financially, every ghostwritten celebrity memoir keeps afloat a whole raft of midlist authors.

Maybe agents and publishers focus too much on "platform." Why should you have to be a speaker/expert/quasi-celebrity? Can't you just write a good book? But if your book is truly fresh

---

111 Most self-published books sell fewer than 100 copies.

and well-written enough to sell without platform, agents and publishers will snap you up. The horrible, unspoken second part of "Sorry, you don't have enough platform..." is "...and your book isn't convincing me it'll be worth the work to overcome that challenge." Excellent and painstaking writers often miss that crucial variable, and it's heartbreaking to pour tremendous time and effort into an unsellable book.

Self- or hybrid publishing might still be right for you.

1) Do you want a long-term writing career?

"At least I'll be published" is the worst possible reason to self-publish. Low first-book numbers make it harder to sell a second book. It's better to have the excitement of being a "debut" author than one who's sold under 10,000 copies[112]—traditional publishers want a positive track record or no track record at all.

Going hybrid, at least one of you thinks you won't sell many copies. If a publisher smells a bestseller, they don't need your money. If you think you can do better, pursue traditional publication or explore self-publishing.

But if you're up for academic tenure, a reputable hybrid press gives you a résumé credit. If you're launching a public-speaking career and will be selling books after every motivational speech, you have built-in readers for a self-published book. If you're busy marketing your coaching or consulting, it can be worth having a hybrid press handle cover design and proofreading.

2) How much energy do you have for marketing?

Even Big-Five-published authors end up marketing their own books. But hybrids (and small literary and university presses) often lack media contacts. Does your press arrange readings or signings at regional book festivals? Do they have a list of radio and podcast producers to contact? Check their social media for links to author interviews and reviews in national media. If a hybrid publisher can't market your book in places that cost money or connections to enter, they aren't doing anything you can't do yourself.

If you're newsworthy in a way related to your book—you just summited Mount Everest without supplementary oxygen or Sherpas; you gave six organs as a living donor; you're a former child star just out of rehab—then marketing isn't your obstacle. Self-publish away!

---

112 Did I mention most self-published books sell fewer than 100 copies?

3) Are you in a hurry?

Traditional publishers take up to three years between contract and printing. With self-publishing, you'll need time to learn key skills and new software, or to research and hire professionals. Good hybrids have an established editing and design pipeline to scoot your book right through in six months or less. If you're dying of cancer or facing a major book-selling event this year, you may want to pay for publishing.

4) Do you know your market and how to reach those readers?

Very few writers create work of transcendent beauty surpassing the need for clear connections to an existing market. Ask yourself, *Is this the best book I can write? Do I know exactly who will want to read it? Do I have a realistic and extensive plan to reach those people?*

Memoirists: do you have substantial personal clout in a field or organization strongly and specifically interested in your topic, with 5000+ members who will purchase your books and evangelize on your behalf?

Novelists: are you active in your genre's communities? Does that subculture exist? Are other books in your genre selling well on Amazon?

Do you have 10-15 hours a week to follow up on press releases, place supporting articles in mass media, chase interviews, and urge friends, family, and strangers to review your book on Amazon and Goodreads?

5) Got money to spend?

Do you have the money/skills for a professional cover that fits the genre and serves as clickbait? Do you have the judgment to let your favorite image go in favor of a cover that sells books?

Do you have the money/skills to design the book interior and handle ebook conversions to multiple formats?

Do you have the money/skills to build a website with a secure e-commerce portal?

Do you have the money/skills for professional-quality PR?

6) Want to make money?

Self-publishing, you control the price and get all the profit.[113] Traditional publishing trades a chunk of the net for marketing

---

113 Most self-published books sell fewer than 100 copies. I can keep saying that all day. What's your plan to sell more?

and reputation. Hybrids take the royalties you agree to give them...on top of the money you already paid to publish.

Will you wholesale to bookstores at the standard discount, even though intuition screams "Why do I have to give up another $2/copy?"

7) Who will edit?

Is your book done? Really, really done? Is there still a nagging feeling in your heart that it could be better? Who are you going to hire to help you and what will that cost?

If you're considering a hybrid, ask what kind of editing will be done, and by whom. "Our in-house editor proofreads" is not the same as helping your prose sing and your story hang together.

8) For hybrids, what are their actual, printed books like?

Order a couple of titles from your prospective hybrid. Is the paper thinner than you expected? Do you see typos, blurry print, bad layout? Is the cover art just plain ugly? Pull out books in the same genre from your shelves and make a table display. Do the hybrid books look like they belong?

9) Due diligence!

- The Independent Book Publishers Association has set guidelines for hybrid presses. This is the bare minimum of legitimacy.

- Search the publisher's name + "scam." Search again on the Absolute Write author forums site (make a free account for better info).

- Check *Writer Beware* Blogs, a wonderful resource that details bad-faith agents and publishers.

- The Science Fiction and Fantasy Writers of America have a list of what to watch out for when approached by a publisher.

- Read Jane Friedman's *The Business of Being a Writer* for a greater understanding of the industry.

Most authors who self-publish or pay a hybrid end up doing the real work anyway. Pounding the pavement to get their book in a few stores. Emailing the target audience.[114] Go in with your eyes open. Self-publishing costs your time and labor. Hybrid publishing is not a "book deal," it's a package of services you purchase. Make sure you're getting your money's worth.

---

114 Key demographic: "everyone I know who has ever read a book, or might need a coaster."

The publishing world is not full of cruel gatekeepers, but people who genuinely value and want to sell good writing. You're one of them. Choose your method carefully.

AWARDS & PRIZES

Maybe you've gotten an email: there's a contest your book is eligible for! If you win, your book will be presented to movie producers and in an ad on Goodreads! Press releases will feature you! You can put shiny gold stickers on your book cover! And it's only $75! Per entry! In as many categories as you want!

Sadly, these "contests" are simply money-making machines for the organizers. "Winning" adds no credibility to your book, doesn't help with sales, and seldom results in any publicity beyond free internet announcements. In fact, there are often so many subcategories that everyone who enters wins. You didn't buy fair consideration and worthy competition—you bought a $75 sticker.[115]

Legitimate contests and meaningful awards are usually ones you've already heard of, or they're affiliated with reputable magazines or organizations that do more than hold contests. You might be part of their mailing list, but they rarely solicit your entry personally. Your book may need to be submitted by your publisher or nominated by librarians or booksellers. The contest judges are published writers or noted agents and editors. Past winners include writers you've heard of, or whose biographies mention MFAs and literary or mass media publications. Entry fees rarely top $50 for a book or $15-20 for a story or essay. Books can only be entered in the year they are released, and in only one category.

Legit contests offer specific, measurable prizes, like "$1000 and a guest lecture at X College," rather than nebulous claims like "promoted to industry insiders." You don't have to purchase your own prize stickers if you win.

Over at the Writer Beware! Blog, Victoria Strauss points out why "winning" may not matter:

> *Profiteer awards and contests don't typically command a lot of name recognition, but if you win or place, you'll be able to tag your book as an "award-winning book" and yourself as an "award-winning author." How much*

---

115 Additional stickers may be purchased at just $25/pack!

readers care about such designations, though, is an open question. With all the fake review scandals, as well as readers' increasing disillusion with authorial self-promotion, I think book buyers have become more cynical in general about what authors say about themselves.

Authors are eager for recognition and that extra something to help their book stand out. Cynical, shady contests recognize and exploit that hunger. Wondering if a contest is legit? Check out the handy chart at The Alliance of Independent Authors website.

Genuine book awards do launch careers. They're also highly competitive and a lot less "rah-rah" about the prizes, because their name *is* the prize (Booker, Pulitzer, Nobel).[116] One day, you'll be in the running. For now, skip the contest entry and use that time to write another essay or short story, something that will draw real attention to your book. Something beautiful. Something more powerful than a $75 sticker.

116 They also offer cash awards of five figures or much more.

QUERYING

You're close to done! It's almost a book! What happens now?

I start querying, I guess?

Great! What agents do you have in mind?

Um...

Finding literary agents is tedious but not difficult. Most of this work can be done at only the cost of your time, and most of the information is free and online.

Start building your agent list even before you finish your book—between drafts, when you're letting your manuscript rest to come back to with fresh eyes. When the time comes, double-check each agent's details, and don't query until the book is DONE.

Build Your List

Yes, you may strike gold right away, but it's more likely you'll query 10-20 agents before revising your query; another 10-20 before revising your first pages; and another 20-50 after that. You may discover after 30 queries that your book is more suited to a university press and you don't need an agent after all, or realize you'd rather self-publish or use a hybrid service. By expecting to query 50-100 agents, in several rounds, you can be pleasantly surprised if Agent #36 is a big "Yes!" rather than moping over rejections #1-35.

100?!?!? How do I find 100 agents?

- Search "literary agent" + [your genre]. Vanity presses like Austin McCaulay and Author Solutions will be right up top, so scroll down past the paid ads. You'll find lists of agents assembled by sources like *Writers Digest*, and agency websites.

- Subscribe to Publishers Marketplace (for a month, if cash is an issue). Agents (not all of them) report their sales (not all of them). Lists of who's selling in your genre include links to agents' profiles with querying instructions. Look up what agents have recently sold. Not all agents looking for X are actually selling X. Focus your time on the agents selling books like yours.

- Look at books like yours. Most authors thank their agents in the acknowledgments. If you like the book, you can include in your query, "I saw you represented Book Name, and I enjoyed [thing about that book]."

Set up a spreadsheet with columns for Agent Name, Agency, Genres They Represent, Open for Queries?, Website, What I Liked About Them, What They Want (pages, attachments, etc.) and any other categories important to you. Online services like Query Tracker also help with this.

Start clicking. Read each agent's website and social media and enter her information. Enter other agents you like at the same agency. Some agencies say, "A no from one is no from the whole agency"; others don't mind if you query all their agents in turn (not at the same time). Note their policy.

If an agent seems like a good fit for your book, write down books she's represented that you enjoyed or are like your book, anything nifty she said on Twitter, quotes from interviews that made you like the agent, etc. You'll use this later for the "personalization" part of your query, where you tell the agent "This is why I'm querying you."

If an agent is clearly NOT right—you hate a book she represented, an interview rubbed you the wrong way—write that down and color-code the entry as a "no" for you. This helps avoid looking up the same agent twice.

Whoa, that's a lot of information.

That's correct.

Like it might take up to 20 minutes per agent, longer if I get sucked into Twitter.

Yes.

I hate Twitter.

You don't have to join Twitter to read it, and agents often post their extremely specific and offbeat interests, like "I'd love to read a travel memoir by a WOC."

After I add an agent to my sheet, do I query her?

No. Research and make entries until you're done for the day. Tomorrow, you'll add more agents. I recommend adding 3-5 agents a day, which will take about an hour if you're reading enough to know if they're a good match. Some agents will be closed to queries or not represent your genre after all.

While you're making your agent list, put your querying materials together.

Write a Query

Searching "how to write a query" will bring up plenty of instructions. Jane Friedman's website is an especially reliable source.

Write a Synopsis

Many agents want one. Summarizing your story in 1-3 pages (1000 words max, shoot for 750) is a great way to see if your plot—or the part of your life you've focused on—is compelling. If it feels unexciting in the synopsis, write a better synopsis...or a better book.

Write a Book Proposal

(If you're writing memoir or nonfiction)

Some memoirs sell on proposal and sample chapters. Some nonfiction sells on platform alone. Writing and assembling a proposal isn't a joyful literary romp, but it is a way to identify your readership and how, specifically, your book will reach those people.

Want to publish traditionally? The publisher wants to know who's going to buy your book.

Want to self-publish? You want to know who's going to buy your book.

You have a soul above social media and filthy lucre? Your readers want to be able to find your powerful, personal, necessary story that will change their lives.

Prepare Your Materials

Agents have individual submissions procedures.

Attach the first 25 pages as a Word doc.

Paste the first 10 pages into the body of the email.

Paste your book proposal into our online web form... but in a different format than you prepared, and with additional information you'll need an hour to write.

Attach a synopsis, paste your bio into the body of the email followed by the first 5 pages and an annotated bibliography, then stand in Warrior II pose while pressing Send.

Prepare the most-requested materials in advance. Format as per Chapter 5. Make a folder on your desktop and save the first 5, 10, 25 and 50 pages of your manuscript as Word docs.

Copy-paste the text of each doc into an email and reformat your spacing and paragraphs (email often wrecks your formatting). Save the emails in your draft folder. Now you can easily copy-paste to query emails or attach requested pages.

Query in Stages

You get one chance per agent, per book. Blasting 100 queries without testing the waters spends your chances poorly.

First, query 10-15 agents who aren't your first choice.

* Getting requests? Keep querying.

* No requests for pages or full manuscripts? Sorry, your query sucks. Revise. Get a professional opinion if you can afford it. Listen to podcasts that analyze queries. Read #10queries / #tenqueries Twitter threads.

* Start querying again.

Agents are requesting your pages...

* ...but sending rejections? Something is wrong with your voice, style, pace, or where the story starts. Stop querying and find the problem. If you want professional help, it's much less expensive to pay for a look at your first 10-25 pages and synopsis. Apply those notes to whole manuscript.

* ...and requesting full manuscripts? Start querying your A-list, now that you know your materials work.

Agents are requesting your full manuscript...

* ...but you've had three requested fulls rejected without personal feedback? Something is wrong with your storytelling/

structure. Stop querying and undertake whatever editing plan works for you, whether that's returning to the Seven Drafts, taking a workshop, or hiring a pro editor.

* ...but you're getting rejections with personal feedback? If you agree with the feedback, revise accordingly and start querying again.

* ...but you're getting encouraging, "great but not for me" feedback? Keep querying until you have 20 rejected fulls. Then either change publication strategies (Maybe this is a direct-to-small-press book? Maybe you need more platform?); ask a publishing professional how to revise your book to be sellable; or put this book in a drawer and write another book. This book might sell later if your topic becomes news or your genre has a boom, or as your second book.

While you're waiting for responses, keep working on your agent list.

This sounds time-consuming.

You're shopping for a long-term professional relationship between two people equally excited about working together. Imagine it as dating, but you're in the traditional "boy" role: yes, you have to be into the other person...but they're getting a lot more messages than you are, so they can be choosy.

What about paid query services? Or websites where I upload my work and agents find me?

Querying is a one-at-a-time job. Agents recognize queries from "We do all the work for you!" companies, and those queries are an automatic rejection. Querying demonstrates "I know how to function in this business," and that includes communicating with agents yourself.

Websites purporting to showcase authors to agents are taking your money and delivering you on a platter to scammers ready to take advantage of a beginner. Agents don't need public slush-piles—they have inboxes.

Query with energy but without hope. Treat it like a trip to the mall. You'd *like* to find a great new jacket, but you're not devastated if your favorite store doesn't have one. Your "dream" agent is the one who loves your book and thinks she can sell it.

Rejections are agents self-selecting out of the pool of "people who can sell your book." Will rejections hurt your feelings? Absolutely. But you're not going to get an agent (or get published) without them. Planning to query widely and setting up systems for tracking your submissions helps you approach querying as a shopper. You need an agent; they need your book. It's a mutual relationship built on trust and the desire to sell a beautiful thing to the people who need it most.

PS on Querying

A few years ago, querying my YA novel was not going well. I had a few requests from conference meetings and Twitter pitchfests, but the actual emailing-agents-I've-never-met process was just not getting responses.

This was deeply puzzling.

I sat down and read my query to two of my writer buddies.

Writer Buddy #1: Huh. I've heard you describe your book and that doesn't sound like it at all.

Writer Buddy #2: I've read your book, and it's not about Controversial and Off-Putting Thing in Your Query at all. Sure, that's a theme, but it's really about More Topical and Less Alienating Thing.

Me: Wait, what?

Me: I just realized...people have read the book, and people have read the query, but I don't think anyone's read both of them.

There wasn't anyone to tell me the book wasn't represented by the query, because I had missed the vital step of having someone read them together. Make sure someone reads both your book and your query, and ask your Friend Readers what they think your book is about.

The answer may surprise even you.

REFERRALS

The first time I queried, I sent to thirty-five agents. Most sent form rejections, or slightly personal rejections, or didn't respond at all. Two agents asked for the full manuscript: both of those agents were referrals.

Referrals are golden tickets to the head of the line. You may not make it out of the chocolate factory, but referred queries get read sooner and more carefully. The agent is more likely to ask for pages even if they don't love the query, but they do love your mutual connection.

A referral is

- a personal recommendation...
- from someone who has read your work...
- preferably the work you're querying right now, and
- knows the agent or editor well enough that their word is trusted.

Sometimes an agent who rejects your query suggests you try another agent, but most referrals come from fellow writers with a business or personal relationship with the editor or agent.

What isn't a referral? Posting to Facebook: "I wrote a memoir about X can anyone tell me what agents might be interested in that subject matter?"

No author wants to offer up a name and have the writer email an agent with "Violet Beauregarde referred me," because giving a name isn't a referral.

Maybe you're already close with someone whose agent is a fit—golden ticket! But most writers need to start unwrapping those Wonka Bars even before they've finished their manuscript. A referral is a big ask, and you need to be 100% ready.

- Starting at least six months before you query, look up the agents who represent your close writer friends and former teachers. If you know someone connected to an agent you'd like to query, buy and review that person's books. Attend their workshops and readings and ask intelligent questions. Join their mailing list. Tweet about their work and retweet (with a positive comment) events and books they promote.[117]

  If you know them in person and they aren't your teacher, offer to read their work. You don't have to be at the same place in your writing careers—newbies can say, "If you're ever looking for a reader, I'd love to practice giving feedback."

- Finish your book. Your work reflects on the person who referred you, so make sure your final draft is proofread and polished. Write and revise your query.

- If your manuscript fits their agent's wishlist, ask your friend if they'd be willing to look at your work and *if they think it's a good fit*, refer you to their agent.

---

117 Don't get stalker-y.

- Make it easy to say no. Your writer-acquaintance may be on deadline, or maybe Violet already referred three people to her agent this month. Use phrases like "I understand you may not have time," or "If you think this might be a fit for Agent Gloop," or "I'm querying widely, but if you're able..." Even if Violet's true feeling is, *This is a dreadful book no way am I referring it*, she might like the next one, so give her a gracious escape. But do ask outright: it takes more time to read between the lines than respond to a clear request.

- Make it easy to say yes. Paste your query and first five pages (or whatever the desired agent's guidelines specify) below your email signature. If Violet's feeling it, she can hit forward and be done. This also lets her skim your work to remember you're a fantastic writer and she'll look good by recommending you. If Violet would rather introduce you in a new email, she knows you're ready to go while the referral is fresh in the agent's mind.

- Send thanks. Referring connects the other writer's reputation to yours, and it takes time from their writing day. Send an email or write a quick note. No gifts that cost, because that feels like pay-to-play. Write the email in a way that requires no additional response: your goal throughout this process is to take as little of the referring writer's time and attention as possible.

Referrals aren't the only way to get attention, but they are a golden gift. Sure, this is literary nepotism, and it's a lot of work. But it's part of being a writer, so get started—those Wonka Bars aren't going to eat themselves.

DEFINING YOUR BOOK

Write your book first, with no regard for how it will be classified or sold. But once you're ready to query, locate your book's place in the world by identifying your comps, genre, and category.

Comps

In your query, give two or three comps. Short for Comparable or Comparative or Competitive Titles, depending on who's defining, but they all mean *books like yours.*

Comps are titles and authors that help the agent understand where your book fits in the market.

Complete at 70,000 words, Plummeting Beats Paperwork: How I Survived Everest and a Million-Dollar Divorce *combines the humor of Tori Spelling's* Unknown TerriTori *with the adrenaline rush of Jon Krakauer's* Into Thin Air.

Gillian Flynn meets Marie Kondo in Spark Terror, *the story of a woman decluttering her own psyche after trauma.*

In a query, pop culture, movies and TV are fair game, *if and only if* you are confident your manuscript will wow the agent like the show does, or your story truly ties into a major cultural moment.

Parking Daniel Craig's Lambo: My Celebrity Assistant Life *will appeal to Bond movie fans with my behind-the-scenes stories from the* Skyfall *set, and to readers of Perez Hilton, for whom I debunk rumors about Dan's underwear, tattoos, and what really happened at the Oscars.*

Big Little Lies *meets* The Parent Trap *in* I Could Have Killed Her, *a domestic thriller about PTA supermom Jenicea mourning the twin sister she hated—and may have murdered.*

Remember when using TV/movie comps, you are literally comparing your work to media with million-dollar budgets and saying, "My book's that good." You'll need a very strong hook to make a non-book comp seem logical, rather than overly aspirational or flat-out deluded.

Genre and Category

Genre describes content. It's the label on the bookshelf. Romance. Thriller. Fantasy. Genre is much less specific than Amazon listings with subrankings like "#3 in Fiction-Animal Stories-Zookeepers-Penguin Specialists."[118]

Category is who will read this book. Young Adult is a category containing the genres YA Mystery, YA Romance and so forth.

The most relevant categories for novelists and memoirists:

Commercial means not too hard to read—usually 7th-10th-grade level—and appealing to a wide range of readers. Think *The DaVinci Code,* James Patterson, Nora Roberts. Commercial books sell in grocery stores and airports as well as bookstores.

---

118 Memoir is its own genre, but usually shelved based on the written experience, such as Travel or Addiction and Recovery.

High-concept books can be summed up in one fresh, intriguing sentence: "A man's wife frames him for her own murder" *(Gone Girl)*. "An autistic boy solves the murder of a dog, told in his own voice" *(Curious Incident of the Dog in the Night-Time)*. *Gone Girl* is high-concept commercial domestic suspense; *Curious Incident* is high-concept upmarket fiction. High-concept books often top libraries' reserved lists and have front-facing displays in bookstores.[119]

Book-club books have themes or plots tying into larger cultural questions. A blurb for Jodi Picoult's *A Spark of Light* (hostage crisis in an abortion clinic from multiple conflicting perspectives) sums this up well: "…a complicated issue in this gripping and nuanced novel." Enough meaty ideas for a discussion, and a compelling read that club members will finish before the next meeting. These books show up in celebrity book-club lists like Oprah's, Reese Witherspoon's, and Emma Watson's, and as community-reading books.

Upmarket means smarter-than-average, but with wider appeal and more action than full-on literary fiction. Upmarket books are less likely to depend on a twist ending and are read for the quality of writing as much as for the story. *Wolf Hall* is upmarket historical fiction. *H Is for Hawk* is upmarket memoir. These books show up in Booker Prize and National Book Award lists.

Literary is a quality of the writer's voice. Literary novels can be "quiet" and character-driven with emphasis on theme and mood, but there are also literary mysteries and other genres. For querying, it can sound arrogant to call one's own work "literary," and it begs judgment of your writing craft. Support your claim with literary comps, mention any previous literary publications, and in your personalization to the agent, stress your attraction to literary books she represents.

Women's fiction means books in any of the above categories that focus on women characters and family issues. But the term is so widely encompassing (Louisa May Alcott! Sophie Kinsella! Toni Morrison!) as to be functionally meaningless. It also presupposes that female authors' work is "women's" before being literary, commercial, etc. "Women's fiction" is still useful to mention in a query, but avoid it if you can. Mostly, the term warehouses and dismisses books by and about women, presuming only women will wish to read them.

---

119 These displays are usually paid for by publishers' marketing budgets, not self-selected by bookstores.

If you're unsure how to classify your book, walk into a book-store and see where your book might be shelved. What's already there? If someone reads the most popular book on the same shelf and picks up your book next, will he feel like he's discovered something amazing in a realm he already loves?

WHAT IF SOMEONE STEALS MY BOOK?

Am I risking plagiarism or idea theft by sharing my manuscript with a writing group, agent, or publisher?

No. Ideas are rarely original (and can't be copyrighted). Execution is what matters. The level of labor, time, and expense needed to skillfully repurpose the plot of a stolen manuscript is unlikely to be taken on by anyone good enough to actually do it.

Plus, every writer has heard from someone, "I have a great idea for a book! You write it and we'll split the money!" Remember how ridiculous it was that the person had absolutely no conception that writing a book is difficult and time-consuming? That puking out ideas is the easy part?

What if I query an agent and she takes my idea and gives it to another writer?

Legitimate agents receive hundreds, even thousands of sub-missions each year—if they like your idea but want a different angle or another writing style, chances are they have already received another query doing exactly that. They may well sell a book that sounds a lot like yours; they almost certainly didn't need to steal it.

What if a publisher prints my book and sells it without paying me?

Scam publishers don't make money by stealing books—they profit by charging authors to publish. If they steal your book, who's going to pay them?

Legitimate publishers don't make enough money from debut authors to bother stealing a first manuscript. Just like agents, they already saw six versions of that story, and they picked the one they liked best.

Should I register a copyright with the Library of Congress?

Only if you really want to.

In North America and Europe (and most other countries), all artistic work is copyrighted from the moment it's created in a fixed form. When you write in a notebook or type into a document, you establish ownership of your creation. Registering copyright allows you to sue for damages, but until your work is actually published (at which point copyright will be registered with the publisher's help, or by you as an indie author), there aren't many damages to sue for.

Putting the copyright symbol on a manuscript submitted to an agent or publisher is the mark of an amateur. While an agent isn't going to turn down a fantastic book because the author jumped the gun on copyright, it is an indicator that the author may have misconceptions about the publishing industry, and the agent will have to educate them as well as trying to sell their book. They will be more work than a savvier author.

Actual piracy—copy-pasting and repackaging the text of a book and selling it as your own—is rare. Book piracy happens primarily in China, India, and Egypt, markets with avid readers and low per-capita incomes. Foreign pirates (or local pirates, if you are Chinese, Indian or Egyptian) do not care about your registered copyright. You will not be able to find and sue them. If you discover a photocopy of your novel in a Cairo souk, your best bet is to figure out how to reach those fans and sell them something else (or at least get a review!).

In North America, most piracy happens with expensive textbooks and in category romance, and pirated copies show up after the book is published. If you're writing one of those genres, by all means do more research, and learn how to file a copyright infringement claim with Amazon. But for memoirists and most novelists, our enemy is not piracy but obscurity.

Our greatest protection as unpublished writers is that nobody wants to steal our work. Yes, that sounds a little sad. But just as "worth publishing" is not "worth stealing," so too, "not worth stealing" does not mean "worthless."

Our second greatest protection is our own voice. What makes our work worth an agent's time, a publisher's investment, and a reader's money, is what we bring to the page, beyond an idea or even a particular plot. *West Side Story* "stole" *Romeo and Juliet*. *Romeo and Juliet* "stole" *The Tragicall History of Romeus and Juliet*. But the transformation of ideas from one author to another resulted each time in something unique...and words so distinct, they are impossible to steal.

REJECTION IS NOT FEEDBACK

Imagine with me: I need a sweater. So I go to the mall.[120]

The first store is showing argyle knitwear this season. Diamond plaids are just not my thing. Do I:

> A) Assume this brand is garbage and everything they will ever make is argyle?
>
> B) Say, "No thank you," and head for another store, dismissing argyle from my mind because hey, someone else is going to love golfing vests?

The second store has a terrific red sweater with those cool thumbhole sleeves. But it's 30% wool, which I am allergic to. Do I:

> A) Laugh heartily at the incompetence of anyone who would dare make a wool sweater?
>
> B) Regretfully decline, and remember the store because they'll probably have something else I like another time?

The third store has a gorgeous blue sweater. Thumbholes, check. No wool, check.

But.

I bought a blue sweater yesterday, from a no-returns store,[121] and today I really want a red one. Do I:

> A) Think whoever made this sweater sucks and should never make another garment?
>
> B) Shake my head sadly and resume the hunt for a red sweater?

You get where I'm going, right?[122]

Rejection is not feedback.

Rejection is not feedback.

No, really. Rejection. Is not. Feedback.

Writers often get mad at themselves or the process when a manuscript is rejected. It's easy to feel, *They thought my work was terrible,* or *I'm a bad writer,* or *They only publish people they already know.*

---

120 The mall is a temple of consumerism with an indoor ski slope overlooked by The Cheesecake Factory, because I live in Dubai.

121 Also a thing in Dubai.

122 Not The Cheesecake Factory.

None of those things can be determined from any single rejection.

When agents and editors read, yes, they are evaluating the overall quality of the work. But they're also asking, *Does this fit our mission? Do I personally like it? Did we accept something similar last week?* They are assessing where your book fits in their business.

Your job is to display our work beautifully, with skilled craft and professional format on the page. To enlist fellow writers and teachers and mentors to give constructive criticism, and incorporate the notes to write the best book you can. To do many drafts until you're truly ready to query. And that's where the writer's control stops. You can't make the customer want your particular sweater—you can only be ready with an excellent sweater for their browsing. You must focus on finding out agents' and publishers' and readers' taste and style and mission and what else they recently bought and what they usually publish—instead of agonizing about why one person didn't want one thing.

Rejection will always sting at least a little. Sometimes it stings a lot. I've gotten plenty of rejections and painful criticism by email and form letter and Submittable and to my face.[123] But I love being published more than I love protecting myself from being hurt. Not instead of—just more. Enough to get back up again.

My worst-ever rejection came from an agent on a requested full. I'd tied a lot of hope into that submission, and her email was kind and thoughtful and had helpful, personal feedback. But that rejection felled me. I felt for the first time what I'd heard other writers describe: *This is it. I'm not a writer anymore. I don't want to write anything again, ever. I'm wasting my time.*

Most writers want to believe that somehow, somewhere, they'll reach a place where rejection doesn't happen, or it doesn't suck.

Nope.

That's writing's nasty little secret. That's the horrible underbelly of great art, the Achilles' heel of incredible physical prowess, the flip side of being good at anything.

Being good doesn't lift you out of failure.

---

123 I once performed on a reality show where Howard Stern got an entire audience to stand up and boo me, personally. In my hometown. In front of my mother. After that, literary rejections are practically hugs.

In fact, the better you get, the more awful failure feels, because you can't let it go with "Oh, I wasn't ready," or "Yeah, that magazine is hard to get into." You start to feel like you've paid your dues, you've put your time in, and when is success going to show up, please, because it's getting late?

Olympic gymnasts still fall hard. World-class runners don't make the team because someone they beat in practice was faster today. Established movie stars don't get cast because the producers don't think they're big enough in the Asian market. Writers don't get published because their book doesn't land on the right person's desk at the right time.

Rejection is market research.

One rejection says "this person couldn't sell this book at this time." Ten or twenty or fifty rejections are enough information to reassess: *Is the book really ready? Have I gotten any personalized feedback? Outside opinions from readers I trust?* We don't get better from nursing hurt feelings. Considering the answers to those questions helps us improve. And every "no thank you" is proof you're doing the work of getting your book out there.

As writers, we're told over and over, "It's hard work. Just keep doing it." We work to believe that, while still hoping it's not true. Sometimes the feeling of writing something wonderful, something we're really proud of, will carry us through rejection and writer's block and ennui.

As it happens, the agent whose rejection devastated me is now my agent. And the book I queried is getting another rewrite—it wasn't ready. But I love it enough to keep going, to make it so.

MAKING A WRITING LIFE

It's easy to forget that Hemingway and the rest went to Paris because it was cheaper than staying at home, and that it was cheaper because a catastrophic war had just laid waste to the continent. These writers produced so much material about each other, in fiction and in letters, that they accidentally crystallized a specific time and place in the American imagination as the essence of what a creative life looks like. This was not only a setting: it was a particular economy. Not only was rent cheap, but print was still the king of mass media. It was possible, for a brief moment in time, to make a living selling pieces to magazines. As a result, the image of the writing life created in this period includes no non-writing day jobs whatsoever.

Rosalie Knecht at *Literary Hub*

The Money Myth

There's a persistent myth that the only thing "real" writers do for money is write. "Real" writers wake up, head for the typewriter, and pound away until their daily word count is complete. Emotionally depleted but happy, they retire to their velvet chaise for the afternoon.

There's something wrong with this picture. For starters, there's a typewriter in it.

It's also (based on every writer I know) inaccurate in every other way.

Yes, I get paid to write,[124] already a huge step, but I wrote for free for years before getting paid, and I still write for free for venues I'm invested in as a literary citizen (hello, *Brevity* readers!). My clients with Big-Five deals still write for free—even authors whose publishers pay for the book tour must write articles and interviews for publicity. Midlist authors—publishing regularly but not bestsellers—mostly have day jobs, or spouses with day jobs. Literary authors often teach full time.

Emerging writers are often working through hardship that shapes their process. Claire Rudy Foster wrote at *The Review Review* about sacrificing to go to an expensive low-residency MFA program. On the first day:

> *The writer leading the group asked us to go around the table and, as an icebreaker, describe our work spaces. I listened carefully as the others talked about their rooms, studies, studios, and offices. They all had computers. They had privacy. Their children were in high school or older, not still in diapers. When it was my turn, I told the truth: that I wrote, one sentence at a time, with whatever was at hand. That I wrote on the bus with my son on my lap, taking him to day care before I went to yet another double shift. That I wrote on my breaks. That I texted sentences to myself. I told them that I wrote when my son went to sleep at night, staying up an extra hour to crank out the draft of another short story.*
>
> *They stared at me as though I was an alien. My ears prickled, and my cheeks flushed. I was ashamed of my poverty—ashamed that I couldn't afford what they had. Finding an apartment with an extra bedroom was beyond my reach. Taking a day off wasn't an option for me—we needed every penny. And then, I looked at my classmates and realized that, regardless of the comforts they possessed, they were not better writers than me. They had yet to be published, much less finish a long project. They didn't know how to work at writing. I did. And I was willing to do anything to keep writing—I had to, if I wanted to produce anything at all.*

---

124 "Getting paid to write" is usually "getting paid to *have written.*" Most writers work for free and hope to get paid.

The Writing All the Time Myth

Many writers love being a good spouse. Parenting well. Keeping a nice home. Excelling at our money-making work—some of us even adore the job itself. That's what we forget when planning our writing lives: it's not the obligations we chafe at that hold us back. It's easy to make writing time by making the kids do their own laundry or grocery shopping only once a week. It's much harder to look at things we love and value, and decide we might love writing more. Especially when we aren't living on our writing money, the time spent can feel like self-indulgence, a frill.

But we'd tell our treasured friend, *you deserve that time.* We'd say, *modeling dedication and focus is also good parenting.* We'd tell them their spouse should be supportive, and applaud the spouses who were.

What feels "real" to me is writing on a me-project four days out of seven. That may not be what works for you—maybe you get ten minutes a day, or chunks of weekend, or early mornings before the kids wake up. Your writing schedule reflects an economy where rent is a much larger percentage of income than it was in 1925, and most health insurance is tied to full-time work. On the upside, we're much less likely to drink or cough ourselves to death or be brutally satirized by Truman Capote.

The Feeling Like You Arrived Myth

I finished a book and sent it to my agent. It felt great for a couple of days; then I spent a month at loose ends. There was a lot of phone-on-sofa time, but not a lot of word count.

I felt like a loser. Like I'd probably never write anything again. That was it, my last good idea, spent. I shame-spiraled into *the book will never sell the agent just felt sorry for me and now she and her interns spend Casual Fridays hoisting Oreo-tinis and reading out choice bits of my manuscript in funny voices.*[125]

So I screwed up my courage and asked a writer I respect a lot, "What do you do after you've written a book?"

"Mooch around the internet, work in my garden, look out the window, and think about how I'll never write anything else ever again."

---

125 Dear agent, please don't tell me if that's true. Let an intern tell me.

Oh.

It's not just me.

It's not just you, either.

Everyone sweats. Everyone slogs. Everyone feels alone and sad, and like they must not be a 'real' writer because real writers have a different/superior/classic process.

You are a real writer when you write. You are still a real writer when you're not writing, when you're sitting and listening for words to come. Maybe your listening is taking long walks, or watching cat videos, or reading wonderful books you admire or trashy books that entertain you. For me, listening is hanging out on the sofa and imagining a little room. I wait in the room, and my ideas are people coming to me with problems. I listen until someone shows up with a problem I want to solve.

I listen for the truth to show up, so I can tell it.

The Validation Myth

But I haven't sold any books, how can I possibly say I'm a writer?

Because our work exists in a recorded and fixed form, we tend to use production of fixed forms—books—as benchmarks of our success. Claiming the title before the accomplishments can feel like misrepresentation. Finishing a piece and publishing a piece and getting an agent and getting a book deal and best-seller lists and prizes and royalty payments are all badges that say "I did it" or "I am it" and each of those things punches our ticket, validation.

But there's no magic graduation ceremony when we're allowed to call ourselves "real" writers. No one ever gives us that permission. Sure, you may not be a published writer. You may not be a full-time writer. But published writers don't get everything they write published. "Full-time" writers almost always teach or edit or freelance on the side. You're never going to feel fully confident in your own work 100% of the time, so don't wait for the Literature Fairy to appear in a cloud of glitter and tell you you're a real writer. Just claim it.

Naming yourself "writer" lets other people help you.

Imagine you're chatting with, say, N. K. Jemisin and your local indie bookstore owner. If they ask if you're a writer, and you say, "Oh, no, not yet," the conversation ends there.

But when you say (modestly), "I'm working on a memoir about my time in the military," or "I've just finished a YA fantasy novel," that opens a door. Sure, they might say, "Oh, nice," and smile blankly. But they might respond with, "I'd love to see a few pages when you're done," or "Make sure you query so-and-so, she loves that genre," or "Do you know about our local authors' reading series?"

"I'm a writer" creates dialogue. Even if you're still learning, even if you're at the very beginning of being good, even if you never sell or publish a word.

Famous writers are doing more than writing what they love. Successful writers may never be household names. Art is not somehow purer if we do nothing else. Do what you love and are good at. Do it when and where you can. Do it often enough to get better.

That's real.

That's enough.

The Code

It may help you feel like a "real writer" to set out what you believe about your work, and why you're doing it. I'm not an especially religious person, but I hold two sacred laws:

1) It is a mortal sin to lie on the page. I can choose not to write something or to tell a different side, but I can only tell the truth. In fiction, this means honestly doing the work to make my characters' choices and actions truthful within their world. In memoir, this means writing the bits that make me look bad. I'm willing to be shitty and selfish and mean on the page, because leaving those things out would be lying.

2) We who are lucky enough to have the desire, ability, and time to write must speak to and for the people who don't or can't. We owe our best telling to those who took the same journey, but can't share it in words. The price of artistic ability is to use it as fully and faithfully as we can.

As long as I keep to those, I'm a writer.

What do you believe about your art?

READING BETTER

Writers must read. You must read to learn what your readers already know and what's going on in your genre, and discover what you have to say that's new. Reading *consciously* also makes you a better writer.

About half of all first-time writers truly, genuinely cannot see the difference between their first draft and a published book.[126] They can't see that the plot is tangled or the description is hackneyed or the story has no tension, because they only know how reading a book makes them *feel*. They've admired the painting without noticing that the people in the park are made of tiny dots, and up close, some of those dots aren't the colors they seem to be from ten feet away.

Rereading builds the ability to read consciously. The first time through a book, relax and enjoy it. Read it again a few months later. This time, follow the clues in the mystery, or pick out particularly nice phrases, or notice how the writer sets up a character to be hated and then loved, or to have our love for them turned to hate.

Think about how we learn to have good sex—sure, we start with fumbling in a car, but we read or watch porn, talk to friends and interact with good partners who teach us. Yes, passion and emotional connection are key, but so are paying attention and being physically precise and learning to do the things our partner loves and teaching them what we enjoy. People often assume sex and writing are innate talents, but they are learned skills.

Conscious reading also develops from reading many books by one author. Notice how their writing matures with experience, particularly authors who started as pure genre writers and crossed into something bigger. Early Dorothy Sayers is almost Agatha Christie—body, detective, killer, guilty. Late Dorothy Sayers (and Jill Paton Walsh's continuation of her work) are glorious tragicomedies of manners and sociopolitical commentary about the nature of marriage and creativity in which the murder victim is almost an aside.[127] Robert Heinlein (bless his

---

126 Until I took "proofreading" off my editorial website, I received at least two Vomit Drafts a month with the author requesting "a quick proofread."

127 *Gaudy Night* has no murder at all, but a great deal about whether women can have both marriage and the pursuit of serious intellectual work.

perverted little heart) went from space westerns to examining how artificial intelligence could foment revolution in a totalitarian society. JK Rowling went from "Whee, we're wizards!" to a powerful moral epic centering on doing good even when it hurts you, and why it's important to make that choice.[128]

Mix your reading. I'm often simultaneously in the middle of research, a fun mealtime book, and a more demanding literary read. This helps me see connections: when writing coach/agent Donald Maass talks about character darkness and scenic moments, or *This American Life* host Ira Glass discusses the entry point for a story, I can see those elements presented in different ways.

The process of learning an art has three stages:

1) Be impressed

2) Identify the tools

3) Learn to use the tools

So copy out that beautiful paragraph and analyze why it works—is it the flow, the voice, the way they anchor sentence endings with strong nouns? Write something parallel—same sentence structure, different nouns and verbs and adjectives. Then write your own version entirely, seeing how that voice or structure or style can influence your own.

WRITING BETTER

Writers edit. More than any other artist (except perhaps painters working in oils), we labor over the fixed form until it's "perfect." Or as close as we can get. Tweaking sentences and swapping out words. Junking the whole thing and starting again, treading the same path, but *better*. Until it wins acceptance, awards, dollars, validation.

You've been editing this whole time, for many pages.

Now stop.

Time to move on. Write something else.

In their 2001 book *Art and Fear*, David Bayles and Ted Orland tell the parable of the pottery class:

---

128 Unfortunately, Rowling has since undercut her own message with her public positions on trans-equality issues.

The ceramics teacher announced on opening day that he was dividing the class into two groups. All those on the left side of the studio, he said, would be graded solely on the quantity of work they produced, all those on the right solely on its quality. His procedure was simple: on the final day of class he would bring in his bathroom scales and weigh the work of the "quantity" group: fifty pound of pots rated an A, forty pounds a B, and so on. Those being graded on "quality", however, needed to produce only one pot—albeit a perfect one—to get an A. Well, came grading time and a curious fact emerged: the works of highest quality were all produced by the group being graded for quantity. It seems that while the "quantity" group was busily churning out piles of work—and learning from their mistakes—the "quality" group had sat theorizing about perfection, and in the end had little more to show for their efforts than grandiose theories and a pile of dead clay.

Write *a lot*. Scribble on napkins at coffee shops when a beautiful sentence arrives in your brain—or a terrible one. Carry a notebook, or a pad of sticky notes, or a folded sheet of paper wrapped around a pen. Use a notes app in your phone. Interrupt your friends and make them say something again. Turn away mid-conversation to write.

Take the chapter that's been tormenting you and shove it in a drawer until ignoring it fixes the problem. Maybe that will be ten days, or a hundred days, or ten years. In the meantime, write some more. Write scraps and crots and pieces of broken structure. Throw them in a pile or a box or even the trash, but write, write, write. Until it's not precious, or special, or *perfect*. It's just what you do.

All the time.

MAKING A WRITING LIFE

What helps us feel like "real" writers are the actions of writing as part of our daily life. You're working to improve your storytelling ability, your technical understanding, and your craft. As a literary citizen, you're a reader, publicist, fan, and critique partner. How does all this fit into your routine?

Write with a plan. Decide what you want to improve about your work. Challenge yourself. Write when it's not easy, when you're not inspired, when you have nothing to say. Write when it isn't fun, when it's a slog up the mountain in the rain. Easy accomplishment is cheap; fighting for the words and winning—even barely, even when it's not your best work—lets you know you can do it again.

Vary your style. Write genres you're not interested in—you may surprise yourself. Write short pieces to show your brevity. Write long pieces to show your staying power. Short attention spans can be your friend; standing out among hundreds can make you shout louder or whisper more piercingly.

Connect. Interact with new and experienced writers in the real world and online, even if only replying to a tweet or commenting on a blog. Share your work with friends outside the literary world, too. Get feedback from writers and readers of every level from "read a cereal box once" to "better writer than you ever dare hope to be."

Be supportive. But when you think someone is ready for it, when you're brave enough, when you've built a relationship of mutual support, give the best critique you can. Give honest feedback. Make your motivations clear. Stay direct even when polite. Tell it like you see it, but tactfully.

Be generous. With your time, your talent, your encouragement and feedback. Read everything you can—strategically, you'll know what you're up against; competitively, you'll be challenged and inspired. Comment on everything you can. We all feel like we're drowning in a lake of obscurity, and even "Enjoyed reading!" is a lifeline from the dock of humanity we're paddling so desperately toward. Being "popular" and being genuinely engaged in the community are the same behavior with different hats.

Be ambitious. Be brave. Be ruthless. Be raw. Write about pomegranates and roller coasters and cement mixers. Write about your relationship and your relationship with your mother and your relationship with your depression. Write to honor your dead. (If you are going to write about the zombie apocalypse, you had better have something damn original to say.)

Put writing first. Stay up late. Get up early. Make it the top of the list, above laundry and getting paid and sometimes above lunch. Skip out on your other responsibilities. If you're an overachiever, narrow your focus. Trust that your children will learn to feed themselves, your life-partner will manage their socks, shaved legs are overrated. And if you can't put writing first, that's OK, too—put it where you can.

This book is about doing the work you must do to be published, but publication is not what makes you a writer. That's not what makes any of us writers—artists—winners. You write, you write, always you write, and in the end, you win because you show up.

Show up to the page. Show up to the community. Show up to your colleagues' writing. Show up to the new writers and the bad writers and the teenage writers and the writers writing only for themselves, but who still need to know they're not alone. Show up with your voice. Show up with your style. Show up with what you love and why it matters, and lay it on the page, naked and alone.

It will be terrifying.

You may feel like you are howling into the void. You are. But there are others in the void, howling back.

And as long as you keep howling, you win.

You win.

You win by being there, and you win by being able to write about it, and by writing about it even when you're not able, when your heart is torn and ragged and the pen in your hand is running dry and all your paper is wet with tears.

You win.

And the cruelest joke the universe plays is that when you win, that's not the end of the game. You're bumped up to a higher level with harder obstacles, and you can never go back and be satisfied playing the level you already beat.

I have one more secret. When you show up, and you reach out with generosity, and you do your best work or your second-best work and summon up the bravery to share it, you create a community. You, a writer, the loneliest of artists, become part of a team. And even when you are home alone, sweating in the Louisiana heat and cursing things that buzz, or walking down 5th and wondering if there might be just one affordable place in this city of strangers and darkness while gearing up to freeze your ass off for the next four months, you are still playing as part of a team. They are in the shadows and they are on the other end of the internet and they are reading your words and saying, *Me, too*.

Me, too.

THE WRITER'S TOOLBOX

You can love the passion of wanting to create, desperate-ly want the feeling of having created, and still have a hard time sitting down to work. Making art is often seen as "play," and writers (and visual artists) often work without any of the tools of a "normal" workday. No set hours, no cubicle where someone will notice if you're watching TikTok. Writers must make their own tools and choose their own coworkers.

Friedrich Nietzsche said of typewriters, "Our writing tools are also working on our thoughts." Tools change their users, and tools to support writing abound. Apps that turn off our internet or blacklist social media sites. Apps to keep writing steadily (or lose your work!).

Writer Dinty W. Moore strongly recommends his workshop students write in-class exercises by hand, because the veins in the hand flow through the arms, connecting to the heart. Many writers prefer a certain notebook, a particular pen. My favorite tool is meeting up with a buddy and writing at the same table. The presence of another person encourage-shames me into typ-ing past the place I'd quit alone. Sure, it's a trick. But the rabbit coming out of the hat is pages.

"Need to post a blog for *Brevity* in an hour" is another strong motivator. So is "I want to finish this book so my publisher will send a check." Or a contest deadline. And sometimes, on a lucky day, "Because I'm passionate about this project and sitting down to work feels good."

But why trust to luck when you can stock a toolbox? Carpenters don't think less of the cabinet that needed a bandsaw as well as a screwdriver. Stockbrokers aren't shy about whipping out calculators and whiteboards. Dancers have mandatory rehearsal as the tool to get work done. They don't look back at the choreography and say, "Yeah, but someone had to tell me to show up to learn that, so it doesn't count."

Writing can feel like a job as well as a joy. And it's OK to need a tool—even one that feels like a trick.

Here are some items you may want in your toolbox.

WRITING GROUPS

Need to jump-start a project? Build a daily or weekly writing habit? Get early-draft feedback? Join a group.

A good writing group gives useful feedback on your work; lets you practice giving feedback to others; and it's free. You may build a relationship with a particular group member and become critique partners, exchanging pages as frequently as you both like.

Plan to shop around—just like a yoga class, the group's purpose, the other members, and the type of leader will make a big difference in your experience. You need writers who

- are at your level of skill or a little better.

- talk the amount of time you want to talk.

- are writing in your genre, or whose understanding of the fundamentals of good writing transcends genre.

Watch out for

- people convinced traditional publishing is a conspiracy against new writers, particularly themselves.[129]

- writers who insist on explaining backstory about their pages (more than a few sentences of context is a waste of time and doesn't reflect the reader's experience).

- writers at wildly different levels—beginners won't have enough to offer; more experienced writers have a hard time limiting critique to what beginners can receive.

My ideal group would contain one person less-skilled than me, so I can practice spotting problems in their work, two people at my level of skill, and one person more skilled and very candid,

---

129 Writers self-publishing because it's their well-researched choice are likely to have insights about story, style, and marketing. Writers whining about gatekeepers and seeing self-publishing as the revenge of an unrecognized genius are unlikely to have useful feedback or an inspiring work ethic.

who can give sharp critique and whose work I have to read very closely to be helpful.

Don't bring your most fragile piece to a first critique. Wait until you know this group is a good fit. (Review Chapter 6: How to Get Useful Feedback for ways to discover whose comments you trust.)

You could find your local writing group (or start one) in one of these places:

* Meetup.com. If there isn't a writing interest group you like, start your own. Write a clear description: is this group for writing together, critique, publishing talk, something else?

* Your local bookstore or library's bulletin board may feature writing group announcements.

* The nearest college or university may have groups open to nonstudents, or students who'd love to be part of an off-campus group.

* Look around your coffee shop—anyone writing alone? Tread carefully if you're a cisgender dude—you may seem like you're hitting on a solo woman. For any gender, keep your approach low-key—drop off your email right before you leave (or as they do). Say you understand if they prefer to focus on themselves, but if they're open to writing together, you'd love to hear from them.

* Coworking spaces usually cost money, but being around other focused, working people helps, even if they're doing another kind of work.

Here's what worked when I started a group:

She who organizes, chooses. First I thought, *Where can people get to...what time of day would be best for the most people....* Then I realized I got to pick. I consulted the writer friend whose presence I valued most; other writers came if they could.

Make it easy to join. I'm part of a local WhatsApp group where anyone can name a time and place. You only write at night? You live on the other end of town? Great, tell us when and where and somebody will join you.

Share your goals. Out-loud goals help with accountability. Feedback is easier when you know the writer's larger purpose.

Be an enforcer. My writing-together group has one rule: come and go quietly. I'm the person popping up in the middle of my own writing to say, "Welcome! Shhhhh! Jump in, we're taking a break in thirty-five minutes and we'll meet you then!" I'm also in charge of "Great break, back to the page everyone!" The structure is appreciated, and setting a good example keeps me focused, too.

Bring a multiplug. Because the coffee shop will have one inconveniently located outlet and everyone needs to charge.

Do your work. Writing locations can be sanctuaries, or they can be (around me as I write this) a swirl of raucous corporate team-building, writers coming and going, the waitress adding more tables. Headphones on. Focus with intent—don't wait until the atmosphere focuses for you.[130]

Use a timer for critique. Divide the meeting duration (minus hello/goodbye time) by the number of writers. That's how many feedback minutes each person gets. Keep your timer audible— hearing the beep is less awkward than cutting in to say, "Wrap it up on Celia!" Without a timer, the first person will get twenty intense minutes and the last person five distracted minutes while everyone pays their tab. Writers who want to share more with each other can stay late.

Stay in tune. Ask writers to (briefly) say what draft they're on and what kind of feedback they're looking for. Rein in free-associators and nitpickers with a compliment-redirect: "Jamie, great point about punctuation, but Riya's focusing on story this week, so let's bring our discussion back to the plot."

Writing is often solitary and sometimes thankless. Fellowship, peer pressure *(I'm running out of steam! But they're all still writing so I can't stop!)* and cupcakes make it warmer and more welcoming.

USEFUL APPS & WEBSITES

Everyone wants the magic bullet—the computer program that can fix our grammar, our spelling, and for good measure, tell us what's wrong with our story.

Sadly, that program does not exist.

However, there are both free and paid applications for different editing tasks. You will still need a discerning eye, whether it's

---

130   Once, my group's writing space was over a ballroom in which a busload of tourists from Hong Kong sang karaoke. We heard every Cantonese lyric. The bass literally shook our chairs. We wrote anyway.

your own that you've sharpened with study and practice, or an outside editor.

Fictionary StoryTeller analyzes characters, scenes, setting, pacing, and story structure and guides authors through a big-picture self-edit of their book. If you need more "tell me what to do in the most helpful sequence" than a book but not quite a professional edit, Fictionary's step-by-step process is a great way to tackle your Story Draft.

Hemingway is available free online and as a paid desktop app. Great for visual learners, the program highlights text: red for excessively complex sentences, yellow for sentences that need shortening or splitting, blue for adverbs, etc. Paste the text you're working on into the app; check the highlights to question and decide what to keep, simplify, or cut.

PerfectIt! from Intelligent Editing is manuscript cleaning software designed for professional editors. Much of its power is for academic editing, but it's also useful for fiction. PerfectIt! catches double spaces, incorrect punctuation, and consistency. If you have "breast feeding" twice, "breast-feeding" once, and "breastfeeding" three times, the program pulls up those instances and asks which one you want. Select the version of the word you wish to keep and PerfectIt! will change them all. Good for misspelled character names, and you can set it to check homophones like to/two/too if needed.

Scrivener is a word-processing program designed specifically to write books. I wrote this book in it, and I also use it for fiction and editorial letters. Most useful is the ability to move between manuscript sections without scrolling, and to see one's entire book as an outline while working on a particular part. If you're self-publishing, Scrivener has powerful formatting tools. I found the learning curve steep but worthwhile.

Purdue OWL, a project of Purdue University's Online Writing Lab, covers grammar, punctuation, and mechanics, and even has a section on writing process and workflow. Purdue OWL is a frequent search result if you're looking up a line or copyediting question, and their answers are reliable and understandable.

Grammar Girl has fun, memorable explanations of rules both simple and complex. If you're having a hard time wrapping your head around a grammar convention, chances are she's explained it. There's also a Grammar Girl podcast.

The Chicago Manual of Style is the bible for editors working in Chicago style (other styles include AP for newspapers and journals, and specific styles for legal, medical, and scientific editing).[131] There's a paid subscription option, but their free searchable site and lively forums cover almost everything you'll need.

Merriam-Webster is the go-to dictionary unless your publisher specifies otherwise. Most words you'll need are free to look up online; there's a paid option for the unabridged dictionary.

Remember **your local library.** Librarians will often be able to direct you to that book you didn't even know you needed. They'll also have newspaper archives, unabridged and specialist dictionaries (gemstones, medicine, entomology), and a climate-controlled location (often with Wi-Fi) where you can sit and type for hours without buying six-dollar coffee.

---

131 More on styles back in Chapter 5, The Personal Copyedit

SELF-EDIT CHECKLIST

If you are sending your manuscript to a professional editor, use the Self-Edit Checklist to send the cleanest possible work and get the most for your money. Or, use these steps as a final polish before beginning your query or self-publication process.

If you finished your manuscript more than two weeks ago, dive back in. Otherwise, let it sit for at least a week and come back with fresh eyes.

You can go through these sections in any order, but I prefer to do the Technical Tune-Up first: I feel like I'm making progress, which gives me a sense of momentum into the next draft, and it helps me notice writing habits and overused words so when I rewrite I'm conscious of addressing those challenges.

TECHNICAL TUNE-UP

1) Format your manuscript for professional submission. If any of these steps are new to you, searching "Word+[thing]" will find instructions. And yes—publishing (for now) uses Word. If you're working in another program, save your manuscript for submissions or the design process as a .doc or .docx.

- ☐ One-inch margins all around
- ☐ Justify left
- ☐ 12-point Times New Roman or a similar unobtrusive serif font
- ☐ Delete any manually added headers and use the Header and Footer tool to put your last name and book title in the header
- ☐ Add automatic page numbers in the header or footer

□ Use Format>Paragraph to double-space text, no spaces between paragraphs. Indent first lines of paragraphs except the first paragraph in each chapter.

□ Remove double spaces after periods in Advanced Find and Replace. Enter two spaces in Find and one space in Replace, then hit Replace All until you reach zero replacements.

2) Run spellcheck with the grammar turned on, but don't assume it's correct. Notoriously among editors, Word's native spell check and Grammarly can see bad grammar as just fine, flag words that are spelled correctly, and suggest some truly terrible sentences. Review each and every change. When in doubt, look up the grammar rule or spelling and make a deliberate choice whether to follow or break the rule.

3) Make a word cloud. Using an app like Wordle, copy-paste your whole document to create a picture of all the words, sized according to their frequency. For overused words (often *that, just, got, around, felt, looked, like*) do a search, and each time the word pops up, ask if it's needed and if it's the right word in that location. Edit ruthlessly.

(The big exception is *said* in dialogue—usually, *said* becomes a neutral word like *the,* and it's better to use *said* than get fancy with dialogue tags.)

Many word clouds don't include *that*—turn off Track Changes and Find-and-Replace *that* with *that.* Hit Replace All for a count of how many *that*s were replaced. If you're a visual person, Replace All *that*s with an unusual word that isn't in your book (maybe *wabisabi* or *wintercearig* or *torschlusspanik*), make a new cloud, and see what size that word is in the cloud. Then hit Undo to put your *that*s back, and address the ones you'd like to remove.

4) Search for said. Is each dialogue tag needed? Can it be deleted or replaced with an action or description tag?

5) Search for "ly[space]." Adverbs aren't quite the Antichrist and they don't all end in -ly, but ask whether you want each one. Remove many.

6) Check pronouns. Search for *it* and see if some can be a more specific noun.

□ If *it* starts a sentence, try to reframe or put in a noun.

□ Search for *he, she, they, them, him, her*—should some be names or descriptors?

7) Root out boring verbs. Search for *began, started, continued* and strengthen the verb instead.

8) Activate passive verbs when possible.

☐ Search for *there was, there are, there were, was being, were being*. Replace them with active verbs and/or move the nouns to the beginning. So instead of "There were six cats on the fence," try "Six cats sat on the fence."

☐ Do a wildcard search for *was verb-ing* and *is verb-ing*. Open Advanced Find and Replace, check the box for Wildcards On and put this (including the <>) in Find: *<was [a-z]@ing>* Repeat with *<is [a-z]@ing>* if you have present-tense verbs. Replace the being-verb+ing constructions unless they are absolutely needed.

☐ Find modal verbs *would* and *could* and change them to more specific verbs unless you want that place to sound hazy.

PLOT CHECK

1) Summarize your story in the "In a world…" format described in Chapter 2: Stasis-Setting-Hero-Mission-Obstacle-Stakes-Theme-Relevance to the Reader. Do you have a story?

2) Check your inciting incident. Does something Simple, Unexpected and Concrete Kick off the story in the first two pages?

3) Make an actions list. if you write out the story as a series of actions, do they logically follow each other? Are there story gaps or unexplained actions? Does the location change randomly? Is your timeline in the order you want?

4) Does each incident in the plot significantly and permanently affect the protagonist? Do they gain a tool or companion, practice or learn, test their preparedness or experience a setback?

PROTAGONIST MASSAGE

You can think through these or write them down.

1) What does the protagonist want? What do the major secondary characters want?

2) What's the main obstacle stopping each one from getting what they want?

3) What's their great, possibly hidden strength that makes them the right person to achieve this goal, or the person who will be able to achieve this goal? If they're an antagonist, what powers, skills or traits help them become an effective obstacle?

4) What's their fatal weakness that will cause difficulty achieving their goal?

5) What must they sacrifice to get to the goal? How much does it cost them?

6) Have you shown the villain's motivation? Is it clear how they believe they are doing the right thing, even if the protagonist believes they are wrong?

7) At the end of the book, how has the protagonist grown or changed? If there's another book coming, what's their new starting place?

WRITING LUBE JOB[132]

1) Check every scene—are you getting in as late as you can, and getting out as early as you can? Does the scene start with forward motion, and impel the reader to the next scene? Do you have a couple of "restful" scenes to allow the reader (and your characters) to breathe/think?

2) Go through the dialogue character by character. Does everyone sound like themselves, and not like anyone else?

3) Look for filtering. Words like *she saw* or *he felt* at the beginning of an action or description can be removed to give the reader a stronger sense of being in the character's head.

4) Search for *explained, discussed* and *told* and see if the words following should be dialogue.

5) Look for As-You-Know-Bob/low-context communication. Is anyone telling someone else things they both already know? Is the narrative telling the reader things they don't have to know right now?

6) Review your world-building. Are customs, history, technology and backstory shown in context or in action rather than told to the reader? If you're writing memoir, can you primarily show your family and friends and the social mores of your world with actions and dialogue instead of description?

7) Check physical action. Are people moving in understandable and humanly possible ways? For fights or sex scenes, act

---

132 I ran out of metaphors.

them out with Barbies or condiment bottles to check physical flow in space and time.

8) Check verb tenses. Is each scene in the same verb tense throughout? Are tense shifts between scenes purposeful? Are the verb tenses clear and consistent through the entire manuscript?

9) Do most sentences end on a strong word? Do most paragraphs end with a strong sentence? Does every chapter end with a sense of forward motion, intrigue, or both?

10) Check point-of-view. For each POV character, check what they see in each scene. What are the physical limits of their area of sight? What are the limits of their vocabulary and understanding? How does their personality, attitude or situation characterize what they see?

BONUS POWER-UP

Go through your manuscript one more time.

1) Is each paragraph necessary?

2) Can you end earlier or start later in each scene?

3) Sentence by sentence: is each sentence saying exactly what you want it to say, in the fewest possible words? Is every word necessary?

4) Chapter by chapter: does each chapter end with a punchline, a button, a hook, or something that makes the reader want to turn the page?

5) For any rule you're breaking or storytelling convention you're violating, is it on purpose and is it working?

6) Does the beginning of the book clearly establish the genre and make a promise to the reader? Does the end of the book fulfill that promise?

7) As a whole. Imagine you are your ideal reader—maybe a famous author, maybe someone who fits the exact profile of a perfect reader for this book. Read it as that person and see if there's anything that makes you cringe.

Breathe deeply.
You got this.

BOOKS & MEDIA MENTIONED

Anderson, Laurie Halse. *Speak.* New York: Farrar, Straus and Giroux, 1999.

Atkinson, Kate. *Life After Life.* New York: Reagan Arthur Books, 2013.

Atwood, Margaret. *The Handmaid's Tale.* [1985] New York: Anchor Books, 1998.

Austen, Jane. *Pride and Prejudice.* [1813] New York: Modern Library, 2000.

Bayles, David, and Ted Orland. *Art and Fear: Observations on the Perils (And Rewards) of Artmaking.* Image Continuum Press, 2001.

Bradbury, Ray. *Fahrenheit 451.* [1953] New York: Simon & Schuster, 2011.

Brecht, Bertolt. *Mother Courage and her Children.* [1941] New York, Arcade Publishing, 1996.

Brontë, Charlotte. *Jane Eyre.* [1847] New York: Penguin Classics, 2003.

Burr-Drysdale, Sky. *Jumpsong.* Work-in-Progress

Burr-Drysdale, Sky. *Wes & Sava.* Work-in-Progress

Campbell, Joseph. *The Hero's Journey: Joseph Campbell on his Life and Work.* San Francisco: New World Library, 2003.

Christie, Agatha. *Murder on the Orient Express.* [1943] New York: HarperCollins, 2007.

Clark, Erin. *If you really love me, throw me off the mountain.* EyeCorner Press, 2020.

Collins, Suzanne. *The Hunger Games.* New York: Scholastic Press, 2008.

Davies, Robertson. *Salterton Trilogy.* [1958] New York: Penguin Books, 1991.

Dreyer, Benjamin. *Dreyer's English: An Utterly Correct Guide to Clarity and Style.* New York: Random House, 2019.

Dubus III, Andre. *House of Sand and Fog.* New York: W. W. Norton & Company, 2018.

Flynn, Gillian. *Gone Girl.* New York: Broadway Books, 2014.

Forster, E.M. *Aspects of the Novel.* [1927] Boston: Mariner Books, 1956.

Forsyth, Mark. *The Elements of Eloquence: How to Turn the Perfect English Phrase*. London: Icon Books, 2013.

Frank, Anne. *The Diary of a Young Girl*. [1947] New York: Bantam, 1993.

Friedman, Jane. *The Business of Being a Writer*. Chicago: University of Chicago Press, 2018.

Gerard, Sarah. *Sunshine State: Essays*. New York: HarperPerennial, 2017.

Gilbert, Elizabeth. *Eat, Pray, Love*. New York: Riverhead Books, 2007.

Grafton, Sue. The Kinsey Millhone Alphabet Series. New York: St. Martin's Press, Putnam & Sons. 1972-2017.

Grisham, John. *The Firm*. New York: Dell, 1999.

Haddon, Mark. *The Curious Incident of the Dog in the Night-Time*. New York: Vintage Contemporaries, 2004.

Israni, Natasha. *Monsoon Gods*. Work-in-Progress.

James, E.L. *Fifty Shades of Grey*. New York: Vintage Books, 2011.

James, P.D. *A Certain Justice*. Toronto: Seal Books, 2006.

Jones, Tayari. *An American Marriage*. New York: Algonquin Books, 2018.

Krantz, Judith. *Scruples*. [1978] New York: Bantam, 2011.

King, Stephen. *On Writing*. New York: Charles Scribner's Sons, 2000.

Lamott, Anne. *Bird by Bird: Some Instructions on Writing and Life*. New York: Anchor Books, 1995.

Lawson, Jenny. *Let's Pretend This Never Happened*. New York: Amy Einhorn/Putnam, 2012.

Lewis, C.S. *The Lion, the Witch and the Wardrobe*. [1950] New York: HarperCollins, 2005.

Lucas, George, director. *Star Wars*. Lucasfilm, 1977.

Luketic, Robert, director. *Legally Blonde*. Metro-Goldwyn-Mayer, 2001.

Macdonald, Helen. *H is for Hawk*. London: Jonathan Cape, 2014.

Mantel, Hilary. *Wolf Hall*. New York: Fourth Estate, 2009.

Marber, Patrick. *Closer*. New York: Dramatists Play Service, 2000.

Martin, George R.R. *Game of Thrones*. New York: Bantam, 1996.

McManus, Karen. *One of Us is Lying*. New York: Delacorte Press, 2017.

Mitchell, Margaret. *Gone With the Wind*. [1936] New York: Warner Books, 1999.

Oliver, Lauren. *Before I Fall*. New York: HarperCollins, 2010.

Picoult, Jodi. *A Spark of Light*. New York: Ballantine Books, 2018.

Pratchett, Terry. *The Truth*. New York: Doubleday, 2000.

Pratchett, Terry. *Going Postal*. New York: HarperCollins, 2004.

Roth, Veronica. *Divergent*. New York: HarperCollins Children's Books, 2011.

Rose, Kathryn. *Ojas*. Work-in-Progress.

Rowling, J.K. *Harry Potter and the Sorcerer's Stone*. New York. Arthur A. Levine Books/Scholastic, 1998.

Rowling, J.K. *Harry Potter and the Prisoner of Azkaban*. London: Bloomsbury, 1999.

Rowling, J. K. *Harry Potter and the Deathly Hallows*. London: Bloomsbury, 2007.

Salesses, Matthew. *Craft in the Real World: Rethinking Fiction Writing and Workshopping*. Portland, OR: Catapult, 2021.

Samuelson, Arnold. *With Hemingway: A Year in Key West and Cuba*. New York: Random House, 1984.

Sayers, Dorothy L. *Gaudy Night*. [1935] New York: HarperTorch, 1995.

Sayers, Dorothy L. and Jill Paton Walsh. *Thrones, Dominations*. New York: St Martin's, 1998.

Sedaris, David. *Me Talk Pretty One Day*. Boston: Little, Brown and Company, 2001.

Shakespeare, William. *Measure for Measure*. [1623] *The Merchant of Venice*. [1596] *Titus Andronicus*. [1594] All Arden Shakespeare Third Series. London: Bloomsbury, 2020.

Snyder, Blake. *Save the Cat: The Last Book on Screenwriting You'll Ever Need*. San Francisco: Michael Wiese Productions, 2005.

Strayed, Cheryl. *Wild: From Lost to Found on the Pacific Crest Trail.* New York: Knopf, 2012.

Tartt, Donna. *The Goldfinch.* Boston: Little, Brown and Company, 2013.

Tartt, Donna. *The Secret History.* New York: Vintage Books, 2004.

Thurston, Baratunde. *How to be Black.* New York: HarperCollins, 2012.

Waller-Bridge, Phoebe, creator. *Killing Eve.* Sid Gentle Films, BBC America, 2018-Present

Walls, Jeannette. *The Glass Castle.* New York: Scribner, 2006.

Walsh, Jill Paton. *Thrones, Dominations.* New York: St. Martin's Press, 1998.

Westover, Tara. *Educated.* New York: Random House, 2018.

Wilder, Laura Ingalls. *By the Shores of Silver Lake.* [1939] New York: HarperTrophy, 2007.

Wilson, W. Brett. *Redefining Success: Still Making Mistakes.* New York: Portfolio, 2012.

Younging, Gregory. *Elements of Indigenous Style: A Guide for Writing By and About Indigenous Peoples.* Edmonton: Brush Education, 2018.

Zinna, Diane. *The All-Night Sun.* New York: Random House, 2020.

Zinsser, William. *On Writing Well: The Classic Guide to Writing Nonfiction.* New York: HarperPerennial, 2016.

ACKNOWLEDGMENTS

Special thanks to Dinty W. Moore and *Brevity*, and Donna Talarico-Beerman, Kevin Beerman, and the Hippocamp Nonfiction Conference for providing me the venues to develop and assemble much of this material, and delightful audiences to test it.

My agent Janet Reid's own writing advice has inspired me since long before we met; I'm thankful for her steady navigation through publishing seas. Publisher Colin Hosten had my attention from the moment I saw him hustling anthologies outside panel events at AWP Portland, and confirmed this book was a good idea. Matt Winkler's good humor and support kept me moving.

A huge shout-out to Sky Burr-Drysdale, without whose encouraging, incisive and speedy feedback I could not have finished this book.

Iobel Andemicael helped shape Chapters 1 & 10 with her editorial comments and inspired me with the depths of her belief in me. Sharp-eyed copyeditor Melanie Gall revived my enthusiasm for this book. Jay Ashworth soldiered into the night setting type, and provided invaluable guidance on consistency, style and interior design. Andrea Schmidt elevated and refined the cover; Heidi Croot caught typos at the eleventh hour; Wendy Savage brilliantly indexed ideas, and Margaret Moore proofread a million hyphens.

Thanks for their support and enthusiasm to my writing buddies Christopher Buehlman, Jenny Currier, Jessica Jarlvi and Hananah Zaheer; to my teachers and mentors Andre Dubus III, Joan Herrington, Laura Williams McCaffrey and Dani Shapiro; and my classmates, colleagues and friends Melissa Ballard, Jocelyn Bartkevicius, Angie Chatman, Lisa Cooper Ellison, Thaddeus Gunn, Natasha Israni, Irene Landsman, Rhiannon Navin, Iris Van Ooyen, Pamela Peterson, Ashleigh Renard, Christianne Sainz, Paul Skenazy and Kristina Stanley.

Thanks also to the authors who have entrusted me with their work and inspired this book through their growth, enthusiasm, excitement, and powerful words, especially the Rebirth Your Book and Rebirth Your Writing alumnae.

Glennis Williams took dictation for my very first story and inspires me every day.

Vick Bain first showed me I was a writer and sustains me with her unwavering belief. Jean Johnson's coaching has supported every success and made me a better person.

The LJ Idol crew first showed me I was an editor: Kathryn Rose, Cislyn Smith, Gary Dreslinski, Katy Pika, HalfshellVenus, Rayaso, and many more.

And more than anything, thank you to my husband, whose faith in me is measureless and means the world.

ABOUT THE AUTHOR

Allison K Williams has edited and coached writers to publishing deals with Penguin Random House, Knopf, Mantle, Spencer Hill, St. Martin's Press and Black Rose as well as hybrid and independent presses. She's guided essayists and humorists to publication in media including the *New Yorker, Time,* the *Guardian, McSweeney's, Refinery29, Brevity, Hippocampus,* the *Belladonna* and TED Talks.

A popular and lively speaker, Allison has appeared at writing conferences, literary festivals, and workshops around the world. As Social Media Editor for *Brevity,* she inspires thousands of writers with weekly blogs on craft and the writing life.

As a memoirist, essayist, playwright and travel journalist, Allison has written craft, culture and comedy for National Public Radio, Canadian Broadcasting Corporation, the *New York Times,* the *Christian Science Monitor, Creative Nonfiction, McSweeney's Internet Tendency, Kenyon Review Online,* the *Prairie Schooner* blog and the *Drum.*

Allison's fiction has appeared in *Crossed Genres, Smokelong Quarterly* and *Deep South,* and her travel stories in *Travelers' Tales* and *Flash Nonfiction Funny.* Her plays include the London Fringe Best of Fringe winner *TRUE STORY* as well as *Drop Dead, Juliet!* and other scripts widely produced in high schools.

Allison holds an MFA from Western Michigan University, and has taught as a guest artist and/or faculty there and at Kalamazoo College, Rollins College, and the University of South Florida.

A former circus aerialist and acrobat, Allison has performed in twenty-three countries and can eat fire, crack a whip, and shut down that drunk in the third row.

Home base is currently Dubai, where the "Pork Shop" is a separate, dimly lit room at the back of the supermarket. It's like buying meat porn.

Exercises

Ability, Weakness, Passion, Foible, 132
Backstory, 151
The Beginning, 108
Character Purpose, 128
Character Voices, 139
Conflict, 80
Dialogue, 137
Dialogue Tags, 210
Events, 94–95
Finding the End of Your Memoir, 98
The Friend Read, 257–258
The Hero of Their Own Story, 136
Necessary Adverbs, 216
One Last Character Polish, 144
Point of View, 169
Scenes, 181
Short Story, 90–91
Starting with SUCK, 72
Structure, 118
Timeline, 119
Trimming the Narrative, 141–143
Verbs, 220
Voice, 165
What's in It for the Reader? 63
In a World, 66
World–Building, 149
Write This as Dialogue, 173

A

action tags, 207–209
actions
  sequence of, 177, 190, 194–196
  story, 43, 58–59, 94–95
active/passive voice, 194, 198, 204–205
adjectives, 216–218
adverbs, 22, 214–216, 318
all right/alright, 222
Alliance of Independent Authors, The, 285
All–Night Sun, The (Zinna), 145
American Marriage, An (Jones), 172, 178–179
Andersen, Stephanie (author), 77
Anderson, Laurie Halse (Speak), 159n68
Antz (film), 39
anymore/any more, 222
apps & websites, 49, 121, 311, 314–315
Art and Fear (Bayles, Orland), 307–308
Ashton, Paul (BBC Writersroom), 59
Aspects of the Novel (Forster), 99, 123
Associated Press (AP), 228
As–You–Know–Bob, 140, 195, 320
Atkinson, Kate (Life After Life), 67, 69, 167, 186, 206
Atwood, Margaret (The Handmaid's Tale), 149
Austen, Jane (Pride and Prejudice), 25n10, 65, 163
awards & prizes, 284–285, 304
awhile/a while, 221

B

backstory, 19, 22, 59, 63, 72–73, 115–116, 120, 121–122, 149–151, 158–159, 267, 312, 320
Bad Tourist (Roberts), 52
bad writers, 53–55, 298, 310
Barber, Nicholas (BBC.com/ culture), 169
Bartkevicius, Jocelyn (author), 120
Battle Royale (film), 40

Bayles, David *(Art and Fear)*, 307–308
BBC Writersroom, 59
BBC.com/culture, 169
Beauty and the Beast (film), 67
Before I Fall (Oliver), 70
beta read, 20, 26, 245
Bird by Bird (Lamott), 34, 275
Bloggess, The (Lawson), 272
book series. *See* series books
Bradbury, Ray *(Fahrenheit 451)*, 222n81
Brecht, Bertolt *(Mother Courage and Her Children)*, 171

Brevity blogs, 52, 113, 311
Broad Street Review (Warren), 273–274
Brontë, Charlotte *(Jane Eyre)*, 108–111
Bug's Life, A (film), 39
Burr–Drysdale, Sky
    (Jumpsong), 150–151
    (Wes & Sava), 141–143, 143n64
Business of Being a Writer, The (Friedman), 283
By the Shores of Silver Lake (Wilder), 146

C

Campbell, Joseph *(The Hero's Journey)*, 100–101, 121
category & genre, 293–296
Certain Justice, A (James, P. D.), 168, 216
chapter breaks, 186–187
Character Draft, 18–19, 21, 26, 34n16, 123–158
characterization, 26, 59, 123–128, 268
characters
    ability/weakness, 130–132, 32
    communication, 139–140
    dialogue, 136–139
    fantasy, 125–126
    Mary Sue, 131, 132–134
    memoirs, 129–130
    passion/foible, 130–132
    Quest & Objective, 65, 66–67, 126–128
    science fiction, 125–126
    series books, 126–128
    villains, 134–136
    voice, 136–139
    world as a character, 145–149
Chekhov, Anton, 83
Chekhov's Gun, 82–83
Chicago Manual of Style (CMOS), 32n13, 228, 315–316

Christie, Agatha, 85, 88, 102, 306
circular structure, 114, 116–117
Clark, Erin
    (If you really love me, throw me off the mountain), 202–203
    (Sex Icon), 201–202
clauses, 162–163, 194, 199–203, 233–235
cliffhangers, 59n30, 127–128, 186–187
Climax, 100n44
    about, 104–105
    eight–point structure, 102, 103–106, 110
    memoirs, 113–114
Closer (Marber), 216
Collins, Suzanne *(The Hunger Games)*. *See* Hunger Games, The
colons/semicolons, 234–237
comma splices, 32n13, 200, 233–234
commas, 231, 233–237
    with adjectives 217
communication, 139–140, 147–148
completing a project. *See* restarting a project
comps, 293–294, 295
concrete (SUCK), 68–71, 101, 319

conflict, 59, 78–80, 131–132, 136, 150, 177
copyediting, 27, 121, 261
copyrights, 153–154, 296–297
Craft in the Real World (Salesses), 252

Crazy Eight. *See* eight–point structure
Critical Choice, 102, 103–104
Curious Incident of the Dog in the Night–Time, The (Haddon), 71, 186–187, 295

D

dashes, 231, 232–233
Davies, Robertson (Salterton Trilogy), 167
dependent clauses, 200, 201–202, 233
details/summaries, 172, 173–174, 191–192, 196
developmental editing, 26, 28, 188, 261, 263, 270
dialogue, 19, 22, 136–140, 169–170, 173, 190, 192, 194–195, 197, 207–210, 215, 231–232, 318, 320
dialogue tags, 139, 143, 185, 207–210, 318
Diary of a Young Girl, The (Frank), 76–77, 78–79
Divergent (Roth), 128n47, 151, 153–155

drama, 73–75, 76–77
dramatic arc
 book length, 100–101
 cliffhangers, 59n30, 127–128, 186–187
 climax, 104–106
 memoirs, 42–43, 98
 mini–dramatic arcs, 102, 105, 160
 series books, 126
 structure, 100–101
drawer book, 242–243
Dreyer, Benjamin (*Dreyer's English*), 27n11, 230
Dubus III, Andre (*House of Sand and Fog*), 50, 175
Dunning–Kruger effect, 16
Dylan, Bob, 16

E

Eat, Pray, Love (Gilbert), 117
editing
 about, 23–27
 copyediting, 27, 121, 261–264
 developmental editing, 26, 188, 261–262, 268–270
 line editing, 26, 188–189
 on paper, 120–121
 proofreading, 24, 27, 121, 263–267
 self–editing, 17, 52, 160, 188, 267, 317
 structural/substantive editing, 17
 types of, 26

Editor Read
 about, 20, 259–260
 cost, 260–262
 editor feedback, 261, 266–268
 hiring an editor, 262–264
 workflow, 268–270
Educated (Westover), 69, 277
eight–point structure
 about, 101–102
 Climax, 102, 104–106
 Critical Choice, 103–104
 Quest, 102–106
 Resolution, 96, 106–108
 Reversal, 102–103, 106

Stasis, 64, 103–108, 319
SUCK, 102–107, 125
Surprises, 102–104
Elements of Eloquence, The (Forsyth), 217–218
Elements of Indigenous Style (Younging), 228
Eliza Doolittle *(My Fair Lady)*, 67–68, 106

Elle Woods *(Legally Blonde)*, 69, 101–107
ellipses, 230–232
Elzbit *(Jumpsong)*, 150–151, 150n65
em dash, 231–235
emotional trauma, 42–44, 273
envy, 243–244
erumpent horn, 82–83
exclamation points, 208, 215, 230

F

fact–checking, 36, 96, 151–153
Fahrenheit 451 (Bradbury), 222n81
fair use (legal principle), 153–154
Fifty Shades of Grey (James, E. L.), 272
fighting & sex, 177–179
filtering language, 203–204, 320
Firm, The (Grisham), 272
first draft, 17–18, 23, 33–35, 42, 48, 53, 113, 306
   See also Vomit Draft
five–act structure, 108–111
Flynn, Gillian *(Gone Girl)*, 79, 119, 295
foreign words, 176–177
Forster, E. M. *(Aspects of the Novel)*, 99, 123
Forsyth, Mark *(Elements of Eloquence)*, 217–218

Foster, Claire Rudy *(The Review Review)*, 302
four–act structure, 112
Francis, Dick, 36, 153
Frank, Anne *(The Diary of a Young Girl)*, 76–77, 78–79
Friedman, Jane *(The Business of Being a Writer)*, 283, 288
Friend Read
   about, 20, 245–246
   criticism, 246–247
   feedback, getting, 247–249
   feedback, giving, 249–251
   patience, 254–256
   writing workshops, 251–254
Friends with Benefits (film), 39, 39n21

G

Game of Thrones (Martin), 99
genre and category, 293–296
Gerard, Sarah *(Sunshine State)*, 117
Gilbert, Elizabeth *(Eat, Pray, Love)*, 117
Ginna, Peter (Bloomsbury Press), 60
GLAAD, 228
Glass Castle, The (Walls), 66, 70
Going Postal (Pratchett), 125
Goldfinch, The (Tartt), 65

Gone Girl (Flynn), 79, 119, 295
Gone With the Wind (Mitchell), 74–75, 125
good writers, 65
Grafton, Sue (The Kinsey Millhone Alphabet Series), 102, 120
Grammar Girl, 230, 315
Grisham, John *(The Firm)*, 272
Guardian, 54, 153

H is for Hawk (Macdonald), 62, 295

Haddon, Mark *(The Curious Incident of the Dog in the Night-Time)*, 71, 186–187, 295

Hamlet (Shakespeare), 44, 69, 78

Handmaid's Tale, The (Atwood), 149

Harry Potter and the Deathly Hallows (Rowling), 117n49

Harry Potter and the Prisoner of Azkaban (Rowling), 92–93

Harry Potter and the Sorcerer's Stone (Rowling), 124, 131–132, 146

Harry Potter (Rowling)
  ability/weakness, 131–132
  Chekhov's Gun, 82–83
  five–act structure, 108–111
  passion/foible, 131–132
  plots, 108–111
  unexpected (SUCK), 69
  world–building, 146

Hemingway, Ernest, 34, 34n17, 301

Hermione Granger (Rowling), 82, 93, 109–111, 124

Hero's Journey, The (Campbell), 100–101, 121

high–context communication, 139–140

Hood (Moke), 33

House of Sand and Fog (Dubus), 50

How to be Black (Thurston), 62

Hunger Games, The (Collins)
  ability/weakness, 131–132
  characterization, 126–127
  cliffhangers, 127, 186
  eight–point structure, 101–102, 107, 108–111
  metaphors, 206
  originality, 40
  passion/foible, 131–132
  Passover Question, 72–73
  sex and fighting, 178
  showing and telling, 172
  SUCK, 130
  world–building, 147

"I Want" song, 67–68, 126

idea theft, 296–297

If you really love me, throw me off the mountain (Clark), 202–203

impartial treatment (in memoir), 44

"In a World"
  about, 64–66
  in fiction, 65
  in nonfiction, 65–66
  Story Draft, 19, 69
  SUCK, 68–72, 393

independent clauses, 200, 202, 233, 235

individuality, 40–41

Ingermanson, Randy (The Snowflake Method), 48

inspiration
  about, 47–48
  suggestions for, 48
  writing process, 43

irregardless, 222

Israni, Natasha *(Monsoon Gods)*, 176

James, E. L. *(Fifty Shades of Grey)*, 272

James, P. D. *(A Certain Justice)*, 85, 168, 199n75, 216

Jane Eyre (Brontë), 108–112
jargon, 158, 176–177
Jones, Tayari *(An American Marriage)*, 25, 172, 178–179

Jumpsong (Burr–Drysdale), 150–151

K

Katniss Everdeen (*Hunger Games, The*), 73, 125, 127
  ability/weakness, 131–132
  characterization, 151, 154–155
  eight–point structure, 101–102, 106–107
  five–act structure, 108–111
  passion/foible, 131–132
kickoffs (SUCK), 69–71, 76, 319

Killing Eve (Waller–Bridge), 88
King, Stephen *(On Writing)*, 214, 271n107
Kinsey Millhone (Grafton), 102, 120
Knecht, Rosalie *(Literary Hub)*, 301
Krantz, Judith *(Scruples)* 116

L

Lamott, Anne *(Bird by Bird)*, 34, 275
Laura Ingalls *(By the Shores of Silver Lake)*, 146
Lawson, Jenny *(Let's Pretend This Never Happened)*, 71, 115, 272
legal action, 275–277
Legally Blonde (Luketic), 69, 101–107
Let's Pretend This Never Happened (Lawson), 71, 115
letter–e structure, 114–116
Lewis, C. S. *(The Lion, the Witch and the Wardrobe)*, 69
Lewis, Kaulie *(The Millions)*, 43–44
Life After Life (Atkinson), 67, 69, 167, 186, 206

line editing, 26, 27n11, 188–196, 197, 223, 225, 260, 270
Lion, the Witch and the Wardrobe, The (Lewis), 69
literary agents, 286–288
Litt, Toby *(Guardian)*, 54
Little Mermaid, The (film), 67
London Review of Books (Mantel), 162–163
low–context communication, 139–140, 195–196, 320
Lucas, George (Star Wars), 68, 101–102, 104, 106–107, 127
Luke Skywalker (Star Wars), 68, 101–102, 104, 106–107, 127
Luketic, Robert (Legally Blonde), 69, 101–107
lyrics, 153–154

M

Macdonald, Helen *(H is for Hawk)*, 62, 295
main story arc *(Legally Blonde)*, 104
Mantel, Hilary *(London Review of Books)*, 162–163

Mantel, Hilary *(Wolf Hall)*, 25, 81, 161–163, 206
manuscript format & style, 227–228
Marber, Patrick *(Closer)*, 216
Martin, George R.R. *(Game of Thrones)*, 99

Mary Sue, 131n56 132–133
McManus, Karen (*One of Us Is Lying*), 119, 159n68
Me Talk Pretty One Day (Sedaris), 117
Measure for Measure (Shakespeare), 236–237
Media Reference Guide (GLAAD), 228
memoir
  characters, 129–130
  drama, 76–77
  dramatic arc, 42–43, 76
  fact–checking, 36, 44
  finding the end, 118
  first draft, 42–43, 48
  impartial treatment, 44
  mystery, 85
  plot, 96–97
  publication, 273–274
  story, 60–62
  structure, 113–114, 115–117
  truth and fairness, 44
Merchant of Venice, The (Shakespeare), 37–39
metaphors/similes, 256–257

Millions, The, 39, 43
Miss Marple (Christie), 102
Mitchell, Margaret (*Gone With the Wind*), 74–75, 125
modal verbs, 213–214, 319
modifiers, repetitive, 219
Moist Von Lipwig (*Going Postal*), 125
Moke, Jenny Elder (*Hood*), 33
moments/things, 174–176
Monsoon Gods (Israni), 176
Moore, Dinty W. (author), 311
Morrison, Blake (*South of the River*), 153
Mother Courage and Her Children (Brecht), 171
multi–act structures
  five–acts, 108–111
  four–acts, 108, 112
  three–acts, 108–111
Murder on the Orient Express (Christie), 88
musicals, 67
My Fair Lady (film), 67–68, 106
mysteries, 36, 57, 59, 80–82, 102, 108, 112, 118, 153, 159, 189, 295

N

NaNoWriMo, 42
narrative, 150, 202, 205
National Novel Writing Month, 42n20
Nick Dunne (*Gone Girl*), 96

Nieman Storyboard, 73
Nietzsche, Friedrich, 391
No Strings Attached (film), 45, 45n21

O

objectives of stories/characters, 81–83, 153–155
Ojas (Rose), 31–35
Oliver, Lauren (*Before I Fall*), 85
On Writing (King), 266
On Writing Well (Zinsser), 266

One of Us Is Lying (McManus), 144, 197n68
Ophelia (Hamlet), 51, 95
Originality of ideas, 45–47
Orland, Ted (*Art and Fear*), 385–386

P

pace, 226–228

paper editing, 144–146, 276–278

passive/active voice, 254–255
Passover Question, 69, 88–90, 93
Personal Copyedit, 21, 281–295
physical editing, 144–146, 276–278
physically possible actions, 20,
    219–222, 404
Picoult, Jodi (*A Spark of Light*), 369
placeholders, 18–19, 147
plots
    about, 111–112
    memoirs, 115–117
    series books, 72
    Story Draft, 69–72
    structure, 71–72, 119–121
point of view. *See* POV
POV
    about, 19–20, 205–208
    character selection, 206–208
    editing of, 234–244
    filtering language, 253–254
    multiple POV, 207
    thoughts, 261–262
Pratchett, Terry
    (*Going Postal*), 152
    (*The Truth*), 207
prepositional phrases, 248–252,
    272, 289n87

Pride and Prejudice (Austen), 80
Prisoner of Azkaban (Rowling), 112
procrastination
    about, 57
    external deadlines, 60
    setting goals and priorities,
    58–60
project selection, 42–45
proofreading, 31, 147, 328, 336,
    365, 383n126
publication
    about, 339–340
    awards & prizes, 355–356
    reparing for, 296–298
    self & hybrid, 348–355
    timelines, 347–348
punctuation, 267
    about, 285
    colons/semicolons, 290–295
    commas, 289–290
    dashes, 288–289
    dialogue tags, 259–260, 261
    ellipses, 286–287
    exclamation points, 285
Purdue OWL, 285, 397

Q

queries, 286–300
Quest
    ability/weakness, 126–128
    about, 65, 90
    eight–point structure, 101–108

passion/foible, 130–132
series books, 59, 102
SUCK, 101
quitting, 241–243
quoting lyrics, 153–154

R

Redefining Success (Wilson), 69
referrals, 364–367
rejections, 373–376
repetitive modifiers, 271–272
research, 36–37. *See also* fact–
    checking

Resolution
    about, 106–107
    five–act structure, 111
    memoirs, 98
restarting a project, 55–56
Reversal
    about, 106
    eight–point structure, 102–103

Review Review, The (Foster), 302
Roberts, Suzanne (Bad Tourist), 52
Romeo and Juliet (Shakespeare),
  40, 253, 297
Rose, Kathryn (Ojas), 27–31
Rowling, J.K., 69, 82–83, 92–93,
  108–111, 117n49, 124, 127,
  131–132, 146, 307n128
Rowling, J.K.
  (Harry Potter and the Deathly
  Hallows), 117n49
  (Harry Potter and the Prisoner of
  Azkaban), 92–93
  (Harry Potter and the Sorcerer's
  Stone), 69, 109–110, 126–127,
  131

Royal Order of Adjectives, The,
  216–218
rules of writing
  editing, 23–25, 26–27
  prescriptivists/descriptivists, 222
  story, plot and structure, 58–59
  stronger sentences, 197–211
  Technical Draft, 155–158
  useful apps & websites, 314–316
  word counts, 158–161
run-on sentences, 199, 201–203,
  233n87

S

Salesses, Matthew (Craft in the Real
  World), 252
Salterton Trilogy (Davies), 167
Samuelson, Arnold (With
  Hemingway), 34, 34n17
Saunders, George (author), 81
Save the Cat (Snyder), 125
Sayers, Dorothy L., 85, 167, 306
Scarlett O'Hara (Gone with the
  Wind), 74–75, 125
scenes
  about, 180
  details, 183–184
  pace, 182–184
  starting and ending, 181–182
  text arrangement, 184–186
  trimming, 180
Scruples (Krantz), 116
Secret History, The (Tartt), 69–70,
  167–168
Sedaris, David (Me Talk Pretty One
  Day), 117
self & hybrid publication, 279–284
self-edit checklist, 317–321
semicolons/colons, 234–238

sentences
  clauses, 200
  length, 199–203
  long and complex, 201–203
  prepositional phrases, 200–201
  word order, 197–199
sequence of actions, 177, 194
series books, 59, 102, 126–127
sex & fighting, 177–179
Sex Icon (Clark), 201–202
Shakespeare, William
  (Hamlet), 44, 69, 78
  (Measure for Measure), 236–237
  (Merchant of Venice, The), 37–39
  monologues, 253
  (Romeo and Juliet), 252–253, 297
  (Titus Andronicus), 238n91
Shapiro, Dani (memoirist), 43–44
showing and telling, 19, 22, 40,
  81,85, 123–124, 140, 144, 162,
  164, 169–172, 173–176, 192, 196,
  204, 214, 240, 320
similarity, 39–41
similes/metaphors, 138, 163,
  206–207
simple (SUCK), 68–71, 101–102,
  319

situation, drama of, 73–74
  memoirs, 76–77
  SUCK, 70–71
Snowflake Method, The
  (Ingermanson), 48
Snyder, Blake (*Save the Cat*), 125
So What Factor, 42, 57, 61–62
Song, DongWon, 72
South of the River (Morrison), 153
Spark of Light, A (Picoult), 295
Speak (Anderson), 159n68
Special Writer Voice, 163–164,
  192–193, 195. See also voice
Star Wars (Lucas), 68, 101, 104,
  106–107
Stasis
  about, 101
  eight–point structure, 101–108
  five–act structure, 108–111
Stein, Gertrude, 64
story
  about, 64–66,
  editing of, 26
  memoir, 60–62
  series books, 59
  starting, 68–73, 108
  structure, 99–101
  Technical Draft, 225
Story Draft
  about, 18, 57–58
  editing of, 18, 121–122
Stranger Than Fiction (film),
  73n39, 182
Strauss, Victoria (*Writer Beware*),
  284–285

Strayed, Cheryl (*Wild*), 40, 62, 65,
  67, 115, 235
structure
  about, 58–59, 99–101
  circular, 116–117
  editing of, 23, 26
  eight–point, 101–108
  letter–e, 115–116
  memoirs, 113–117
  multi–act, 108–112
  playwriting, 22–23
  series books, 59
  Technical Draft, 225
style sheets, 27, 27n12, 32, 227,
  268
SUCK
  about, 68,
  action, 70
  concrete, 68–71, 101, 319
  eight–point structure, 101–108,
  examples, 68–71, 102, 125
  kickoffs, 69–71, 76, 319
  series books, 102
  simple, 68–71, 101–102, 319
  situation, 70–71
  unexpected, 68–71, 101, 319
  voice, 71
suing. See legal action
summaries/details, 172, 173–174,
  191–192, 196
Sunshine State (Gerard), 117
Surprises
  about, 102–103
  eight–point structure, 102–105

T

tags. *See* dialogue tags
Talking to Strangers, 65
Tartt, Donna
  (*The Goldfinch*), 65, 326
  (*The Secret History*), 69–70, 167,
  326

Technical Draft
  about, 19, 26, 155–158, 268
  final check, 225
  scene trimming, 180
telling and showing, 19, 22, 40,
  81,85, 123–124, 140, 144, 162,
  164, 169–172, 173–176, 192, 196,
  204, 214, 240, 320

text arrangement, 184–186
texts and thoughts, 210–211
that, 220–221
that/which, 220–221
theft of ideas, 296–297
themes, 86–89
things/moments, 174–176
three–act structure, 111
Thrones, Dominations (Sayers, Walsh), 167

Thurston, Baratunde *(How to be Black)*, 62
timelines, 118–119, 278–279
Titus Andronicus (Shakespeare), 238n91
Tris Prior *(Divergent)*, 125, 127
Truth, The (Pratchett), 167
truth and fairness, 44

u

unexpected (SUCK), 68–71, 101, 319
Unkind Editor, The, 21

Updegrave, Samantha Claire (author), 113

v

verbs
  modal, 213–214
  tenses, 121, 190, 212–213
villains, 123, 134–136
voice
  about, 161–163
  character voices, 136–139
  editing of, 225
  passive/active, 204–205
  special writer voice, 163–164, 192–196
  SUCK, 68–72

Vomit Draft. See also first draft
  about, 18, 33–35
  fact–checking, 151–153
  memoirs, 42
  physical editing of, 120

w

Walk in the Woods, A, 40
Waller–Bridge, Phoebe *(Killing Eve)*, 88
Walls, Jeannette *(The Glass Castle)*, 66, 70
Walsh, Jill Paton *(Thrones, Dominations)*, 167, 335
Warren, Roz *(Broad Street Review)*, 273–274
websites & apps, 314–316
Wendig, Chuck, 136, 145, 155, 207
Wes & Sava (Burr-Drysdale), 141–143, 143n64

West Side Story (film), 40, 297
Westover, Tara *(Educated)*, 69, 277
what's happening/what's not happening, 205–206
Where'd You Go, Bernadette? 186
which/that, 220–221
Wild (Strayed), 40, 62, 65, 67, 115, 235
Wilder, Laura Ingalls *(By the Shores of Silver Lake)*, 146
Williams, Laura Jane (author), 53
Williams, William Carlos (poet), 174

Wilson, W. Brett *(Redefining Success)*, 69

With Hemingway (Samuelson), 34n17

Wolf Hall (Mantel), 25, 161–163, 186, 206, 233n87, 295

word counts
  about, 158
  guidelines, 158–159
  too long, 160
  too short, 160

world–building
  about, 145–146
  names, 149
  physical world, 147
  political hierarchy, 149
  privacy, 148
  religion, 148
  social rules, 148
  technology, 147–148
  time, 147

Writer Beware (Strauss), 240, 283–284

writers as readers, 306–307

writers as writers, 307–310

writer's toolbox, 391–395

writing, rules of. See rules of writing

writing for a living, 301–305

writing from experience, 36–37

writing groups, 392–395

writing process
  about, 45–46
  are you good enough? 53–55
  editing, 51–53
  inspiration, 47–48
  personal restrictions, 45–47
  procrastination, 49–51
  restarting, 55–56

writing queries, 286–291

Y

Younging, Gregory *(Elements of Indigenous Style)*, 283

Z

Zinna, Diane *(The All–Night Sun)*, 177–178

Zinsser, William *(On Writing Well)*, 266

Made in the USA
Monee, IL
12 September 2023

42607893R00199